A Herstory of Economics

A Herstory of Economics

Edith Kuiper

polity

First published in 2022 by Polity Press

Polity Press
65 Bridge Street
Cambridge CB2 1UR, UK

Polity Press
101 Station Landing
Suite 300
Medford, MA 02155, USA

ISBN-13: 978-1-5095-3842-3
ISBN-13: 978-1-5095-3843-0 (pb)

A catalogue record for this book is available from the British Library.

Library of Congress Control Number: 2021946894

Typeset in 10.5 on 12 pt Sabon
by Fakenham Prepress Solutions, Fakenham, Norfolk NR21 8NL
Printed and bound in Great Britain by TJ Books Ltd, Padstow, Cornwall

For further information on Polity, visit our website:
politybooks.com

Contents

Women Economic Writers

Edith Abbott (1876–1957)
Abigail Adams (1744–1818)
Sadie Tanner Mossell Alexander (1898–1989)
Mary Astell (1666–1731)
Mabel Atkinson (1876–1958)
Jane Austen (1775–1817)
Sarah Bagley (1806–89)
Martha Moore Ballard (1785–1812)
Grisell Baillie (1665–1746)
Anna Laetitia Barbauld (1743–1825)
Catharine Esther Beecher (1800–78)
Barbara Bergmann (1925–2015)
Annie Besant (1847–1933)
Ada Heather Bigg (1855–1944)
Barbara Leigh Smith Bodichon (1827–91)
Ester Boserup (1910–99)
Jessie Boucherett (1825–1905)
Sophonisba P. Breckinridge (1866–1948)
Emma Brooke (1844–1926)
Frances (Fanny) Burney (1752–1840)
Hester Mulso Chapone (1695–1730)
Sarah Chapone (1699–1764)
Émilie du Châtelet (1706–49)
Frances Power Cobbe (1822–1904)
Kezia Folger Coffin (1723–98)
Clara Collet (1860–1948)

Mary Collier (*c*.1688–1762)
Sophie de Grouchy de Condorcet (1764–1822)
Anna Julie Cooper (1858–1964)
Caroline Healey Dall (1822–1912)
Julie-Victoire Daubié (1824–74)
Marie Dessauer-Meinhardt (1901–86)
Maria Edgeworth (1768–1849)
Millicent Garrett Fawcett (1847–1929)
Betty Friedan (1921–2006)
Elizabeth Cleghorn Gaskell (1810–65)
Charlotte Perkins Gilman (1860–1935)
Olympe de Gouges (1748–93)
Angelina Grimké (1805–79
Sarah Grimké (1792–1873)
Glückel von Hameln (1646–1724)
Elizabeth Ellis Hoyt (1893–1980)
Elizabeth Leigh Hutchins (1858–1935)
Mary Hays (1759–1843)
Harriet Jacobs (1813–97)
Alexandra Kollontai (1872–1952)
Hazel Kyrk (1886–1957)
Anne-Thérèse, marquise de Lambert (1647–1733)
Rosa Luxemburg (1871–1919)
Mary Lyon (1797–1849)
Jane Haldimand Marcet (1769–1858)
Harriet Martineau (1802–76)
Mary Masters (1694?–1759?)
Harriet Taylor Mill (1807–58)
Elizabeth Montagu (1718–1800)
Hannah More (1745–1833)
Judith Sargent Murray (1751–1820)
Alva Myrdal (1902–86)
Elinor Ostrom (1933–2012)
Mary Paley Marshall (1850–1944)
Etta Palm, Baroness d'Aelders (1743–99)
Bessie Rayner Parkes (1829–1925)
Virginia Penny (1826–1913)
Eliza Lucas Pinckney (1722–93)
Mary Prince (1788–1833)
Ann Radcliffe (1764–1823)
Ayn Rand (1905–82)
Eleanor Rathbone (1872–1946)
Clara Reeve (1729–97)

Maud Pember Reeves (1865–1953)
Margaret Gilpin Reid (1896–1991)
Harriet Hanson Robinson (1825–1911)
Joan Robinson (1903–83)
Margaret Higgins Sanger (1879–1966)
Janet Schaw (*c*.1731–*c*.1801)
Olive Schreiner (1855–1920)
Anna Maria van Schuurman (1607–78)
Sarah Robinson Scott (1720–95)
Ann Stephens (1810–86)
Marion Talbot (1858–1948)
Ida Minerva Tarbell (1857–1944)
Elizabeth Church Terrell (1863–1954)
Charlotte Elizabeth Tonna (1790–1846)
Sarah Trimmer (1741–1810)
Flora Tristan (1803–44)
Sojourner Truth (*c*. 1797–1783)
Priscilla Wakefield (1751–1832)
Beatrice Potter Webb (1858–1943)
Ida B. Wells-Barnett (1862–1931)
Anna Doyle Wheeler (1785–1848)
Helen Maria Williams (1759–1827)
Mary Wollstonecraft (1759–97)
Victoria Woodhull (1838–1927)
Helen Woodward (1882–1960)
Virginia Woolf (1882–1941)
Frances Wright (1795–1852)
Ann Yearsley (1753–1806)
Clara Zetkin (1857–1933)

Preface and Acknowledgments

Being part of the history I have been writing about has been a mixed pleasure, I can tell you that. As a philosopher and historian of economic thought, my research on the invisible women economic writers and economists in the history of economic thought quite literally cost me my job, as this topic was considered "not core to the field." This book tells the larger history, or perhaps better, the herstory of economic thought. It tells the story of women, a long line of women who wrote about economic topics, theories, insights, and their experiences – the story of women economic writers and women economists and their work. Because they were women and because they wrote about women, their work was ignored and left to gather dust.

This book will put a spotlight on these women, most of them still unknown even to scholars of the history of economic thought. Many of them were impressive and insightful people, who stepped forward and wrote about what they considered to be highly relevant and important, what they thought needed to be said. Occasionally their writing made them rich and famous, but, in other cases, these women faced dire consequences for publishing their thoughts. This book aims to show that their work is worth reading and that they can teach us about crucial aspects of an economy.

Losing my job worked out well for me in the end. I found a position that provided me with the support and opportunity to gather together the essays, letters, pamphlets, and books of eighteenth-century women economic writers (see Barker and Kuiper, 2010; Kuiper, 2014) and to teach on the topic. It also enabled me, subsequently, to write this book about these women. This book presents a selection of voices that tell us about how women lived in eighteenth- and nineteenth-century England and France, and in the nineteenth- and twentieth-century US; about the economic problems they encountered, the solutions they proposed and fought for, and the way they viewed the economy. This book will provide you with a new perspective on the history of economic thought. Be warned, though: once read, there is no going back …

I would like to thank the Dutch Organization of Scientific Research (NWO) for supporting my initial research on women's writing in the history of economic thought with their VENI grant, which enabled me to do four years of research, to change my mind, and to receive the institutional support that I needed. I would also like to thank the International Association for Feminist Economics (IAFFE) and all the friends and colleagues I had the chance to work with over the years and who provided me with an inspiring and supportive professional environment. I warmly thank my colleagues of the State University of New York (SUNY) at New Paltz's Economics Department – Mona Ali, Hamid Azari-Rad, Laura Ebert, and Simin Mozayeni – who so wholeheartedly supported me in writing this book, and the Women's, Gender, and Sexuality Studies Department – Karl Bryant, Meg Devlin, Heather Hewitt, Kathleen Dowley, and Jess Pabon – who taught me so much, and also the students in my History of Economic Thought courses, who pushed me to be more articulate and to sharpen my thoughts and narratives. I would also like to thank my friends and dear colleagues for their time, comments, discussions, and inspiration, especially Drucilla Barker, Ann Davis, Koen Bron, Hettie Pott-Buter, and Jolande Sap for their support in this lengthy endeavor. I would particularly like to thank my students Adrienne Springer, Claudia Garcia-Robles, and Yili Hasandjekaj for their research, respectively, on Émilie du Châtelet, Elizabeth Montagu, and Sadie Alexander.

Finally, in the words of Mary Lee Chudleigh (1701), I do "beg your pardon for the length of this Address, and for the liberty I have taken to speak my Thoughts so freely, which I do not doubt but you will readily grant to one, who has no other Design but that of doing you Justice."

Enjoy the read!

Introduction

What is a herstory of economics? And why do we need it?

As it is taught today, the history of economic thought consists of a chain of intriguing and engaging stories about great economists, with a focus on a fixed set of male Western economists. Political economy emerged in Western Europe during the second half of the eighteenth century, and, during British economic hegemony, it was centered at the University of Cambridge in England. The history of economic science was traditionally taught using an internalist approach. This meant that teaching focused on the rational considerations of great minds like Adam Smith (1723–90), Karl Marx (1818–83), and John Maynard Keynes (1883–1946) (rhymes with 'brains,' as US economist Deirdre McCloskey would say), and the debates between them and their contemporaries. Recently, historians of economics have become more and more interested in applying an externalist approach, paying attention to facts not directly related to political economy – for example wars, revolutions and political backlashes, economic crises, as well as personal friendships, mental health issues, class, and personal hang-ups – to better understand the development of economic concepts, models, and theories. As part of this, there is an emerging interest in the role of women, as well as norms, values, and institutional practices around gender and women's voices in economic science. Historians of economic thought have started to turn their eyes to the role of gender in economics (see Pujol, 1992; Groenewegen, 1994; Folbre, 2009), the work of female economists (see Thomson, 1973; Libby, 1990; Dimand et al., 2000; Madden et al., 2004), and the reasons for the low representation of women in the history of economic thought (see Dimand, 1995; Madden, 2002). Collections of texts by women economic writers and feminist economists have been compiled (Barker and Kuiper, 2010; Kuiper, 2014) and women's economic writings are being analyzed (see Madden and Dimand, 2019; Rostek, 2021). This book is a logical follow-up to this work and makes grateful use of it.

In the overall discipline, however, most women economic writers and women who were professional economists, including those who were once well known and engaged in the economic science of their time, have been forgotten and excluded from the narrative of the history of economic science. Even those who were very famous in their lifetime – Oprah Winfrey-like famous – were, mostly by default, excluded from accounts of the history of economics. It is still the case that few historians of economics, let alone other economists, have heard about the work of Mary Astell, Sarah Chapone, Priscilla Wakefield, Elizabeth Hutchins, or Hazel Kyrk. Those who put together lists, websites, posters, and calendars of economists generally overlook women economic writers and economists. At best, their number is reduced to one, Joan Robinson, or two, Joan Robinson and Rosa Luxemburg, as women economists who somehow made it to the surface. Joan Robinson (1903–83) and Rosa Luxemburg (1871–1919) were both fine economists. Robinson wrote about monopolistic markets and price discrimination and she had the dubious honor of being the woman who "should have received the Nobel Prize for Economics" but never did. Luxemburg described and analyzed imperialism: why and how the capitalist system spreads more and more widely over the globe. The history of women economists generally stops here, as if mentioning two women in the history of economic thought is enough – more than enough. That these two economists did not write about women is not a coincidence. They were part of a male-dominated tradition of economics in which women's concerns and interests did not have a place. Although Luxemburg and Robinson themselves had little to do with it, their place in the field as token women takes the light away from other women who wrote about their economic views, experiences, concerns, and interests and who thus missed out on the attention they deserved. It took until only a few decades ago for this to change.

This book is not about *why* women have been excluded from the annals of the history of economic thought and exactly *how* this process of their exclusion from the history of economic thought worked. Although these questions will come up, this book's main aim is to introduce the reader to a selection of women economic writers and economists who engaged in substantial work on economic issues yet fell through the cracks of history because of their gender. In doing so, this book aims to show that these omissions impact our understanding of the economy and the history of economic thought.

The book introduces the reader to a wealth of works by both women economic writers and women economists, the difference being that the former wrote about economic topics but did not have an academic status. For many of these women, their lack of academic status was caused by the fact that universities were closed to them. This only changed at the end of the nineteenth century, after which female economists were able to enter the discipline and start to publish in academic journals. The reader will meet a diverse group of women who put their economic thoughts and experiences on record; their insights are out there waiting to be rediscovered. Synthesizing my extended exploration of their works, I highlight a set of themes that emerged from bringing these writings back into the limelight.

This book aims to meet the need for a more accessible text on women's economic writing that can be used in courses on the history of economic thought – a book that introduces students, as well as a general audience interested in the development of our economic thinking, to the work of women economic writers and economists. Each of the nine chapters of the book addresses a theme, while telling the stories of these women and analyzing their work along chronological lines. It has not been possible, by any means, to cover all women economic writers and economists in the UK and the US. To maintain some coherency, I had to step away from discussing the work of some of the great women whom you might expect to appear in these pages; Mary Robinson, Madame De Staël, Helen Bosanquet, and Emma Goldman come to mind, but there are (many) others. This does show, though, that there is still more work out there that deserves to be analyzed and brought into the herstory of economics.

The themes distilled from these women's economic writings coincide with some of the main debates in the academic field of political economy, which, by the end of the nineteenth century, came to be known as "economics" or "economic science." Together, the chapters in this book cover the period from 1700 to 2020. While the story in each one unfolds in a chronological manner, each chapter also focuses on a specific period in which the main theme of that chapter surfaced in economic debates inside and outside academia. The last chapter brings the main findings together, thereby collating some of the lessons that can be learned by listening to our foremothers and reading their work.

Most of the women economic writers and economists who come forward in this book led fascinating lives. The reader will be introduced to these women and to their main economic works. Most of them come from the UK and, in a later time period, the US; it was, after all, in England and Scotland that political economy emerged and that makes these women particularly relevant for this herstory of economics. After the global economic hegemony had shifted to the US – following World War II – the center of gravity in the field of economics moved from Cambridge, UK to Cambridge, Massachusetts. This book aims to break open and disrupt the settled story of the history of economic thought that has been written from the perspective of European – and, later, American – middle-class white men. As the author of this book, I am aware that the consideration of women's experiences and feminist perspectives is only a start and that much more work needs to be done to bring in economic contributions from Asian Americans, Native Americans, and the economic writers and economists from countries in the South.

Presented in this book is a rarefied group of women. In the eighteenth century, even those upper-class and aristocratic women who had learned to read and write saw their lives strictly regulated by laws and social norms that limited their ability to study, write, and publish. Practically all women in the UK were excluded from higher education and universities over most of the past four centuries, and it was against the law to teach enslaved people to read and write in the US. Because of these restrictions, most of the women who were able to read and write and who left economic texts for posterity were upper-class and aristocratic women. Some working-class and enslaved women did manage, against all the odds, to learn how to read and write, including on economic issues, and some of their texts are included in this overview.

Women economic writers wrote predominantly in non-academic genres: pamphlets, letters, diaries, household books, poems, etc. Quite a few of them commented on, translated, and engaged with the work of the male academic economists of their time. Again others focused fully on the day-to-day interests and concerns of women, which they wanted to become more widely known. Others were involved in politics, activism, and public debates. Rather than aiming to make a name for themselves, these women articulated their views in order to make their point as a contribution to their cause.

The topics these women wrote about differed from those addressed by academic economists, such as money, trade, government policies, competition, and investment. In much the same way that gender norms have set the focus of male economists, women economic writers have proceeded from their own experiences, which were highly impacted by contemporary gender expectations. These impacts were considerable, especially in the eighteenth and nineteenth centuries, when gender norms set strict limits on behavior in most West European countries. Rather than engaging in the abstract reasoning that some of their male contemporaries excelled in, it was women's daily experiences that led them to write about how to run a household or estate, their lack of economic rights, their particular roles in production and consumption, their social and economic dependence on their husbands, their limited rights to earn and keep a wage, the difference between women's and men's wages, and other topics. These women developed perspectives on social and political institutions, moral behavior, and care, and thus provided a broad perspective on the economy, if one only cared to read their work and listen to their message. In this book, you will learn about these economic writers' views on the issues they were concerned about, fought for, risked a prison or mental-hospital sentence for, or, like Olympe de Gouges during the French Revolution, lost their life over. This book will also make extensive use of women's economic writings as background, as secondary sources, and as illustration. We will see that including their analyses in the history of economic thought will shift the focus, change the main narrative in this field, and, as an intended consequence, restructure the story of the history of economic thought with which some of you are already familiar.

Some context and central concepts

The writings of the economic authors discussed here have to be seen against the historical background of the emergence and growth of industrial society and the capitalist system. To give the reader a brief, rough sketch of the women's and gender history from which these texts originate and to which they refer, I would like to start by stressing the profound shift brought about by the change from an agricultural and feudal society to an industrial society dominated by money values and market relations. For women of the lower and middle classes this change meant that the productive work they used to do was increasingly pulled out of the home to be conducted in workshops and factories. Women and girls who were part of the working class were forced to work outside the home and earn a subsistence wage. Most middle-class women remained in the home where their productive tasks were reduced to raising children and running the household, while their economic dependence on their husbands increased substantially. Low wages for women's work and a lack of decent jobs open to women made it impossible for them to live independently, and the insufficient number of men available on the marriage market meant that this arrangement failed large groups of women who strived for economic security over their lifetime (Atkinson, 1987 [1914]). The emergence and strengthening of abolitionist, labor, and women's movements, the increasing role of the government in the economy, and, more generally, the growth in productivity and technology led over the nineteenth century in Europe and the US to changes in marriage laws and property rights. As middle-class women emerged onto the labor market over the twentieth century, their participation in the workforce grew from about 20 percent in 1900 to around 50 percent in 1980 (Goldin, 1990). Although the shift of productive activities from the household to the market is still ongoing, the increase of female labor force participation has by now maxed out, stalled, and, with the onset of the COVID-19 pandemic in 2020, reversed into a decline. Thus far, the twenty-first century has brought some severe economic crises, and industrial society faces limits in various other respects, such as the exhaustion of resources, climate change, and the unsustainability of white male dominance.

Talking about some central concepts where the herstory of economics is concerned, the first and often primary question that feminist scholars ask is: "Where are the women?" This question is particularly relevant where the history of economic thought is concerned because of the absence of women on various levels; as economists, as topics of research, and in terms of their specific interests. To answer this question, one needs to dive deep into the story and bring in perspectives other than the ones usually presented by historians. After addressing that initial question, which focuses on women as a group, we also need to identify and address the differences in experience among women, including the conflicted interests between them, given that they are not all positioned equally. White women in positions of power, for instance, often sided with men in the silencing of enslaved women, thus sustaining if not joining the cruel behavior of the men in their vicinity. Women of privilege exploited domestic workers, as in the case of Hannah More, a member of the Bluestocking Society in England who appropriated the intellectual work of her servant, Ann Yearsley, under the cover of philanthropy. These conflicts and opposing interests deserve attention and inclusion in the assessment of the work under scrutiny.

Scientists and scholars, including economists, tend to build on the work of their teachers and predecessors, and work within the theoretical framework or research program within which they were trained. Many of the stories, assumptions, and values that made women invisible became part of the basic notions of these research programs and thus have implicitly taken over the field. Therefore, after decades, if not centuries, during which women were left out by the authorities in the field, it takes conscious action – with a risk to reputation and career – to bring them back in, as this means going against both the theoretical framework and the academic norms and values of the times. The absence of women in the room to ask the question "Where are the women?" has made it easier to normalize the invisibility of women in science, including economic science. This, of course, was the same, if not more so, for people of color. Their absence protected those who were present – white male economists – from having to acknowledge their privilege and enabled them to rationalize the absence of women, and women of color in particular, as a matter of merit.

By the 1980s, the absence of women and their economic interests had become a defining part of economic scientific reasoning, norms, and values that seemed to be confirmed by facts and other empirical evidence. Rational Economic Man, the central character in economic theory, was considered as generic in describing humans' behavior, men and women alike. The analysis of labor market behavior was based on that of men only, but that limitation was not problematized. Women's economic behavior, on the other hand, was assumed to be captured by the analysis of "family behavior," and those who invested their career in research on women's economic behavior were pushed to the fringes of the discipline. More generally, economic behavior and agency were defined by a conceptualization of rational behavior – choosing between two best options based on your own self-interest – that was associated with American notions of masculinity. It was when finally, as an increasing number of women and feminist economists entered economics departments and published their research in established economic journals, that women came to the table, asked their questions, and pursued them in search of answers.

Before we turn to the structure of the book, I would like to take a step back and discuss some basic notions that might be new to some. Underlying the focus on women's economic writing, for instance, is the question of what being "a woman" means for their writing and to what extent their gender determines what they write. To answer this question in the context of this book, let us start with dissecting the concepts "woman" and "man." These two terms are less straightforward and obvious in their meaning than most of us think and have been taught. In daily life, women and men are often seen as obviously different, not least because women give birth and men do not. Some people view women and men as so different that they are opposites, albeit complementary to each other; in this view, women are emotional and men are rational, women are weak and need protection, and men are strong – "real men" because they protect "their woman." This implies more or less that women and men cannot live without each other and are even seen by some as, together, merging as one individual. Think, for instance, of how married couples were, and sometimes still are, addressed as Mr. and Mrs. John Jones. This set of ideas pairs with an understanding of the differences between women and men as "natural" or mainly biologically based.

Research and experience over the past few decades, however, have contradicted this view of the differences between women and men. Women and men are not opposites – as in A and not-A – but can be perceived as being on a spectrum with respect to their DNA, physical reproductive organs, and their individual experience of gender identity (Reis, 2009). Some of us are very feminine; others have various traits traditionally considered masculine or identify as men despite being raised as women. The wide variety of gender identities cannot be captured using a binary; on the contrary, trying to do that is harmful, particularly to those who do not "fit." To be clear, we are not talking here about "sexual orientation." Sexual orientation refers to who you are sexually attracted to; if you are heterosexual, gay, pan-, bi- or a-sexual. That is a separate matter, which I would like to leave aside for now. Let me also clarify that men, who have masculine biological traits (DNA and hormones) do not, of course, "naturally" show signs of toxic masculinity, such as dominating and assaulting women. How one deals with being a man is a matter of nurture, not nature. Even though some try to claim that assaulting women is a "natural" thing to do, such behavior in no way makes them a "real" or "good" man.

Feminist scholars have found that ideas of what it means to be "a good man" or "a real woman" differ from country to country, from culture to culture, and from century to century. They differ even between groups of people. Among American football players, for instance, it is considered very masculine to be physically strong, to not mind getting hit hard, and to engage in strong teamwork. These are not the same qualities seen as manly by economists. What is seen as "tough," "cool," and "hot" in the field of economics is, for instance, coming up with smooth and "charming" solutions or complex mathematical models all by oneself and beating one's competitor on the magnitude of a variable. So feminist scholars unlinked "gender" from "sex difference," which meant that gender could be investigated separately from biology. Feminist economist Julie Nelson describes gender as "the associations, stereotypes, and social patterns that a culture constructs on the basis of actual or perceived differences between women and men" (1995: 132). Feminist theory developed further and this gender concept was criticized by feminist scholars like Judith Butler (1990), who pointed out that "sex differences" also contained a cultural component. Parents of children born with genitals that were not straightforwardly either male or female, more often than not would ask doctors to interfere to "fix" any ambiguity. Thus, cultural perceptions of gender impact physical and biological differences, and sex differences also become gender differences. Judith Butler and others perceived gender identity as much more fluid, as a process in which individuals "performed" their gender. More recently, women and men who identify as being of a different gender from the one they were assigned at birth – trans individuals – have criticized the woman/man binary as well as the fundamental pattern of binary thinking that is linked to it. As we will see, binary thinking is also deeply ingrained in economic thought, but more about that later. This book focuses on the work of "cis-women" – those women who identified as female, which was for them the gender they were assigned at birth.

As I mentioned before, and as we all know, women are not a homogeneous group; they differ in class, skin color, education, age, health, religion, physical ability, and location. Because women do not all automatically have the same interests, and have widely different experiences, one cannot obviously speak on behalf of another. Moreover, some women face discrimination not only based on their gender, but also, and at the same time, because they are women of color, because they face physical limitations, and/or because they are young or older. Kimberlé Crenshaw (1993) referred to this overlapping of "systems of oppression" as "intersectionality." A woman of color will experience both sexism and racism, and these forms of discrimination may well reinforce each other.

This book focuses on women's writing on economic issues, and not, for instance, on economists' writing on women's issues, because it is *here* – on the basis of their gender – that women economic writers and economists have been excluded. For the former, it was a *physical* exclusion, for they, *as women*, were not allowed to take up any sort of position at universities. Later, it was the historical exclusion of the invisible work of these economic writers and of many economists *as*

women that became part of the silencing of women in economic texts
and theories. This exclusion has assisted in maintaining the division
between, on the one hand, "pure economics" – that part of the
science in which economists engaged in "value-free" reasoning – and,
on the other, "women's issues," which were generally considered as
normative economics, based on explicit or implicit value judgments.
This book focuses on the work of people who, *as women*, developed
a perspective on the economy that was and is very different from
that developed by men *as men*. It brings together a variety of voices
of women who were excluded and silenced because, *as women*, they
had little or no access to the resources and liberties men had, and
even when they did produce work, this did not make it into the
literature on the history of economics. It is those hidden stories and
those silenced voices that I want to go back to, learn from, and use
to reassess the economic concepts, ideas, and theories that men have
developed over the centuries.

   To be explicit about our concepts, we need also to address the
questions "What is economics?" and "What is the economy?" The
economy – like notions of gender – has to be considered as a social
construct; there is nothing we can point to and definitively say:
"THAT is the economy." What has become part of "the economy"
has been constructed socially, culturally, politically, and economically over the past centuries. Therefore, what is considered part of
"the economy" is neither "natural" nor a politically neutral given, as
we will see in particular when we talk about women's work.

   Political economy, which acknowledged the role of power, morals,
and the conflict of interest between classes, became redefined by the
end of the nineteenth century. The theoretical approach of political
economists such as Adam Smith, David Ricardo, and Thomas
Malthus is often also referred to as "Classical Economics," a term
coined by Karl Marx. Economists started to refer to the new set of
theories that was based on a quantitative methodology dominant
in physics at the time, and that focused on individual behavior
(of men), as "Economics." Consequently, alongside "œconomia,"
which concerns economic thinking that preceded political economy,
this book will refer to either "political economy" or "economics,"
depending on the time period under discussion. Finally, and just
to be clear, the economy and economics are not one and the same
thing. Economics is a field of study that includes concepts, theories,
economic journals and books, and the economists doing the research.
This field of study may be influential, but only indirectly influences
what is happening in what we call "the economy" in the much
broader sense.

This means that the questions "What is economics?" and "Who is to do economics?" are both relevant given that they are both concerned with whose questions deserve attention and further investigation, and who gets to decide whether the answers are satisfactory. Until recently the issues and questions of women and women of color, in particular, clearly did not count for much, and many of the answers that economists came up with left a lot of women economic writers and economists in the dark.

Themes and structure of the book

As already stated, this book is structured around a set of themes distilled from women's economic writings over the period 1700–2020: one or more theme per chapter, eight chapters in total, plus a concluding chapter. While each chapter unfolds in a chronological manner, each theme is addressed in more detail for the period in which it became central in the economists' debates. The theme of morality, for instance, was extensively discussed by early political economists like Bernard Mandeville and Adam Smith during the eighteenth century; one of the two themes addressed in Chapter 1 is women's economic writing on a new morality during that time period. These themes are foundations to be built upon in subsequent chapters, as they continue to play roles in the herstory of economic thinking of later periods. In subsequent chapters, the reader will see returns to time periods addressed previously, as the themes of focus shift through time and through the chapters. The sequence of the chapters follows the sequence of these theme periods through the herstory of economic thought, as is outlined in the rest of this Introduction.

Chapter 1, "The Emergence of Political Economy," goes back to the origins of political economy and the times during which the field was referred to as "œconomia," or the study of the household. In later texts, a lot of women economic writers and Greek philosophers like Xenophon and Socrates address their experiences in running a household. In this chapter, we meet Grisell Baillie of Jarviswood (1665–1746), who kept household books over a period of more than thirty years over the first decades of the eighteenth century; the chapter brings into focus the tradition of books on household management, increasingly perceived, in England and elsewhere, as women's exclusive realm. After political economy emerges and redefines the field to focus on the individual engaging in exchange relations, the tradition of household management continues, but outside academia. In the early twentieth century, this tradition gets replaced by the more scientific analysis of Home Economics, which includes, for instance, *Economics of Household Production* (1934) by Margaret G. Reid (1896–1991). This tradition resurfaced as New Home Economics in the 1960s and 1970s, applying mainstream, neoclassical economic theory to household behavior.

From the period during which scientific study became institutionalized, we will meet Émilie du Châtelet (1706–49) who lived in France, translated the poem *The Fable of the Bees* (1714) by Bernard Mandeville (1670–1733), and contributed to the new moral system that came with the emerging industrial society. She was a central figure in the French Enlightenment as she gathered free thinkers, both aristocrats and bourgeois, around her to discuss mathematics, natural science, and philosophy. We will also read about Elizabeth Montagu (1718–1800), leader of the Bluestocking Society and a very visible personality in British society. The ideas of both du Châtelet and Montagu on the new daily morality in France and England will be related to Adam Smith's *Theory of Moral Sentiments* (1759). The remaining part of this first chapter will introduce Maria Edgeworth (1768–1849), who described the change in culture and morality from feudal relations to early capitalist in *Castle Rackrent* (1800), and Mary Hays (1759–1843), whose message and tone are more urgent, as she addresses the threats of poverty and moral downfall faced by women. Closing off this chapter is Sophie de Grouchy de Condorcet (1764–1822), who translated Adam Smith's *Theory of Moral Sentiments* (1759) into French and contributed her views on moral decision-making and the role of institutions. The relation between morality and economic science will remain a recurring theme throughout the history of economic thought.

Chapter 2, "Power, Agency, and Property Rights," lays bare some other cornerstones of political economy. With the growth of bourgeois society, the legal and political position of women became redefined, acknowledging fathers, brothers, and husbands as women's legal guardians in a legal system that dispossessed married women from control over their fortunes, their children, and their futures. Sarah Chapone (1699–1764) sounded the alarm bell about the loss of legal rights for women in 1735. Later in the eighteenth century, women economic and legal writers claimed and fought for women's rights to full citizenship, marriage laws based on equality, and for the right to divorce. The French Olympe de Gouges (1748–93), the Dutch Etta Palm, Baroness d'Aelders (1743–99), and the English Mary Wollstonecraft (1759–97) will tell us more. This chapter goes into depth discussing their ideas, comparing them with the concepts and principles of the founders of political economy, like Cesare di Beccaria, Anne-Robert-Jacques Turgot, and Adam Smith.

Chapter 3, "Education," addresses what functioned as the gateway for both women and men to become full members of society and be able to contribute to social, economic, and cultural developments. Education was, therefore, a central and recurring theme in the women's movement. Mary Astell (1666–1731), Anne-Thérèse, marquise de Lambert (1647–1733), and Maria Edgeworth, amongst others, wrote about the importance of a sound education and training for girls. Mary Church Terrell (1863–1954) spoke in 1898 about the way black women in the US had made large strides and had caught up with respect to the level of their education, and about the progress the black community had made by that time, building their own colleges and universities.

Elizabeth Montagu, whom we already met in Chapter 1, was an early contributor to the emerging school movement in England. To support the improvement of the education of girls, she started her own schools, thus setting an example that many women economic writers would follow. Sarah Trimmer (1741–1810), who also started her own school, wrote a handbook on how to start and run a school, *The Oeconomy of Charity; or, an Address to Ladies Concerning Sunday-Schools* (1787). Trimmer was one of the many economic writers who wrote about their experiences and views on improving education for girls, Mary Wollstonecraft being another of them.

More specifically, on economic literacy and education, Hannah More (1745–1833), Jane Haldimand Marcet (1769–1858), Harriet Martineau (1802–76), and Millicent Garrett Fawcett (1847–1929) wrote works that rendered political economic principles and concepts about daily life into accessible language. The last writer addressed under this theme is Ayn Rand (1905–82), who became famous for her novels in which she brings economic ideas to life that have substantially influenced the Tea Party movement in the US.

Chapter 4, "Women's Relation to Wealth: Capital, Money, and Finance," points out that women's loss of control over their capital, their labor, and their land rights contributed to the rise of the (Gothic) novel at the end of the eighteenth century. Ann Radcliffe (1764–1823), for instance, contributed in a major way to this genre and provided a venue for women to vent their economic ideas and experiences, and gave witness to women's concerns, if not plain anxieties, that their complete dependency on men brought about. This development is strengthened by changes in social norms around women dealing with money that rationalized and accommodated the distancing of women from their economic assets. Novels remain an important venue for women to express ideas about the role of money in their lives, as Jane Austen (1775–1817) shows in her books. A few decades later, with the economic crises of 1837 and 1857 hitting the US, we again see the emergence of a wave of women's economic novel writing. The reclaiming of control over economic assets and means of production continues to this day, which we see reflected in, for instance, Bina Agarwal's (1994) pathbreaking empirical research on women's control and use of land in India. The chapter ends with an account of women's role in the financialization of the economy and the more recent work of economists such as Susan George (1988), Gary Dymski and Maria Floro (2000), and Libby Assassi (2009).

"Production," the theme of Chapter 5, has always had a gendered meaning in economic theory. Economic writers such as Mary Collier (c.1688–1762), Eliza Lucas Pinckney (1722–93), and Priscilla Wakefield (1751–1832) provide us with their personal experiences as, respectively, washer woman, farmer and merchant, and author and banker. Over the course of the nineteenth century, economic historians such as Elizabeth Hutchins, Olive Schreiner, Edith Abbott, and Ivy Pinchbeck wrote about the history of women in industry. Focusing on women's labor force participation, the first section of this chapter reports on the work of the Langham Place group in London, headed by Barbara Leigh Smith Bodichon (1827–91), which examined women's work and education and engaged in activism to change the laws that kept women back, using data as presented in the census to back up their statements. The next section discusses the work of the Fabian Women's Group, founded in 1907 in London, which was engaged in the debate about occupational segregation based on gender. This chapter ends with an exploration of the experiences and views of women economic writers and economists concerning running one's own business.

Chapter 6, "Distribution," discusses work by Charlotte Perkins Gilman (1860–1935), Eleanor Rathbone (1872–1946), and others who criticized and suggested various gender and income distribution arrangements or social contracts. It lays out the initial emergence of the abolitionist and labor movements that preceded the women's movement. Women contributed to the early labor movement and wrote pamphlets and in magazines to make their point – as did, for example, Harriet Hanson Robinson (1825–1911).

This chapter also describes the debate in *The Economic Journal* between several male and female economists on the demand for equal pay for equal work. As the patriarchal social contract had turned into a middle-class ideal, this gender ideology would also take over in economics, as is shown for instance in Gary Becker's *A Treatise on the Family* (1981). The increase in the number of women economists in the 1960s and 1970s brings about a new literature in which Paula England, Francine Blau, Claudia Goldin, and many others apply neoclassical analysis and other economic theories to explain the gender and racial wage gaps.

Chapter 7, "Consumption," outlines a field in which women had a lot of daily experience. Consumerism, in which women have played a central role, developed alongside production in industrial society. Novelists like Elizabeth Cleghorn Gaskell (1810–65) describe the impact of the increase of consumerism on women's lives in British middle-class households. In the first decades of the twentieth century, Hazel Kyrk (1886–1957) and Margaret G. Reid articulate, respectively, theories of consumption and household production. Marion Talbot (1858–1948) and Sophonisba Breckinridge (1866–1948) further develop the study of household administration; Helen Woodward (1882–1960) was one of the founders of the study of marketing, in which she took the perspective of the consumer. Political economists and, later, economists left the study of marketing and consumer behavior to business economists, leaving the consumer underinformed. More recently, consumer choice has become the focus of Behavioral Economics, the analysis of non-rational consumer choice behavior.

The provision of goods and services formerly produced in the household has been in part taken over by local and national governments. Chapter 8, "Government Policies," addresses the increase in tasks and responsibilities of national governments due to the monetization and marketization of production of what used to be seen as "women's work" and took place in the household. The chapter starts with the debates about the role of governments with respect to population and birth control, followed by a discussion on the work of authors such as Elizabeth Leigh Hutchins (1858–1935), who described the slow but consistent increase in factory legislation in England. After outlining the emergence of large-scale policy research in the early years of the twentieth century, the focus shifts to the development of policy analysis by feminist economists, and of gender responsive budgeting in particular. The chapter ends with a discussion on the limits of the government provision of women's former production in the household, such as care work, waste reduction, and conservation of the natural environment.

Chapter 9, "Findings, Feminist Economics, and Further Explorations," briefly outlines the main findings that emerge as different from the traditional narrative of the history of economic thought. In addition, the chapter provides a brief account of the development of the field of feminist economics, and ends with an exploration of directions for future economic research that takes gender, race, and the conservation of the environment into account.

1

The Emergence of Political Economy

Introduction

One possible point at which to start this herstory of economics could be the publication of Adam Smith's *An Inquiry into the Nature and Causes of the Wealth of Nations* (1776). Smith (1723–90) is generally considered to be the founder, or father, of political economy. To find the women in political economy, however, we need to dig deeper. We need to go back to the first texts in the tradition that brings about political economy in the second half of eighteenth-century England and Scotland. In doing this, we will find ourselves reading texts by Ancient Greek philosophers and medieval writers who focused on the economy of the household, the field of study referred to as "œconomia."

This chapter will shed light on the early texts by Greek philosophers and later texts by women economic writers on the economy of the household. The second thread in this chapter explores women's economic writing in the 1700s, engaging with a new morality that emerged with the growth of the middle class. I will describe the cradle of political economy and some major shifts that define the field over the centuries that follow.

Œconomia or the study of household management

Most of the very early women's economic writings are lost in the mists of history. Only a few phrases of, for instance, Aspasia

(470–400 BC), the Ancient Greek political philosopher, have been retained. Xenophon (431–354 BC) and Aristotle (384–322 BC), whose writings did survive, wrote quite extensively about women and gender. A large part of Xenophon's *Œconomicus* (362 BC), which translates to "the man who manages the household" (Ekelund and Hébert, 1997), reports on Socrates' dialogues. Socrates talks about setting up a household, the division of tasks between husband and wife, and the use of training a young wife to become a prudent housewife. He tells us that having a good housewife is crucial for the wealth of the household. "And I can show that some so treat their wedded wives also as to have them as fellow workers in helping to increase their estates, and that others treat them in a way in which most of those who do so bring themselves to ruin" (Xenophon, 2021: 13). Socrates also explains his marriage to Xanthippe, with whom he quarreled on a constant basis, by the fact that she was a strong woman. His remarks are sharp and teasing; in other words, *Œconomicus* is a good read. Most textbooks on the history of economic thought that point out the importance of the division of labor in Xenophon's text, like Ekelund and Hébert's book, referred to above, do so, however, without mentioning his focus on the original division of labor: that between husband and wife, men and women.

The focus on household economy made sense in Greece, which was in those times an agrarian society divided into a number of city-states. In Athens and Sparta, cities that were frequently engaged in warfare, the estate was the central economic unit. Such estates generally contained large, self-sufficient communities of families, servants, slaves, horses, and other animals. Aristotle, whose influence on economic thinking has been substantial and ongoing, had a negative view of women. They were, according to him, merely incomplete men and – using his binary logic – cold and passive, in contrast to men, who were seen as hot and active.

Aristotle distinguished between two kinds of economy. The kind that aimed at sustenance for members of the household by providing food, clothes, and shelter, and that took place within the estate; he called this the "natural economy" or *œconomia*. He considered the dealings and trades that took place outside the household and that aimed at making a profit, including lending money against an interest, to be part of the "unnatural economy" or *chrematistikè*. The unnatural economy was a necessary evil that needed to be contained and kept on the margins of society, otherwise, according to Aristotle, it would lead society to chaos (Ekelund and Hébert, 1997).

The household would remain center stage in economic thinking over the centuries to come. At the end of the Middle Ages (1500–1600s)

Europe was still an agrarian society and the early Renaissance literature on husbandry described methods of farming: when to sow, when and how best to harvest, how to deal with animal sickness, etc. Books on husbandry, as Keith Tribe (1978) explains, were mainly based on biblical images and religious concepts, recounting the vertical, hierarchical relations between Adam and the Earth, God and Man, and so on. In this context, when biblical stories and some local folklore were the main narratives that the general populace had access to, just as paintings in the church dominated the imagery they had access to, Eve was pictured as the woman who seduced Adam. Women – as daughters of Eve – played either a negative role in these stories or were simply left out. Some scholastic political philosophers and early economic writers, like Jean Bodin (*c.*1530–96), for instance, took this perception of women so far that they contributed to the witch hunts that raged throughout Europe from about 1450 to 1750 (see, e.g., Federici, 2014).

During the Middle Ages, many learned women lived in monasteries and wrote religious and philosophical texts. Christine de Pisan, for instance, was a prolific writer in many genres and the first woman in Western Europe to express herself in the vernacular language about women's issues. In her view, women should be educated and they had the virtues, interests, and potential to contribute to many fields and excel in many professions. In her *Book of the City of Ladies* (1405), she described many negative myths about women and told of women's strengths, using the allegory of the building of a city based on women's virtues – a city in which women could be safe and respected (Richards, 1982). A few centuries later, Anna Maria van Schuurman (1607–78), in her day an acknowledged genius who spoke at least twelve languages, wrote a scientific thesis, *The Learned Maid, or Whether a Maid May Be a Scholar* (1638). Schuurman also stood up for women's rights to be educated and to study. Moreover, she claimed that women's minds and the daily schedule of privileged women enabled them particularly to engage in scientific study. De Pisan and Schuurman, however, were viewed as exceptions, and, luckily for them, they were accepted as such.

With the rise of Protestantism and a new class of merchants and middlemen, the household became more and more ideologically perceived as "a man's castle" in which women were domesticated and kept as housewives. Until the sixteenth century, and even into the seventeenth, aristocratic women in Europe still had a say in political matters, but over the course of the eighteenth century, especially in the UK, even these women were increasingly kept out of the public sphere. Rising in importance, politics, trade, and industrial endeavors became exclusively male territory, and the household the realm of women. Whereas earlier, keeping the household account books was mainly a task for men, women over time developed their knowledge of running a household and many of them kept their own household books.

Educated and upper-class women started to document their skills in running extended households. Lady Grisell Baillie (1665–1746) turned the art of running a household practically into a science. Hundreds of people lived and worked at the Baillie estates in Edinburgh, London, and at the large Mellerstain House in Berwickshire in southern Scotland. Grisell Baillie was a celebrity in Scotland at the time, known and famous for her heroic behavior as a 12-year-old, when she secretly visited her father in prison and brought him food. Her father, a political prisoner and religious agitator for the Covenanters, would later escape from prison and flee to Holland with his family. After they returned to Scotland in the wake of William III and his wife Mary II claiming the English throne in 1692, Grisell and her family were restored to their property. Grisell married the love of her youth, George Baillie, and, in the years that followed, she and her husband played a central role in the Scottish aristocracy.

Grisell Baillie was so successful in keeping the books in her own household that both her father and her brother-in-law let her run their estates as well. *The Household Book of Lady Grisell Baillie, 1692–1733,* published in 1911, provides insight into the management of these three households, including the rules for personnel, extensive menus for large dinners, money spent on weaponry, hunting, traveling, the wages of domestic servants, and additional funds spent in support of these workers. As such, Baillie's books paint a detailed image of the way such households were run. Marion Lochhead (1948), for instance, used it as the basis for her analysis of the wealth development of the Baillie household. Similar account books have recently been revisited as a source of economic information and as such are becoming part of the history of economics (see, e.g., Maas, 2016).

This literature on household management developed over the course of the seventeenth and eighteenth centuries in England and Scotland into a library of books that dealt with a range of aspects of household management. Consistently ignored by economists and historians of economics alike, it is a large literature on how to best run a household, including how to deal with personnel and sickness, how to remove stains, use herbs for food and medicine, and maintain and repair various kinds of woodwork, tapestry, and clothing, and, of course, how to do the conservation and cooking. Books like Martha Bradley's *The British Housewife; or, the Cook, Housekeeper's, and Gardiner's Companion* (1758), Mrs. Smith's *The Female Economist; or A Plain System of Cookery: For the Use of Families* (1810), and Catharine Beecher's *A Treatise on Domestic Economy* (1841) were meant specifically for middle- and upper-class young women who started and ran their own households. Note that Mrs. Smith closes her introduction by stating that her book is well adapted to the purposes of domestic economy, considering "moral attitudes such as economy, cleanliness, and propriety as inherently part" of these household management books. It is *Mrs. Beeton's Book of Household Management* (1861) that becomes more or less the standard work and that it is still being reprinted and sold today.

As the household became more and more the exclusive realm of women in Western Europe, the gendered divide in public and private domains also became part of the political philosophy of the time (Habermas, 1989 [1962]; Fraser, 1992 [1990]). In the tradition of earlier thinkers like Aristotle, Jean-Jacques Rousseau (1712–78) focused on "men" and assumed that citizens were exclusively male. In *A Discourse on Inequality* (2016 [1755]), he put forward a history of society in which he articulated a divide between the state of nature and the state of society. Rousseau philosophized that man's natural state was single and independent and that women and "savages" lived in the state of nature. Over time, civilized and educated men built a society of men and the family, located "outside culture," was characterized by Rousseau as a remnant of natural relationships. The natural state was healthy, according to Rousseau, and had little to do with property rights and other economic laws that were part and parcel of culture and politics and as such corrupted. Rousseau, a friend of David Hume, had a profound influence on the thinking of Adam Smith, who applied these ideas about the gendered nature of private and public life as building blocks to his *Wealth of Nations* (1976 [1776]) (see Rendall, 1987).

Smith built his monumental work on the early industrial economic system on the work of other scholars too – for example, the work of Isaac Newton (1642–1727), whose comprehensive theory of gravity and the application of natural laws gave Smith a model for his theoretical framework. William Petty (1623–87), who started the Royal Society in London and measured the national income of both Ireland and England, provided the groundwork for macroeconomic analysis. French philosophers and economists, including François Quesnay, Anne-Robert-Jacques Turgot, and Pierre le Pesant, sieur de

Boiguilbert, provided Smith with important tools for his analysis of the economy.

In his works, Smith made a silent but crucial move: he shifted attention away from the household. Changing the focus 180 degrees, he turned his back on the household, and put the autonomous male individuals center stage. He made this move silently in the sense that he simply excluded women and the household from his works. He used the term "œconomy" for what we would call Home Economics or Household Management, thereby separating it from "the economy," the term he uses for productivity and wealth in the public realm.

In the two books Smith published during his lifetime, *The Theory of Moral Sentiments* (1759) and the *Wealth of Nations* (1776), it is the (male) individual who represents the household in the contexts of the law and market exchange. It is these individuals who have "the propensity to truck, barter, and exchange goods one thing for another" (1976 [1776]: 25). It is this male individual who becomes the basic unit of economic analysis – also known as Rational Economic Man – and, as such, the focus for generations of economists to come.

These specific binary notions of private and public, nature and society, femininity and masculinity thus became part of political economy at a fundamental level. Smith perceived manhood and masculinity in terms of self-control, individuality, the ability to make decisions on one's own account, and the freedom to pursue one's own interest. Femininity, on the other hand, was defined merely by default and in negative terms, such as "effeminate," "economically dependent," "driven by strong passions," "sexually teasing," and so on (Kuiper, 2003). These notions of masculinity and femininity are still with us today. Take, for instance, a basic macroeconomic model: the Circular Flow Model. The idea of public and private as fundamentally distinct realms still informs the definition of the main actors in this model. It is the firm that produces, the firm that is active and makes the economy grow, while the household is perceived as having a more passive role, consuming goods, choosing between goods and services supplied to them, and providing labor, land, and capital, which are then used by firms in a "productive manner." It is not until the publication of *Beyond Economic Man* in 1993, as part of the emergence of feminist economics as a field of study, that we get a thorough critique of the use of binary concepts in economics. In this book, edited by Marianne Ferber and Julie Nelson, a group of economists identify binary concepts such as productive/unproductive, investment/savings, culture/nature, public/private, linking them to notions of masculinity/femininity and, as such, structuring mainstream economic theories.

Since the household and women had become excluded from political economy, it was mostly women who further developed the literature on household management over the course of the nineteenth century and into the twentieth century. Retaining the traditional focus on how to run an efficient household, the growth of this field of economic study gravitated outside academia. By the end of the nineteenth century, part of this research was being conducted by women as a subfield of economics, which became known as Home Economics. In the US it was the only field in which women could obtain a position within economics departments (Le Tollec, 2020). Hazel Kyrk (1886–1957) would restructure the home economics department she was heading by applying the scientific method to her research on the household, and by theorizing the consumption process in her 1923 book *A Theory of Consumption*. Her PhD student Margaret G. Reid (1896–1991) focused her attention on productive activities in the household, and published *Economics of Household Production* (1934). Reid defined unpaid household production here as – in brief – those unpaid activities in the household which *can be* (but are not) replaced by market goods or paid services. Using this so-called "third person criterion" enabled her to make a clear distinction between unpaid household production and personal care. It would later enable economists to investigate productive activities conducted in the household and to develop a method to estimate the value of unpaid production in the household in monetary terms (see UNDP, 1995).

In the 1960s, Gary S. Becker (1930–2014), then an economist at the University of Chicago, picked up where Kyrk and Reid left off and applied neoclassical economic theory to explain household behavior. In his 1965 article "A Theory of the Allocation of Time," he perceived women's unpaid work in the household as productive and reasoned along the lines of Reid. Later, others like Marilyn Manser and Murray Brown (1979) and Marjorie McElroy and Mary Horney (1981) would apply game theory to explain intra-household decision-making. The application of neoclassical and game theoretical models in the analysis of household economic decision-making tended to provide explanations of hierarchical gender relations as being rational and as producing efficient outcomes.

When, in the 1970s and 1980s, greater numbers of women entered academia, including the field of economics, feminist economists started to ask questions, and to measure, conceptualize, and theorize the value and role of "domestic work," "household

production," "unpaid labor," and "care work." To achieve acknowledgment of unpaid household production, some demanded pay for
this work (see, e.g., Dalla Costa and James, 1972; Federici, 2012
[1975]). Others, like Himmelweit and Mohun (1977), Humphries
(1977), and Folbre (1982), criticized Marxian theory in what
became referred to as the domestic labor debate about the role and
gendered nature of unpaid household production and its function in
capitalism.

Feminist economists moved beyond "bashing Becker" and
gathered new data, coining new concepts and coming up with new
theories and models. Marilyn Waring (1988), for instance, developed
a method to measure the unpaid household production. Making use
of time–use surveys (TUS) and an average wage per hour to assign
a monetary value to the time spent on producing goods and services
in the household (the so-called "input method"), she estimated the
amount of unpaid production by women. This research showed
that about 30–35 percent of all productive work worldwide is done
unpaid, which exposes the limits of current economic analysis that
still focuses on economic growth in terms of Gross Domestic Product
(GDP).

The United Nations Development Programme (UNDP) used the
input method in its comparison of the value of household production
in nations worldwide. The results showed that, globally, women
do 51–53 percent of all unpaid work, and that, in industrialized
countries, women tend to account for two-thirds and, in the South,
three-quarters of the unpaid working hours. Men, on the other
hand, generally conduct 66 percent of all paid work in the North
and 75 percent of all paid work in the South. Rania Antonopoulos
and Indira Hirway (2009) brought into focus the link between the
level of household production and the poverty rate in countries in
the South.

Nancy Folbre has criticized neoclassical or mainstream economic
theory for not including unpaid care work in the household in their
models, the Circular Flow Model in particular. Folbre argues (2008)
that what happens inside the household remains invisible for economists, even though, in line with Reid (1934), households produce as
well as consume. Besides contributing to the production of goods and
services, the household, according to Folbre, also produces workers,
and this production remains unpaid and unaccounted for. Besides
raising children who become workers, the production of workers also
generates positive externalities. Thus, after having been pushed out
of the sight of economists for so long, it looks like the household is
back, and moving more center stage.

Morality of the middle classes

Going back to the early days of political economy, to when the rise of the new middle class became increasingly evident, we are looking at a time period during which there was a lot of social turmoil. The old moral regime supported by the aristocracy and the Roman Catholic Church came under pressure as new forms of production emerged. Middle-class or bourgeois men opened up a new space where "men were equal" and where their debates were based on rational arguments and empirical research. Although in early Enlightenment France it was women of the aristocratic class who created these spaces at their dinner tables, they themselves were excluded from the academies where scholars and artists presented their work and explored the latest scientific discoveries, philosophies, and moral considerations. This newly emerging morality that evolved and accommodated the experience of bourgeois men would become part and parcel of the new science of political economy.

Political economy, and later economics, has always had a complicated relationship with moral reasoning, with explicit or implicit judgments about what is right and what is wrong. Aiming to be a "real" science, most political economists and economists tried to stay away from claims about, for instance, what a preferable income and wealth distribution would look like. The moral content of economics was and continues to be a highly contested topic. From the early days of political economy, however, female economic writers contributed to the debates about the newly emerging morality, reflecting on their own experiences, articulating their views, presenting their moral philosophies and critiques on contemporary economic ideas. Let us meet some of the women who made such contributions in France and England.

Émilie du Châtelet (1706–49) – her full name was Gabrielle Émilie le Tonnelier de Breteuil, Marquise du Châtelet – grew up in the highest echelons of French aristocracy to become a natural philosopher, famous mathematician, physicist, essayist, and the French translator of Bernard Mandeville's *The Fable of the Bees* (1714). Over the course of her life, she engaged in various academic debates, among which were those on the origin of fire, the morality of pursuing happiness, and commercial society more broadly. She frequented dinners in Paris and hosted her own gatherings in Cirey, her husband's country house. Her salons were attended by aristocrats and bourgeois, philosophers and artists. Judith Zinsser (2006), du Châtelet's biographer, describes her life at Cirey and the community of prominent mathematicians and philosophers she brought together. In the conversations during gatherings, dinners, and walks, people such as the mathematician Pierre Louis Maupertuis, the famous novelist, playwright, and philosopher Voltaire, salon host Madame de Graffigny, and the Italian philosopher Francesco Algarotti reported on their studies of nature and mathematics, the laws of nature, and the right to happiness. As in other salons where political issues came to the table and "*le querelle du femme*" (the woman question) was discussed, those present often critiqued the status quo and those in power, even at the risk of receiving a "*lettre du cachet*" that would send them to prison. Voltaire and Diderot, among others, experienced that more than once (Zinsser, 2006).

When Bernard Mandeville (1670–1733) claimed that Christian moral behavior is not a good basis for a flourishing economy, but instead would probably mean the end of it, du Châtelet was intrigued. Mandeville, a doctor born in Leiden, the Netherlands, who lived in Scotland, made the daring point that you cannot have it both ways; that is, a population of all good people living by the teachings of the Bible and, at the same time, a thriving economy. His poem *The Fable of the Bees, or, Private Vices, Publick Benefits* (first published in 1705, and as a book in 1714) caused a shockwave in intellectual circles. Here was an educated man, who claimed that private vices – like greed, indulging in luxury, drinking, etc. – are actually public benefits, as they are the basis of a thriving economy. His poem was widely read and became hugely popular, causing a ripple effect all over England and beyond.

Du Châtelet decided to translate Mandeville's poem into French, as, in her words, "it is, I believe, the best book of ethics ever written, that is to say, the one that most leads men to the true source of the feelings of which they abandon themselves almost without examining them" (Zinsser, 2009: 50) In her article on this translation of Mandeville's poem, Felicia Gottman (2011) mentions that du Châtelet did much more than just translate this text and that "transformation" would be a better term to describe what she does with Mandeville's poem. Her own philosophical stance, according to Gottman, was informed by the ancient Greek philosophers Epicurus and Lucretius, who had claimed that man by nature becomes a social being by loving a woman and having a family, and by living in mutual dependence with his neighbors. Mandeville, on the other hand, considered man first and foremost an autonomous and solitary creature, who is oftentimes driven by his passions. These passions were seen by Mandeville in a negative light. In her translation and comments, du Châtelet shifted the balance in Mandeville's reasoning, reimagining humans as capable of rational reasoning and of seeing passions as a positive and necessary part of being human. Her ideas about a secular ethics would inspire Voltaire's work as well. Du Châtelet and Voltaire were involved in an intimate relationship for a period of time, which is how most people first learn about and are introduced to Émilie du Châtelet.

In "transforming" Mandeville's text, du Châtelet stood in a broader tradition. Women writers often engaged in translating academic texts; in addition to this, they would write their own introductions, and many would also provide comments on the translation itself, expressing their personal views. In her introduction to Mandeville's text, du Châtelet addresses both the role of the translator of a work of genius, and also gender as being a possible issue for some. In the Translator's Preface, which is as beautifully written as it is critical, du Châtelet claims her voice and the right to contribute to scientific reasoning and to further develop her capacity to think: "I feel the full weight of prejudice that excludes us [women] so universally from the sciences, this being one of the contradictions of this world, which has always astonished me, as there are great countries whose laws allow us to decide their destiny, but none where we are brought up to think" (Zinsser, 2009: 48).

Besides a comment on the Bible, du Châtelet also wrote *Discours sur le bonheur* (*Discourse on Happiness*) (2009 [1779]) in which she elaborated her views on a secular ethics (see also Kuiper and Springer, 2013; Zinsser, 2006). Implicitly contradicting the teachings of the Roman Catholic Church, du Châtelet shares Mandeville's recognition of the importance of passions and the pursuit of happiness in one's life. The *Discourse* is an intriguing essay in which the author starts out making a set of rational arguments for the right to live a happy life, followed by some instructions of how to achieve happiness and arguments about the importance of love. The text ends in what can be read as a reflection on her relationship with Voltaire.

Du Châtelet's major work, however, was the translation of Newton's *Philosophiæ Naturalis Principia Mathematica* (1687), or the *Principia* in short, into French. As this work contained complex mathematical arguments, no French translation had yet become available. Where others tried and failed, du Châtelet completed the work, while pregnant with her second daughter. Zinsser (2006) recounts the pressure du Châtelet was under to finish it in time. Time was limited, since du Châtelet, informed by her doctor, knew for a while that there was little chance that she would survive having a second child. She completed the work just days before dying in childbirth in 1749. Her contribution to the Enlightenment and to a new bourgeois perception of morality that would come to be part of the foundation of political economy remained, was lost sometime in the nineteenth century, only to be recovered in the twenty-first century.

The debate on a secular ethics, or the new morality of commercial society, also took place on the other side of the Channel. In Scotland, an important center of the Enlightenment movement, David Hume (1711–76) published *A Treatise of Human Nature* (1739). He was known as an atheist, which prevented him from ever holding an academic position (Carlyle, 1973). Francis Hutcheson (1694–1746), Adam Smith's predecessor at the University of Glasgow, stressed the tendency in human beings to engage in benevolent actions. The second part of his *An Inquiry into the Original of our Idea of Beauty and Virtue* (2004 [1726]) addressed "the moral good and evil" and described benevolence as a driving motive in human behavior. These discussions were all part of the larger debate on "the nature of man" that evolved around David Hume at the time. Although they did not have access to academic institutions, women writers made substantial contributions to these debates anyway. Elizabeth Montagu (1718–1800), for example, critiqued and compared Shakespeare's and Voltaire's works and the morals ingrained in them, deciding – of course – in favor of Shakespeare. So, who was this Elizabeth Montagu?

Elizabeth Robinson was born into a gentry family in Yorkshire in 1718 and was the older sister of Sarah Robinson Scott, author of *A Description of Millennium Hall* (1762). Elizabeth was a smart, spirited young woman who obtained most of her education from her grandfather, a librarian at the University of Cambridge (Kuiper and Robles-García, 2012). In her early twenties, she married money: the 54-year-old landowner and scholar Edward Montagu, owner of several coalmines and large estates. Elizabeth Montagu would become a well-known member of London society. Until a few decades ago, we only knew her as the Queen of the Bluestockings. The Bluestocking Society was a group of women and a few men who gathered over dinner to discuss culture, politics, and their writings. After the death of her husband in 1776, Elizabeth took over the management of the coalmines and estates, which she ran successfully for the rest of her life; indeed, so successfully that, at her death, she was the richest woman in England.

Elizabeth Montagu wrote a few essays that brought her literary and academic recognition; her main work was an *Essay on the Writings and Genius of Shakespear*, published in 1769. Her arguments go back to Epicurus, the ancient Greek philosopher (and yes, the same philosopher who influenced Émilie du Châtelet), who was also popular in cultured circles in London at the time. Montagu is merciless in her criticism of Voltaire, French's most famous and respected philosopher and playwright. According to Montagu (1769), his "translations often, and ... criticism still oftener, prove he did not perfectly understand the Words of the Author; and therefore, it is certain he could not enter into its Meaning." She counterpointed Shakespeare's historical approach to drama, the wide range of characters that figure in his plays, and his use of language, to the French theatric tradition in which, according to Montagu, the characters used eloquent but often pompous rhetoric and the historical accounts tended to be romanticized. Her daring essay caused a diplomatic row between England and France. It also brought her an invitation from the Académie Française to attend one of their meetings (on the balcony – as a woman she did not have full access) during which her essay was read out (Kuiper and Robles-García, 2012).

Montagu stressed particularly Shakespeare's extraordinary ability to let the audience sympathize with his main characters, rich or poor. She did this against a background in which sympathy was a widely discussed concept and the authority on the topic was Adam Smith. The two had met on a trip to Scotland in 1766 and both had pleasant memories of their conversations, but they did not keep in contact.

At that point in time, Smith had already completed his work on morality, the result of his years of teaching moral philosophy to the students (all male) at Glasgow University. It was his perception of moral behavior that precedes in terms of both time and argument his *Wealth of Nations* (1976 [1776]). In his *Theory of Moral Sentiments* (1984 [1759]), Smith describes and reconstructs the process through which individual middle-class men and boys develop self-consciousness and begin to achieve independent moral standing, and thus obtain the right to moral judgment and decision-making. Smith conceptualizes this process as an internal and rational process in which sympathy, or the ability to place oneself in another person's shoes, plays a crucial part, as does "the impartial spectator," the imaginary independent bystander through whose eyes one can reflect on one's own behavior. Smith saw sympathy as the means for the individual to obtain insight into his own passions and to understand the behavior of other humans, or not – in the latter case passing a negative judgment. To make a well-based judgment, the individual would need to fully identify with the impartial spectator. In the absence of God and the Bible, the individual had to imagine how an impartial spectator would look at any given situation and then take that judgment into account when assessing his own behavior and that of the other in the situation, and thus be guided in deciding what to do. By identifying fully with the impartial spectator, the individual could also obtain a strong sense of self-command and suppress his personal passions, particularly his fears and anger. Women do not play a role in this treatise on moral behavior and only incidentally figure as foil for Smith's arguments on the development of the moral behavior of men.

In articulating his moral philosophy, Smith applied and defined a specific conceptualization of masculinity. Both Stewart Justman (1993) and I (Kuiper, 2003) have analyzed Smith's *Theory of Moral Sentiments* as a gendered text, a text that is structured by a specific definition of masculinity and femininity. Justman sees Smith's reasoning as an attempt to retain male autonomy in the context of the emerging commercial society, which was generally perceived as feminine. Applying a psychological framework, I describe Smith's reasoning throughout his book as a way to construct a masculine identity by identification with an imaginary father. For Smith, who never met his father since he died a few months before his son was born, it is the identification with the impartial spectator that provides a man with the moral authority to make decisions: "The man of real constancy and firmness, the wise and just man who has been thoroughly bred in the great school of self-command ... He does not merely affect the sentiments of the impartial spectator. He really adopts them. He almost identifies himself with, he almost becomes himself that impartial spectator, and scarce even feels but as that great arbiter of his conduct directs him to feel" (1984 [1759]: 146–7)

Although Smith's *Theory of Moral Sentiments* is an impressive account of the process through which men develop a conscience, the perception of this process is limited to modern standards, and women play hardly any role in the book. It is, nevertheless, Smith's understanding of human nature and his perception of masculinity or "manhood" that would become ingrained in political economy as the moral basis for economic decision-making – or rational choice, which is how individual economic behavior came to be defined. In the context of Smith's *Theory of Moral Sentiments*, women were neither considered rational nor legally able to make contracts (see, e.g., Folbre, 2009).

Smith's book found its way across the Channel where it was widely read in intellectual circles in France. A leading *salonnière* in Paris, Sophie de Grouchy de Condorcet (1764–1822), translated the treatise into French, and this became the standard French translation for the next two centuries. Like Émilie du Châtelet's comments on Mandeville's *Fable of the Bees*, Sophie de Grouchy articulated criticism on the text she worked on, and these were added as a set of eight letters to the 1798 edition of her translation. These letters contain remarkable comments by a central figure in French society at the time, but it would take until 2008 for them to be fully translated into the English language (see Brown, 2008).

De Grouchy started her work on the *Theory of Moral Sentiments* after the death of her husband, the famous philosopher and mathematician Nicolas Caritat, Marquis de Condorcet. Sophie de Grouchy de Condorcet organized her salons and befriended radical thinkers such as Thomas Paine, whose letters and speeches she also translated into French. After the French Revolution broke out in 1789 and turned sour a few years later, her husband fled persecution, and moved to live in hiding. De Grouchy visited him in secret and they discussed his work on *Sketch for a Picture of the Historical Progress of the Human Mind* (published posthumously in 1822). After nine months of hiding, Marquis de Condorcet was arrested in 1794; he died in his cell a few months later (Brown, 2008). Sophie de Grouchy was thirty years old at the time, and it was in the years that followed that she focused her attention on translating Adam Smith's treatise on moral behavior.

In her *Letters on Sympathy* (1798), de Grouchy entered into a conversation with her brother-in-law, P. J. G. Cabanis, about Smith's ideas on the origins and nature of moral behavior and her own views on political economy. She criticizes Smith for not fully seeing his conceptualization of sympathy through. In her view, sympathy is not only a rational process of the imagination, but also has a physical basis; she describes the physical response and connection from one human to all other beings – men, women, children, and animals. Where Smith stops short of discussing policy implications in his *Theory of Moral Sentiments*, de Grouchy, a social reformer and feminist, points out that society should design its institutions in such a way that, instead of normalizing self-interested behavior, behavior based on sympathy should be supported by the way institutions are built. Social institutions, according to her, are built on the presumption of self-interested behavior, thereby supporting and condoning such behavior, which makes it hard to pursue a life of merit and sincerity. De Grouchy ends her last letter, Letter VIII, with a striking and timely attack on social institutions that create and reproduce class and other social divides, and argues that "by means of the unnatural needs institutions have created, they have weakened a powerful motive that can lead to upright conduct, namely the lure of domestic tranquility" (1798: 181).

Although constrained, due to their gender, women like Émilie du Châtelet, Elizabeth Montagu, and Sophie de Grouchy de Condorcet had the means and support enabling them to write, get their work published, and receive acknowledgment. Elizabeth Montagu may have provoked substantial criticism because of her outgoing personality, but her wealth and connections provided her with opportunities to make substantial contributions to cultured life in London and to the communities on her estates. For most women writers, however, including economic writers, life looked rather different. Some self-taught intellectuals, like Mary Hays (1759–1843), raised their voice against the gender hierarchy and the dark sides of capitalism that brought moral decay to thousands of women. Hays spoke from an economic and political position that was impacted by economic insecurity and poverty. Speaking to the better selves of those in power, she wrote an *Appeal to the Men of Great Britain on Behalf of Women* (1798), arguing forcefully that women had little or no possibility of pursuing their ambitions and improving their own economic situation. She argued that women faced a limited set of professions that were, therefore, overcrowded and thus underpaid. As a result, "want of fortune, and want of appropriate employment, leave them open to the attempts of those who can afford to bribe them from the paths of virtue" (1798: 279). Hays is referring here to the many women who ended up so destitute that prostitution was the only way they could earn a living for themselves and their children. She stresses that the behavior of such women was driven by dire circumstances rather than by "moral weakness," and she argues that, given their financial circumstances, these women were forced to pursue their economic self-interest in this way. Middle-class political economists, however, neglected these women and their circumstances and failed to include them in their academic economic theorizing, limiting themselves to making moral judgments and rejecting alternative arguments, such as those presented by Mary Hays.

Maria Edgeworth (1768–1849), a contemporary of Hays, lived in better circumstances. She received a decent education and her social environment provided her with support and acknowledgment of her writing. Edgeworth wrote first with her father on education matters, and later, on her own, a number of novels. Famous for her writing and experienced in managing her father's estate, the circle of people around the political economist David Ricardo (1772–1823), including Thomas Malthus (1766–1834), James Mill (1773–1836), and Jane Haldimand Marcet (1769–1858) (Heilbroner, 1999 [1981]: 86; Kern, 1998), opened up to her. Edgeworth engaged in an ongoing discussion and correspondence with Ricardo on the causes of rent increases, which she saw as based on lack of innovation in agricultural methods and mismanagement by landlords. Her most famous work, *Castle Rackrent* (1800), contains an entertaining story about the shift in culture from the patriarchal, agricultural setting, in which landlords had a moral obligation to their tenants, to a world in which relations became impersonal, and in which profit-seeking and personal enrichment became more important than moral obligations. Edgeworth describes here the era in which landlords left their estates to go and entertain themselves in cities like Edinburgh, Glasgow, and London, appointing stewards in their absence. Often, these stewards, while their boss was away, would suppress and exploit the tenants and even manage to keep large parts of the revenues for themselves. In other words, it was a world where economic relations ceased to be modeled after the family, but became rational, transactional, and driven by self-interest and the pursuit of profits. Although an insightful description of the changing economic relations and morals of her time, *Castle Rackrent* did not address the shifts in gender relations that were part of this process.

The role of implicit moral and value judgments in economic theory was dealt with in various way by economists. Jeremy Bentham (1748–1832), for example, aimed in his *Introduction to the Principles of Morals and Legislation* (1789) to stop political economists from making moral judgments by adopting, instead, quantitative reasoning. On the other hand, economists like John Stuart Mill (1806–73) described political economy as partly a positive and partly a normative science. Neoclassical economists like William Stanley Jevons (1835–82) and Alfred Marshall (1842–1924) explicitly claimed that their science was, or at least should be, a positivist one. According to Marshall, "political economy or economics is a study of mankind in the ordinary business of life" (1890: 1) and economics should be based on observations, definitions, classification, induction, and deduction to "reach the knowledge of the interdependence of economic phenomena" (1890: 29). By basing themselves on rational reasoning and facts, economists were able to provide answers to policy issues and analyses of topics that were the subject of heated political debates, claiming scientific status and objectivity for their studies and solutions.

Other economists pointed out the particular morality implicit in economic concepts and theories that had long been taken for granted by economists. Women economic writers and economists can predominantly be found in this last group (see Madden, 2002). Feminist economists in particular criticized the implicit gender notions, male bias, and other value judgments that structure economic theorizing. Sandra Harding, a feminist philosopher, published "Can Feminist Thought Make Economics More Objective?" (1995) in the first issue of the *Feminist Economics* journal. She made the point that value neutrality based on shared values do not make for an objective statement. The fact that these values are shared only makes them invisible. One way to counter the invisibility of shared values is by bringing in a wider and more diverse set of voices, as this introduces different views that will contest – and as such make visible – the formerly shared values. Taking a feminist perspective, for instance, brings to light patriarchal values implicit in mainstream economic thinking.

2

Power, Agency, and Property Rights

Introduction

The emergence of political economy was closely linked to the emergence and growth of industrial society in England. Within the social sciences though, political economy was a late arrival. Trade, money, profits, and interests were not considered topics of serious academic study, as merchants and bankers had not been highly respected in society. This started to change in the second half of the eighteenth century in England when industrialization took off. Joseph Schumpeter (1883–1950), economist and historian of economic thought, identified three founders of political economy: Cesare Bonesana, marchese di Beccaria (1738–94), Anne-Robert-Jacques Turgot, baron de l'Aulne (1727–81), and Adam Smith (1723–90). These men were, as Schumpeter indicates, strikingly similar in terms of background and personal interests; they read widely and had a broad vision, they demonstrated "single minded devotion to the duty in hand," and they stood outside the realm of politics and business (1954: 238). These well-educated, middle- and upper-class men, from Italy, France, and Scotland respectively, showed a considerable unity of ideas, which they developed together with many other men with similar interests in the decades running up to 1776, the date of publication of Smith's *Wealth of Nations* (Groenewegen, 2002: 5): "All three economists regarded the reproduction and increase of wealth as the primary objective of their inquiries." Where Xenophon discussed in detail the distribution between husband and wife as the first division of labor that makes specialization possible, Beccaria, Turgot, and Smith started from the experience of men – men as the producers of wealth. These early political economists coined and developed their concepts, theories, and principles within an academic environment, in which women were notoriously absent; this absence was not incidental, but a foundational part of the design of academic institutions (see e.g. Keller, 1985; Noble, 1992; Schiebinger, 1989).

Universities all over Europe were built – sometimes literally – on the ruins of Roman Catholic monasteries. The universities of Oxford and Cambridge primarily educated men to become clergy. Cambridge, for instance, required its fellows who lived on campus to remain unmarried, or else to leave, and Oxford prohibited women from accessing the premises until far into the twentieth century. Similar to the French salons and modeled after the older scientific societies in France and England, men interested in economic debates started societies for, for instance, "*les économists*" in Switzerland and "*les philosophes*" in France. England also had its clubs, as did Scotland. Glasgow and Edinburgh were full of them, providing social spaces outside the otherwise small and crowded living quarters; they ranged widely in kind and the rules they set for their members. Rules – often awkward and humorous in kind – defined who had access to these clubs using names such as "the Hodge Podge Club," "the Accidental Club," and "the Beefsteak Club" (Strang, 1856). Being essentially fraternities, "No women allowed" was another of those rules. Adam Smith, who lived both in Edinburgh and in Glasgow, was very involved in attending and even starting clubs, such as the Poker Club (Ross, 1995), all of which excluded women. The political economic discussions between legislators, merchants, and academics reflected the absence of women and did not reckon their economic behavior or interests to be worth considering, or even to be within the limits of the field.

In this chapter, we will focus on the economic writing of women who speak out against patriarchy and the hierarchical notions of gender that were structuring political economic concepts. Gendered conceptualizations of power, agency, and property rights referred at the time differently to women than to men, while non-Western people were characterized as "other," as "savages," and as "primitive," which legitimized treating these people as less than human. With the basic concepts and principles in place, political economy conceptualized economic relations in ways that accommodated the perspective and interests of white middle-class Western men, in whose service the field developed further.

The power of economic reasoning

As scientific reasoning, research, and results increasingly took the place of institutionalized religion, the claim to scientific truth, the use of the laws of nature, and the development of new technologies all provided academic men with increasing levels of social and political respect. At the same time, this gave them greater access to power. Traditional bulwarks of scholastic knowledge, such as the Church of England, dominated by the universities of Oxford and Cambridge, were no longer at the center of this new science. Dissenting academies such as Leyden and Utrecht in the Netherlands, and the universities of Edinburgh and Glasgow in Scotland, where Isaac Newton's philosophy was taught, provided a more open learning environment. The latter were the centers of the Scottish Enlightenment.

Women writers did speak out for the right to engage in scientific research and study. A few generations after Anna Maria van Schuurman, the seventeenth-century Dutch genius discussed in Chapter 1, Anne-Thérèse, marquise de Lambert (1647–1733), then a central figure in early Parisian salon life, who opened her salon doors to bourgeois intellectuals and aristocrats in 1710, spoke in favor of a woman's right to engage in scientific inquiry. De Lambert, a writer herself, published the philosophical essay *New Reflections on the Fair Sex* (1729), in which she develops a philosophy of love and makes a similar point to that made earlier by van Schuurman, namely that women's upbringing and minds are particularly suited to scientific reasoning and study. De Lambert claimed:

> Those who have thought fit to level their pens against women, have pretended, that the action of the mind, which consists of contemplating an object, was much less perfect in the female sex; and that because the sensation or impulse, which governs them, distracts their minds, and bears them along with it. Attention is certainly necessary; it makes light spring up as it were; brings the ideas of the mind nearer, and places them within our reach: but in women, ideas arise spontaneously, and range themselves in order, which is done rather by sensation, or the intuitive faculty, than reflection: nature itself argues for them, and saves them the labour of forming long series of arguments. (1729: 22)

De Lambert's book on the education of both boys and girls, *Letters to her Son and Daughter* (1749), was widely read and even found its way into Adam Smith's library. These voices, however, were not reflected in the early science of political economy. An exception in this respect was Jeremy Bentham (1748–1832), founder of utilitarianism and advisor to many governments, who was a free thinker about sexual practices and a feminist (Williford, 1975). He famously argued for the greatest happiness for the greatest number of individuals: "A measure of government ... may be said to be conformable to or dictated by the principle of utility, when in like manner the tendency which it has to augment the happiness of the community is greater than any which it has to diminish it" (1789: 8). Bentham also argued for animal rights, for full gender equality, and for women's right to vote, acknowledging that the reason women had few rights was because they lacked representation and access to the legislative process. He himself, however, when in a position to do so, refrained from providing women with constitutional rights because, in his assessment, "the prepossession against their admission, is at present too general, and too intense to afford any chance in favour of a proposal for their admission" (Bentham 1827, *Constitutional Code*, quoted in Williford, 1975: 169).

Early political economy treatises, such as those by Adam Smith, Jeremy Bentham and David Ricardo, were written for legislators in a language they would understand and could use. The lack of attention to women and their economic issues and interests was, at least initially, not accidental but constituent of a society in which women were controlled by men. In the debates over men's rights to liberty and freedom, women's rights were articulated, but only as an afterthought. Sarah Chapone (1699–1764) had already signaled the serious problems that English laws posed for women. Published anonymously in 1735, but identified by twentieth-century feminist scholars as having been written by Chapone, *The Hardships of the English Laws in Relation to Wives* argued and pleaded with legislators, warning them about the profound effects of the emerging new regime of manmade legislation and natural philosophy:

> But since some Men by then extraordinary Flights of Conceit have thought fit to assail the Almighty, and are endeavouring to bring over the rest of their Sex, as fast as they can, it is Time for Us to look about us, and to use all justifiable Methods to provide against the impending Danger: For since we seem to be hastening into a *State of Nature,* in which there can be no appeal but to the Laws of our Country, and the Authority of the Scripture is going down, which directs a Man erect a private Court of Equity in his own Breast, what shall restrain the Strong from oppressing the *Weak,* if the Laws of our Country do not, they being in such a State the only established Rules of Society? (Chapone, 1735: 5; emphasis in original)

In this text, Chapone lays out in great detail the vulnerable situation of married women, who lacked protection under the law. She submits a complaint that consists of three main articles:

I   That the Estate of Wives is more disadvantageous than Slavery itself.

II   That Wives may be made Prisoners for Life at the Discretion of their Domestick Governors, whose Power, as we at present apprehend, bears no Manner or Proportion to that Degree of Authority, which is vested in any other Set of Men in *England*. ...

III That Wives have no Property, neither *in their own Persons, Children,* or *Fortunes*.

(1735: 7; emphasis in original)

Outspoken from a young age, and influenced by feminist writer Mary Astell's (1666–1731) pamphlet, *Some Reflections upon Marriage* (1700), Chapone took her argument further in her polemic on women's legal rights. Joanna Rostek (2021) analyzes the economic content of *Hardships of the English Laws*. She points out that Chapone brings her concerns about the deterioration of the economic position of women to the fore, especially with respect to their freedoms and the effect of discrimination on their ability to engage in paid work. Chapone states with a sense of urgency the general impacts of economic dependence of married women on their husbands. In addition, she exposed with a clear eye the double standards where sexual rights were concerned, the male bias in custody regulations, and the vulnerable position of rich heiresses, who, with the new laws, lost control over their inheritance (Rostek, 2021: 103).

Chapone did not live to see the day when William Blackstone (1723–80) published his *Commentaries on the Laws of England* (1765–69), in which he articulated the rights of married women in terms of "coverture." Coverture meant that, once married, the wife would become "a feme covert"; in other words:

> By marriage the husband and wife are one person in the law: that is, the very being or legal existence of the woman is suspended during the marriage, or at least, is incorporated and consolidated into that of the husband: under whose wing, protection, and cover, she performs every thing. (Blackstone 1765: 430; quoted in Rostek 2021: 90)

This indeed meant that women became excluded from all legislative language, laws, and policies, as they were assumed to be represented by their husband, father, or son, and, upon marriage, they lost all agency before the law.

The process of the redefinition of property rights described by Chapone was referred to, variously, by Adam Smith, Karl Marx, Rosa Luxemburg, and Hannah Arendt, in terms such as "accumulation by dispossession" and "primitive accumulation" (see Harvey, 2003; Wood, 1999; Perelman, 2000). David Harvey identified a range of examples of what he refers to as "accumulation by dispossession," including commodification and privatization of land; the conversion of various forms of property rights (common, collective, state, etc.) into exclusive private property rights; the commodification of labor power; the colonial, neocolonial, and imperial processes of appropriation of assets (including natural resources); the monetization of exchange and taxation; the slave trade; and the credit system (2003: 145). The accumulation by dispossession that took place in England as a result of marriage laws may well have contributed directly to the development of a money economy, "and to the development of complex legal and financial instruments to go with a money economy," as Amy Louise Erickson has argued (2005: 2). This and other processes of dispossession, such as slavery and the enclosure movement, provided industrial society, or capitalism, with the initial capital that made further accumulation possible.

As men dominated legal power – whether it was as landowner or clergyman, or as part of the newly emerging middle class – women of all classes lacked leverage. Elizabeth Montagu could control and manage her lands, houses, and mines – as we saw in Chapter 1 – but only due to a special arrangement made by her husband during his lifetime. Similarly, Émilie du Châtelet could invite her intellectual friends over, but only due to the leniency of her husband.

Olympe de Gouges (1748–93) was a French revolutionary, playwright, and author of many political tracts, among which was her *Déclaration des Droits de la Femme et de la Citoyenne* [*Declaration of the Rights of Women and of the Female Citizen*] (1791), which she addressed to Queen Marie-Antoinette (Schröder, 1989). Born and raised as Marie Gouze, the daughter of a butcher, she was actually the illegitimate daughter of Marquis Le Franc de Pompignan and Anne-Olympe Moiset. In her declaration, de Gouges outlines a list of demands that sound radical even today. She demanded the right to vote for women – a year before Mary Wollstonecraft would do the same in 1792 – as well as the right to get a divorce, access to professions for women, and equal wages for women and men:

Article I: Woman is born free and lives equal to man in her rights. Social distinctions can be based only on the common utility. ...

Article XIII: For the support of the public force and the expense of administration, the contributions of woman and men are equal, she shares all the duties [*corvées*] and all the painful tasks, therefore, she must have the same share in the distribution of positions, employment, office, honors, and jobs [*industrie*] ...

Article XVII: Property belongs to both sexes whether united or separate, for each it is an inviable and sacred right, no one can be deprived of it, since it is the true patrimony of nature, unless the legally determined public need obviously dictates it, and then only with a just and prior indemnity. (1791: 92)

De Gouges became victim to the Revolution. She ended up in prison and, after a farcical trial, died by guillotine at the hands of the revolutionaries. The French Revolution did not bring French women full citizenship. In the end, the National Assemblée confirmed the civil rights of the middle classes, but for men only. The exclusion of married women from citizenship would be affirmed in the Code Napoléon and thus become a foundational aspect of many legislative systems in Europe.

It is Mary Wollstonecraft (1759–97) who raised her voice in England and claimed voting rights for women. In 1792, Wollstonecraft published, in response to Edward Burke's *Reflections on the Revolution in France* (1790), her most famous book, *A Vindication of the Rights of Woman*, which makes an extended case for the improvement of the education of women. This book had a huge impact, and was widely read and talked about; here was a woman demanding the right to vote! Wollstonecraft is mostly known for being a political activist and novelist, but, as we will see in later chapters, she also addressed economic issues head on. She had traveled to France to join the Revolution early on, but returned to England after becoming disappointed by the turn the Revolution took. Her independent lifestyle was widely critiqued as scandalous, especially after her husband, William Godwin, posthumously published her biography (1798).

As Sarah Chapone had foreseen, natural law provided scientific reasoning – and political economy more particularly – with a new bedrock to build upon, a foundation, separate from religious dogma and political intrigue. The early political economists, especially in France, placed themselves outside or even above the political debates of the times, claiming a basis of rational reasoning and natural law. Thus, political economy, while taking the sexual division in the household as a given, and building on the ideology of separated spheres, focused on what was considered the male realm and thereby naturalized the production and distribution of goods as "the economy." Placing white middle-class men at the center of attention, political economy focused on the labor of male workers and the exchanges between men, who were considered basically equal, while using language that excluded women and children and portrayed nonwhite people as "the Other." As such, political economists provided the language, concepts, and theories to explain the increase of the wealth of nations as a natural process and to design policies to further economic growth. Taking the dispossession of women, workers, and enslaved people as a given, political economy was silent on the processes of primitive accumulation that were, nevertheless, part and parcel of the industrialization process. The new institution of property rights articulated the relation between "Man" and "Nature" in binary terms as a relationship between the owner and the "things" he owned as commodities (goods he has the rights to both use and sell). Capital, land (at home and in the colonies), and labor (in factories, mines, and in the household) were thus made available for use and contributed to the accumulation of capital in Western Europe and, later, the US. The cost and damage done to women, children, colonized people, and the natural environment were not considered or taken into account. As we go on to listen to women's voices in this process, we will notice that their stories differed substantially from those articulated by the men of the emerging middle class in England and Scotland.

Women's economic agency

Eighteenth-century British women, married women in particular, lacked political power as well as economic agency; they could neither make contracts by themselves nor inherit property, and they were not perceived as rational by most men. Pursuing self-interest, regarded by political economists as a "natural" behavioral feature of men, was, on the other hand, considered distinctly unnatural and unattractive in women (Folbre, 2009).

Adam Smith's *Wealth of Nations* (1776), like his *Theory of Moral Sentiments* (1984 [1759]), hardly mentioned women, and where women do appear in the text, they lack substantive economic agency. Smith perceived services like those of artists, doctors, and civil servants as nonproductive. While applying the gendered division of public and private (see Rendall, 1987; Shah, 2006), he did not perceive a wife's services in the household or a mother's contribution to the education of her children as productive either. Smith's "Introduction and Plan of the Work" that precedes the main text of *Wealth of Nations* provides some interesting language about what, in his view, determined the wealth of a nation: (a) the labor available in a nation, i.e. the skill and dexterity of useful labor put to work, and (b) the "proportion between the number of those who are employed in useful labour, and that of those who are not so employed" (1976 [1776]: 10). Those "who do not labour at all" are thus perceived by Smith as being a burden for those who are engaged in useful labor.

Although works by Smith, Malthus, Ricardo, and other political economists focused on the exchange that takes place between men – laborers, farmers, merchants, etc. – this did not mean that in real life there were no women in these trades. About 25 percent of English women were active as, for example, inn-keepers, printers, and weavers (Pinchbeck, 1930). With the exception of their work as spinners – basic to the wool industry, which was basic to England's industrialization process – in general women's economic contributions were hardly, if ever, acknowledged by these political economists, who followed the legal language of the times, denying married women all agency including the right to enter into contracts independently.

Priscilla Wakefield (1751–1832), a contemporary of Jeremy Bentham and Thomas Malthus, published the pamphlet *Reflections on the Present Condition of the Female Sex; with Suggestions for Its Improvement* (1798). Wakefield had her own experiences with earning money and competition in the labor market. As her husband had a tendency to sink the family's funds into fruitless investments, she had taken up writing for a living, covering a wide range of topics; she produced the first ever textbook on botany and published various children's books. *Reflections* starts with a critical remark about the representation of women in Smith's work; Wakefield refers to the preface to the *Wealth of Nations*:

[It] is asserted by Doctor Adam Smith, that every individual is a burthen upon the society to which he belongs, who does not contribute his share of productive labour for the good of the whole. The Doctor, when he lays down this principle, speaks in general terms of man, as a being capable of forming a social compact for mutual defence, and the advantage of the community at large. He does not absolutely specify, that both sexes, in order to render themselves beneficial members of society, are equally required to comply with these terms; but since the female sex is included in the idea of the species, and as women possess the same qualities as men, though perhaps in a different degree, their sex cannot free them from the claim of the public for their proportion of usefulness. (1798: 1–2)

Although both strategic and sarcastic in content, this statement on the equality of the sexes was a hard claim to make at the time. By linking her work this way to that of Smith, while critiquing Smith on a fundamental level, Wakefield used this assertion here as the very starting point for her pamphlet and the arguments she set out to make – which we will discuss in more detail in Chapter 5. Nevertheless, economists would long default to the concept of "Man" in political economy (and later in economics) as a generic concept, assuming it referred to all human beings.

Women's lack of legal and economic agency, especially when married, their background of homemaking, living with and working alongside their neighbors, and their vulnerability when standing alone may have been reasons why several women economic writers articulated the importance of community. Sarah Robinson Scott (1720–95), the younger sister of Elizabeth Montagu, lived and wrote at the border of two worlds: the feudal and the early industrial. Sarah was more withdrawn than the outgoing Elizabeth. She became a writer, publishing *A Description of Millennium Hall, and the Country Adjacent* (1762). This book tells the story of a visit to a community of women living independently from men, an ideal that was seldom attained by women in England. It describes, for instance, an infirmary and a drawing-room, as well as the inhabitants of these spaces.

> I was so filled with astonishment, at characters so new, and so curious to know by what steps women thus qualified both by nature and fortune to have the world almost at command, were brought thus to seclude themselves from it, and make as it were a new one for themselves, constituted on such very new principles from that I had hitherto lived in, that I longed to be alone with my cousin, in hopes I might from her receive some account of this wonder. (1762: 29)

Millennium Hall became the signature text of the Bluestocking Society that was led by her sister Elizabeth. Elizabeth Montagu took up Scott's idea of community, and, so to speak, ran with it, mainly in her letters. She described her estates and factories as communities of the people working there, in contrast to the factories of her colleagues in the mining industry who, in her view, were mainly in the business for profit and who were keen to exploit their workers. Later in life, Sarah Scott would herself, alongside others, found a community that was inspired by the ideas expressed in *Millennium Hall*.

Thirty years later, Clara Reeve (1729–97), also a member of the Bluestocking Society, drew another blueprint for a secular community of independent living for women in her *Plans of Education* (1792), which contained a description of a "Seminary of Female Education." These works by Montagu, Scott, and Reeve preceded those of early socialists like Robert Owen (1771–1858) and Charles Fourier (1772–1837), and would stress the importance of education, acknowledged women's agency in the economy, and started and propagated the founding of communities. Since Elizabeth Montagu, Robert Owen, and Frances Wright (1795–1852), who would start her own community in the US and will be discussed later in this chapter, were all part of the same social circles, Sarah Scott's *Millennium Hall* and Clara Reeve's *Plans of Education* may well have been an inspiration to them and other early socialists.

In general, however, the working classes and the poor did not have a voice either in politics or in business. Thomas Malthus's *Essay on Population* (1798) can be seen as mainly siding with the landowning class and expressed concerns about the rise of the middle class. In a context, in which it was out of the question for "civilized" people to refer – even in the slightest – to sexuality, pleasure, sexual attraction, or intercourse, Malthus described man, and the working man in particular, as being driven by two main biological urges: the need for food and sexual drives. He elaborated on Smith's principles of population, arguing that when wages go up above the rate of sustenance, the working class was likely to reproduce itself at a higher pace, thus bringing wages down again. To keep "the power of population" in check, Malthus suggested sexual restraint in the form of late marriages and sexual abstinence. His recognition of two main urges in man's life is addressed, however, from a male perspective, leaving it to others to articulate a female perspective on her agency in these matters (Rostek, 2021).

Political economists, among others, perceived workers as lazy, so their argument was that making them live on the verge of destitution would keep them going. Workers were not considered to be economic agents, but were like slaves in that they were seen as things for use, as commodities. David Ricardo, the economist known for his abstract reasoning in his analysis of the impact of distribution on economic growth in *The Principles of Political Economy and Taxation* (1817), mostly speaks about "labour," "rent," "capital," etc. The principles he discusses refer to male workers, as in: "Suppose two men employ one hundred men each for a year in the construction of two machines, and another man employs the same number of men in cultivating corn, ..." (1911 [1817]: 20). Though there were women working in factories and in agriculture, they were excluded from his analyses and became invisible in this process of abstraction.

William Thompson (1775–1833) and Anna Doyle Wheeler (1785–1848) critiqued utilitarianism, and James Mill in particular, in their *Appeal of One Half of the Human Race, Women, Against the Pretensions of the Other Half* (1825). They contradicted James Mill's claim that men could and should represent women assuming that this would result in "the greatest quantity of human happiness" by positing that men in England had abused their power and that women's economic interests had been vastly neglected (Nyland and Heenan, 2003; see also Madden and Persky, 2021). To achieve the identity of interests between husband and wife, political economy should move to acknowledge mutual self-interest, instead of the narrow notion of self-interest that originated in and ended with the individual. It was Mill's notion of self-interest, however, that would become applied to model the labor relations between the capitalist and the worker.

Nassau Senior (1790–1864), an economist, lawyer, and government advisor, not a progressive thinker by any stretch of the imagination, argued in one of his lectures in 1830 that workers could not have it both ways; that is to say, they could not be free and retain "the rights" of a slave. In Senior's view, a slave is entitled to food and shelter and owes his owner his labor. The "freeman," however, is free: free to sell his labor or not, with the employer having no obligation to maintain him. As they were no longer the responsibility of their owner, freemen would have to take care of themselves and enter into wage negotiations with their boss (Senior, 1830). This transition made workers responsible for their own housing and for feeding their family, with their wages set by the market. If they thought their wages were too low, they were "free" to go elsewhere. Workers thus became economic agents by selling their own labor to the highest bidder – at least that was the argument. Meet the modern labor market.

The labor activist, traveler, and writer Flora Tristan (1803–44), born of a Peruvian aristocratic father and a French mother, is a well-known historical figure in Latin America, even though she lived most of her life in France and England. Tristan spent her entire adult life writing on class issues and giving speeches to workers; she addressed them as rational people and her lectures were very popular. She was inspired by the early socialist Charles Fourier and had a vision: workers needed to form unions, set up workers' funds, and build hospitals or, even better, community buildings. Tristan died in her early forties, exhausted by traveling and lecturing.

In *The Workers' Union*, published in 1843, Tristan presents her plan to the workers; the book includes various templates for letters they could use to address the authorities. She called them to action: "Workers, you must leave behind this division and isolation as quickly as possible and march courageously and fraternally down the only appropriate path – *unity*. My union plan rests upon a broad base, and its spirit is capable of fully satisfying the moral and material needs of a great people" (1983 [1843]: 51; emphasis in original). Like various other thinkers in the early socialist movement – "utopian socialist" was the degrading name foisted upon these thinkers by Karl Marx – she also talked about women workers, and in doing so she does not hold back: "Up to now, woman has counted for nothing in human society. What has been the result of this? That the priest, the lawmaker, and the philosopher have treated her as a true *pariah*" (1983 [1843]: 76; emphasis in original). Tristan presses husbands to respect their wives and treat them well in order to bring happiness to the household:

> Knowing that his wife has rights equal to this, the husband would not treat her anymore with the disdain and scorn shown to inferiors. On the contrary, he would treat her with the respect and deference one grants to equals. Then the woman will no longer have cause for irritation; and once that is destroyed, she will no longer appear brutal, devious, grouchy, angry, exasperated, or mean. No longer considered her husband's servant at home, but his associate, friend, and companion, she will naturally take an interest in the association and do all she can to make the little household flourish. (1983 [1843]: 84)

In 1848 protests ran rampant all over Europe and in this year of revolutions workers and the middles classes rose up, dethroned kings, and extended their power. It was also the year that Karl Marx and Friedrich Engels published their *Communist Manifesto*. Marx positioned himself within political economy and claimed scientific status for his analysis of capitalism; the prediction of socialism is not political ideology or wishful thinking, according to Marx, but based on scientific analysis of the contradictions of the capitalist system. The increasing commodification of human beings and nature – turning these into things that can be used and sold through the market – is a consequence of capitalism taking its course. Socialists would argue in the years to come that the exploitation of women and children would end once socialism came about – that was the reasoning at least. Also in 1848, women in the US took things in their own hands and organized the first women's conference in Seneca Falls.

Later, the lack of economic agency of married women, including the lack of access to the labor market, was critically addressed by

Charlotte Perkins Gilman (1860–1935). Gilman was a famous American feminist, a prolific writer and columnist who applied the modern scientific notions of Darwinism to her economic analysis of the position of women in the economy. She distinguishes between the sex-relation, the biological urge to reproduce, and the race-relation, the urge to sustain humanity as a species. Gilman argues that the economic dependence of women, who married young without the ability to actively choose their life partner, was a problem, as it made young women over-sexed: "because of the economic dependence of the human female on her mate, she is modified to sex to an excessive degree" (1998 [1898]: 19–20). Gilman questioned the male wage-earner model by claiming that it was unnatural, because under the model of the male-breadwinner household women by marriage became economically dependent on their husbands for the rest of their lives.

Gilman's short story "The Yellow Wallpaper" (1892) is an account of the experience of a woman with depression caught in a web of economic dependency on men (her husband and her doctors in this case). Gilman tells the story of a young married couple in which the wife develops mental health problems – in those days often referred to as "hysteria." Her doctor and husband force her into a life of passivity and make her stay in her room as the best way to become healthy again. Instead, this treatment leads her to go mad. The lack of agency and physical exercise, the feeling of uselessness, and sheer isolation characterize the tragic stories of many of the middle- and upper-class women in Gilman's day.

After decades of struggle and winning state-by-state victories, the women's movement achieved a major coup in 1920, when women won full voting rights in the US, but it lost its focus soon after that. Alongside the fight for reproductive rights, economic topics such as the right to work, labor protection, and access to financial independence resurfaced during what became known as "the second feminist wave" of the 1960s and 1970s. It is then that women's economic writing started to be acknowledged, as feminist scholars put women center stage and claimed attention for their economic experience and economic agency. Even with a much larger female labor participation rate and with women climbing the corporate ladders, their concerns were still largely ranked as "women's issues." It would take into the 1990s and 2000s before the relevance and importance of their insights, traditions, and economic contributions to the economy, and thus to the field of economics, would start to be recognized (see, e.g., World Bank, 2001).

Property rights: Marriage as an economic institution

Adam Smith, and later Karl Marx, perceived the development of the institution of property rights as central to the distinction of stages in economic development. Industrial society, or capitalism, was based on the most complex property rights, legislative institutions, and markets for the exchange of property rights on capital, land, and labor. As we discussed earlier in this chapter, the reformulation of property rights in the 1700s into exclusive rights of men to make contracts forced women and colonized people to lose control over assets such as capital and land. The British marriage laws played a substantial role in this process, not least because these laws concerned a large part of the population.

The marriage agreement was a central contract in the lives of most women and determined their access to assets, income, wealth, and, more generally, to economic security. England was extreme, in comparison to other European countries, during the emergence of the industrialization process, in the way married women lost any property rights they may previously have had. By signing the marriage contract, women relinquished their rights to be a legal agent.

Today, the romantic perception of marriage as mostly a matter of the heart may dominate, but for aristocratic families and other people of wealth marriage has always been first and foremost about exchange: bringing a bride into the family in exchange for a fortune to be paid or received. For such families, marrying off their children was often an extension and strengthening of their social and political networks and a sensible alternative to going to war. Women economic writers evidently assigned great importance to marriage, its laws, its economic and physical impacts, and to the ways it limited the freedom of women. This was in striking contrast to male economists, who considered marriage merely part of the private realm. Moreover, these economists perceived marriage as a social institution more than an economic one, even though it played a major part in determining the distribution of resources in the household between husband, wife, and children, and between generations.

Mary Astell (1666–1731), an early feminist who was financially independent, wrote the pamphlet *Some Reflections upon Marriage* (1700). She addressed a range of aspects of marriage, analyzing its foundations and socioeconomic importance for women. In this pamphlet, Astell provides advice to married women on how to survive a lifelong connection to a man, especially those who behave nastily and violently. Ruth Perry (2005) tells us about Astell's life as an intellectual who, supported by patrons, worked with a circle of like-minded women, like Elizabeth Elstob and Lady Mary Wortley Montagu. In her analysis, Astell focused on the meaning of marriage for middle- and upper-class and aristocratic women, rather than for working-class women, who often did not marry and occasionally were sold into marriage.

Sarah Chapone, whom we met earlier, had warned that with the new marriage laws wives would have no property rights – in their own persons, in their children, or in their fortunes (1735: 7). As Chapone pointed out:

> The Laws of *England* allow a Wife no such Privilege [ensuring the wife to put a hold on (part of) the fortune of her husband]; for if a Man having no real Estate, marries a Woman with any Fortune in Money, and covenants to leave her such a Part of it at his Death, if afterwards she perceives that he designs to spend the whole in his Life-time, she cannot take any Method to prevent it, the Law allowing her no Remedy. (1735: 30; emphasis in original)

Mary Wollstonecraft, who tried to stay away from marriage in her personal life, wrote *Mary: A Fiction* (1788), about the life of a woman who is stuck in a marriage with a violent husband. The novel describes her miserable journey, in which her children are used against her and she ends up in one of the madhouses in England, a fate that befell many of her gender. At the end of her short life, Wollstonecraft married the radical philosopher William Godwin. She died days after giving birth to her daughter Mary Shelley (later, author of *Frankenstein*) at the age of thirty-eight. In *Vindication* (1792), Wollstonecraft does not so much question the marriage legislation itself; her focus is more on women's lack of education. The hierarchical character of the relation between husband and wife, an integral part of the marriage arrangement at the time – which, when forced upon a woman, Wollstonecraft considered as "legal prostitution" – made, in her view, a true and sincere relationship between husband and wife impossible (see also Rostek, 2021).

Divorce was a solution to a bad marriage that was available only to upper-class women, and even then, only in exceptional situations. Arguing for the right to divorce, Olympe de Gouges composed a new *"contrat social"* in her letter to Queen Marie-Antoinette, in which women's and men's respective rights were to be included. Her *contrat social* would protect women from the profligate behavior of men by requesting financial help from fathers and compensation for exploited and deserted women (Schröder, 1989: 78). De Gouges was part of a movement of women who supported these demands, as was Etta Palm, Baroness d'Aelders (1743–99). D'Aelders, a Dutch woman who was born as Etta Palm, had left her husband and child to go to Paris. There, she changed her name and gave herself the title of Baroness so she could function at the French Court. She built a name for herself and got involved in starting a French women's movement, and it was she who presented the argument for the right to divorce before the Assemblée Nationale Législative on 1 April 1792. When she aged and lost her beauty, which was her capital in the environment of the court, she decided to become a spy for the Dutch government at the French Court. When the French army annexed the Netherlands, d'Aelders ended up a prisoner in the Castle of Woerden. Freed in 1798, she died a few months after her release (Hardenberg, 1962). Although her battle for the right to divorce was successful, the war was lost as the right would only stand for a short amount of time: in 1804, it was killed off by the Code Napoléon.

Jean-Baptiste Say (1767–1832), a respected French economist, who was in correspondence with Thomas Malthus and David Ricardo, supported the right to divorce, which enabled husband and wife to divorce by mutual consent or on the basis of incompatibility requested by one of the partners (Forget, 1999: 99). Exploring its origin, Say considered the social order to be mainly brought about and maintained by the legislator. He shared with the English political economists the ideas that self-interested behavior is central in the economy, and that the interests of the family are represented by those of the father, stating that:

> If we set aside the interior relations between the members of a family that can be considered as forming a single individual because their interests are common, and the purely personal relationship of a man with his Creator that one can hardly consider as part of the social body, all social questions reduce to the valuations of reciprocal interests. (Quoted in Forget, 1999: 6)

Marriage was a legal contract that differed from other contracts in that one of the partners in the contract agreed to dissolve their legal agency, which enabled them to enter into the marriage contract in the first place. This was problematic in legal terms. Harriet Taylor Mill (1807–58) addressed the legal basis of marriage in "The Enfranchisement of Women" (1851). This essay was originally published under her husband's name – John Stuart Mill – and was only later ascribed to Taylor Mill (see Bodkin, 1999). John Stuart

Mill was supportive of the feminist ideas of Harriet Taylor, who was at first his longtime friend and, after the death of her husband, became his wife. After her death, when Mill was briefly a Member of Parliament, he submitted an amendment to the Second Reform Act that would loosen the property requirements for men to vote in 1867. He proposed changing the terms "man" and "men" to "person(s)," which would enable women with property to vote – but he was unsuccessful in getting this accepted.

An elaboration of the arguments published in Taylor Mill's 1851 essay, in which she reports on the Women's Rights Convention in October 1850 in Worcester, Massachusetts, was published as *The Subjection of Women* (1869) under her husband's name (see Jacobs and Payne, 1998). This book aimed to show that the principle of legal subordination of one sex to the other was wrong in itself and hindered human improvement. John Stuart Mill and Harriet Taylor Mill argued for this principle to be replaced by a principle of perfect equality. Marriage is here characterized as a remnant of primitive power relations that provide the husband with freedom and power and leave the wife as dependent on and controlled by the husband. *The Subjection of Women* compared the legal status of married women to those of slaves, pointing out that, in marriage, women are expected to obey willingly. The Mills considered women's role as mother and head of the household instead as a profession, chosen by women who married. They saw no sensible rationale for limiting the access to professions and jobs to women who did not marry, but they were concerned that married women could be forced to take up paid work by their husbands, who could then step back and enjoy a life of leisure. In his *Autobiography* (1873), John Stuart Mill acknowledges that not only *The Subjection of Women* but also many of his other works, including his *Principles of Political Economy* (1848), which became the most important textbook in the field for decades to come, were inspired by conversations with his wife.

Socialist thinkers like Friedrich Engels, in his *The Origin of the Family, Private Property, and the State* (1884), and August Bebel, in *Women in the Past, Present & Future* (1879), provided an overview of the institution of marriage in various cultures over the centuries, taking an analytical and therein radical approach to this institution. For both Engels and Bebel, the patriarchal marriage contract was an essential constitutive element of capitalist society. The relation between husband and wife was, in their view, comparable to the exploitative relation between the owner of capital and the worker. These relations would change and become more open and equal with the emergence of socialism, though. Feminists in the socialist movement, however, including many women economic writers and economists, were, if anything, less and less willing to wait and endure the neglect and denial of women's demands in the meantime.

During the second half of the nineteenth century, the rights of married women in Britain improved. Barbara Leigh Smith Bodichon (1827–91) and the Langham Place group fought for and were instrumental in getting the Married Women's Property Bill brought before Parliament in 1857, though it was not finally passed until 1870. This act gave a married woman the right to "be capable of acquiring, holding, and disposing by will or otherwise," to earn and keep her own wages and buy stocks without requiring her husband's signature (Holcombe, 1983: 246). These changes in women's property rights and marriage laws, together with technological change, led to new professions opening up for women. Until far into the twentieth century, however, married women still lacked the right to enter into contract by themselves. They could not take out a loan, for example, without their husband cosigning and, by implication, they were not considered (fully) liable for their actions either. While the laws limiting women in their legal or contractual capacity were repealed in Germany in 1953, in the Netherlands in 1957, in Belgium in 1958, and in France in 1965, the US took until 2006 for Congress to accept the Legal Capacity of Married Persons Act (Pott-Buter, 1992; Cornell Law School, 2021). In practice, however, US state and local courts already in a "vast majority of cases" upheld contracts signed by married women (Ehrenzweig, 1959). As the family still retained its character as a private realm and outside the reach of the government, rape and violence within the marriage continued to be seen as "a private matter" until far into the twentieth century. In economics, however, the male-headed wage-earner household would remain firmly in place, and the increase of female labor force participation in the early 1960s was met with surprise and perceived as an exceptional phenomenon.

Property rights: Slavery and colonialization

There were indeed, as Sarah Chapone had claimed, parallels between the way capitalist property rights and contract theory dispossessed married women and the way the law was used to take away native and enslaved people's agency, their land, and the control over their children. Though the exploitation and abuse of enslaved people and Native Americans was much more severe, the process through which oppression and submission was enforced through the use of force backed-up by the law was comparable: the appropriation of the fruits of their labor, the loss of control over their land and other assets, the lack of agency before the law, and lack of protection of their person, bodies, and possessions. Native American women with their tribes suffered the loss of land and often a loss of control over their children. Enslaved women could not protect their bodies from abuse by their enslavers, bodily punishments, and murder.

The voices of enslaved women provide us with insights into their experiences, which were very different from those of white women in Europe and the US. It is only recently that historians of economics and economists start to recognize the extent to which slave labor contributed to the tax revenues of the Southern states and to the wealth of the US more generally. This section focuses on the experience of enslaved women who, while being producers of goods and/or services, had their agency taken away.

Most readers will be familiar with the names of Phyllis Wheatley, Harriet Tubman, and Sojourner Truth, all of whom who were part of the struggle to end slavery. Truth (*c.*1797–1883) gave speeches and wrote, or rather dictated, her life story: *The Narrative of Sojourner Truth* (1850). This is the story of Isabella – Sojourner Truth's birth name – and of her early years, the auction where she was sold, her relationships with the slaveowners, and her marriage. Isabella was promised freedom in 1827, but that promise was broken, and she escaped. The narrative subsequently covers her struggle to keep her son out of slavery and her religious training, and contains some reflections on her situations. It also recounts the rationalizations of the slaveholders for their treatment of slaves, all told with a light tone of sarcasm and irony – their slaves would love them, cruelties against slaves would exist only in the imagination, and slaves were supposed to be *grateful* for their chains (Truth, 1993 [1850]: 66; emphasis in original). Sojourner Truth, a name of her own choosing, a very tall woman, was a strong public speaker. She traveled and spoke about the wrongs of slavery and about her religion. At the Akron's Women's Rights Convention in 1851, she told her audience "but the women are coming up blessed be God and a few of the men are coming up with them. But man is in a tight place, the poor slave is on him, woman is coming on him, and he is surely between a hawk and a buzzard" (1993 [1850]: 118).

Other writings by enslaved women include *The History of Mary Prince* (1831), *Religious Experience and Journal of Mrs. Jarena Lee* (1861), *Incidents in the Life of a Slave Girl* (Jacobs, 1861), and *A Slave Girl's Story* (Drumgoold, 1898). These texts give the reader a bare and bold, often shocking, report of the life experiences of black women in the US, who speak from the perspective of a person who is "owned" and reduced to a commodity used to make profits. These (formerly) enslaved women tell the stories of mothers who were separated from their husbands and children, who were raped and abused by their captors, and who tried to survive under these harsh circumstances.

The double position of white women with respect to slavery entailed that they shared the oppression by white men, while, at the same time, profiting from slavery, siding with their privileged husband and family. A similar problematic stand was often taken by white women with respect to Native Americans. A few women economic writers report on their experiences in the colonies and their interactions with the indigenous population. Eliza Lucas Pinckney (1722–93), who set up and developed the indigo trade in the Carolinas, is one of them. She ran the estate while her father traveled around the Caribbean, and she reported the daily events to him and the progress she made in her endeavors, which included her dealings with "the Negroes." Her experience with Native Americans did not go much further than hearing of and writing about what she reported as attacks on the city. The travel story of Janet Schaw (c.1731–c.1801), published around 1778 under the title *Journal of a Lady of Quality. Being the Narrative of a Journey from Scotland to the West Indies, North Carolina, and Portugal, in the Years 1774 to 1776*, gives accounts of her relationship with indigenous people. Schaw questions their treatment. These women, who were members of the plantation owners' community, at most express concerns about the conditions their workers were living under, while still enjoying the advantages and privileges these conditions brought them.

Back in the "mother country" a group of female economic writers spoke out and worked toward ending slavery. Anna Laetitia Barbauld (1743–1825), who was a central figure in the women's movement at the time, started her writing career with the publication of children's books, but over the years her writing became more political. She expressed her stance on slavery in her poem *Epistle to William Wilberforce, Esq. on the Rejection of the Bill for Abolishing the Slave Trade* (1791), in which she denounces Britain for its role in the slave trade:

> She [England] knows and she persists–Still Afric bleeds,
> Uncheck'd, the human traffic still proceeds;
> She stamps her infamy to future time,
> And on her harden'd forehead seals the crime.

Barbauld zooms in here on the institution of slavery and the gains it brought to the slaveowners as a reason for its sustenance. Others, like Helen Maria Williams (1759–1827), a novelist and poet, and Hannah More (1745–1833), a prominent member of the Bluestocking Society and an active member of the abolitionist movement in London, made humanitarian arguments that appealed to people's fellow feeling. It was Frances (Fanny) Wright, who, after writing about the practice of slavery, moved to the US and took concrete action to end it. Wright, who was born in Dundee, Scotland, was part of the upper-class intellectual circle around Jeremy Bentham and John Millar, and had family ties to Elizabeth Montagu. During a four-year stay in France, she befriended and gained the respect of General Lafayette and became enthusiastic about the US as a political experiment. After her first visit to the US, she wrote *Views of Society and Manners in America* (1821), an enthusiastic account of her travels (Eckhardt, 1984).

When Wright traveled to the US a second time and visited the South, she witnessed the practice of slavery and was shocked. Her experiences made her decide to join the abolitionist movement. Following the example of Robert Owen, she took the initiative to start her own Nashoba community in Tennessee, in 1825. One of her main aims was to show Southern slaveowners that freeing slaves was financially sustainable; enslaved people could work and earn an income from which to pay the slaveowner for their loss due to the enslaved person gaining their freedom. Wright bought and freed a group of enslaved people, who worked in the grounds in her community to "earn their freedom." Though problematic in its ethics, this way of enslaved people compensating slaveowners later became an established practice in many states in the South. Although Robert Owen, an enthusiastic utilitarian, "always remained perfectly cold to negro emancipation [and] his efforts for the reform of social evil and injustice were confined to the white race, to the point even that people of color were excluded from membership in his community" (Perkins and Wolfson, 1939: 127), Wright resisted this racism and saw the principles of Owenite cooperatives as applicable to plantations in the South.

While fighting for the survival of her community, Wright became sick – be reminded that she had never done this kind of work before – and needed a break. During this break she visited Owen's son, Robert Dale, at the New Harmony community, wrote (a lot) and gave lectures, only to find Neshoba in a bad state upon her return. In her memoir, she explains the breakdown of her community by the fact that her brother-in-law took over during her absence, but lacked the "great force of character [that] was needed for the prosecution of such an enterprise" (2020 [1855]: 29). Wright then traveled with the group of former slaves from Neshoba to Haiti to guarantee their safety and freedom and returned to Paris herself. She was an early socialist thinker and writer, who was very committed to putting her ideas into practice with the goal of ending, in her words, "the monstrous anomaly – Negro Slavery" (2020 [1855]: 20).

Harriet Martineau (1802–76), a prolific English writer we will learn more about in the next chapter, was also an active abolitionist. She traveled to the US, where she met with American abolitionists in Boston in 1835. In *Society in America* (1837), she pointed out the hypocrisy of the founding fathers who claimed that the government's power was derived from those governed, but who themselves owned slaves who lacked agency (Folbre, 2009: 78). In the book, Martineau provides a detailed report of the ethics, manners, and practices of Southern slaveholders and gives her own take on a variety of aspects of that economic system, discussing the circumstances under which it could and should be ended.

Sarah Grimké (1792–1873) and her sister Angelina (1805–79), who grew up in a patriarchal slaveowning family in Charleston, South Carolina, later in their lives became pioneers in the abolitionist and women's movement in the US. Both lived a life of lecturing and traveling in a time that this was uncommon for women. In her *Letters on the Equality of the Sexes* (1838) Sarah lays out her concerns about women's legal, educational, and economic status and that of enslaved women in particular. Enslaved women, Grimké points out, were not only exploited for their labor and considered property, but were also used as "broodmares" by the slaveowners. Sarah described the poignant consequences, stating: "It is an occurrence of no uncommon nature to see a Christian father sell his own daughter, and the brother his own sister" (1838: 60).

After the official end of slavery in the US in 1865, the situation of Black Americans improved only marginally. Initially, they were assigned plots of land, but this practice only lasted a few years. Violence against black people was paramount, in the South especially, and lynching was widespread. The murder of a good friend led Ida B. Wells-Barnett (1862–1931) to get involved and become a founder of the National Association for the Advancement of Colored People (NAACP) as well as a vocal activist in the women's movement. In 1892 she published *Southern Horrors: Lynch Law in All Its Phases* and in 1895 *The Red Record*, in which she documented lynchings in much detail. One of the points she made was that the victims of these lynchings were not criminals as was claimed but, rather, successful business people who increased competition for the white business community. *The Red Record* provides extensive data on and descriptions of lynchings during the period 1892–5. Wells-Barnett notes that, just as enslaved people had lost their value to the slaveowners, so black people were hunted down to maintain the dominance of whites in the South.

Strongly analytical and modern in content is *A Voice from the South* (1892) by Anna Julie Cooper (1858–1964) who would go on to receive a PhD from the Sorbonne in Paris in 1924. Cooper links gender and racial issues, addressing the double role of white women as oppressed in their relationship with their husbands and other white men, on the one hand, and as oppressor in their relations with African American women and Native American women on the other. Her analysis of white supremacy in relation to the intersectional experience of women of color is remarkably modern. She discusses in depth the importance of education, and higher education for women of color in particular. Phrasing the issues in a way that may sound sadly familiar to a woman of the twenty-first century, Cooper addresses the changes in power relations emerging at the end of the nineteenth century for women and people of color, stressing the opportunities these bring. She is optimistic in that she believes that prospective dictators do not have a chance in the US, due to its diversity and "opposition tones," but adds that "the last monster that shall be throttled forever methinks is race prejudice" (2016 [1892]: 79–80). It would take until 1921 for the first African American woman, Sadie Tanner Mossell Alexander (1898–1989), to receive a PhD in Economics.

As Jim Crow laws and racist violence continued to hamper the ability and opportunity of the black community in the US to accumulate wealth, African American women faced the double jeopardy of being a woman in the civil rights movement and being black in the women's movement. Patricia Hill Collins (2000) reports on the emergence of black women economic historians in the 1980s, who described black women's work under slavery and later in the agricultural and domestic sectors. Collins mentions three dimensions of the oppression of African American women: the exploitation of their labor, the lack of political rights such as voting rights and the right to run for office, and the colonialization of black women's minds by controlling the images that had their origin in the slave era, and preventing black women from knowing their own history and culture. Amott and Matthaei (1991) include the economic histories of Black American, Native American, and Asian American women to compile a more comprehensive narrative of economic development in the US. That the economic work of Sadie Alexander has only recently been published for the first time (Banks, 2021) is an indication of all the work that still needs to be done in this respect.

Closing this chapter on power, agency, and property rights, the dispossession of nature deserves at least brief attention. Through comparable processes as applied to women and people of color, industrial society has been using natural resources and the environment for its own ends without recognizing nature's own value and generally without compensating, replacing, or cleaning up after the damage is done. Backed up by political economic theory and later economics, the costs of, for instance, the extraction of copper or wood in the colonies (and elsewhere) has been computed by including only the costs of the use of machines and labor involved in the mining of these resources, not the damage done to nature. By externalizing these costs, and thus making them invisible, the assumption that nature (like women) had an unlimited power to regenerate itself became integrated into economic concepts and theories.

Women, most famously Native American women, who worked directly with the land and resources, have spoken out about their practices and detailed their concerns about the industrial manner of extracting resources, often leaving devastation behind: land ravaged, mountains hollowed out, and rivers polluted. In European economic writing by women, we find concern for limiting waste cropping up in household management books and in the works of Charlotte Perkins Gilman, Hazel Kyrk, and others. Preventing waste as part of efficient use of resources, however, vanished from the economic dictionary after that.

3

Education

Introduction

The exclusion of women, girls, and colonialized and enslaved people from getting a decent education prevented them not only from learning to read and write, but also from obtaining better-paid positions and from contributing to culture – their culture. Their lack of education kept these groups effectively out of centers of power. Not being able to read and write is a serious social handicap. Colonized people who were able to go to school were often forced to speak the language of the colonizers; they were taught details about the colonizing country, including its history and even its local geography, without learning about their own history and culture. Women of all classes endured this colonialization of the mind.

This chapter's first section presents women economic writers who considered obtaining access to education their highest priority as a first step to women's emancipation. Given that, in the early days of industrial society, few schools were open to girls, quite a few women economic writers decided to start and run a school of their own. The second section gives an overview of their writing on this topic. Absent accessible books on political economy, women economic writers composed their own such books in which they addressed women and girls in particular, to explain basic economic principles while referring to the lives of common people. The third and last section of this chapter outlines this tradition in economic writing.

Education as women's portal to culture and society

Women who wanted to live a life of learning and had the means to do so could, in medieval times, either receive tutoring at home or enter into a convent that accommodated learning. With the rise of universities, however, this latter option for women declined (Schiebinger, 1989). Others, from the gentry or of aristocratic birth, worked at home while corresponding with fellow philosophers and other like-minded people. For simpler mortals, however, the lack of education presented a major hurdle for contributing to society and for protecting one's interests. Mary Astell, who not only wrote about marriage (see Chapter 2), also published (anonymously), in two parts, *A Serious Proposal to the Ladies* (1695 and 1697). In these pamphlets, Astell makes a strong plea to young women to turn their mind away from frivolous behavior and concerns about dress, and instead to train their mind and build their character.

These pamphlets were widely read in England and Astell entered into public debates with John Locke, John Norris, and others about the role of education and the formation of character. John Locke (1632–1704) had argued that a newborn child's mind resembled a *tabula rasa*, a blank slate. This perception of human nature puts a lot of responsibility on the educator, as human nature is considered malleable and fully formed by its environment. In her pamphlets, Astell lays out in great detail the importance of an education for women in support of their religion and in the raising of their children. Young women, she argues, should develop their minds, which would bring out their "real beauty," and they should focus on finding a good husband instead of an attractive one, as "such an education will put the stability of marriage on a basis not furnished by the charms of the wife, but on a basis furnished by veneration and esteem" (1695: 99). In opposition to Locke, Astell believed that some ideas are innate. In her view, women and men were basically equal (Smith, 1966 [1916]: 60). Astell may have confirmed the status quo where marriage was concerned, yet the fact that she spoke up in public, supported women, and engaged in a public religious conversation meant that her work was contentious and often considered scandalous.

In France, Anne-Thérèse, marquise de Lambert, makes a similar case for the education of children, especially women. Her *Lettres de l'Éducation* (1748) addresses the education of boys and the education of girls as two different matters. The impact of Jean-Jacques Rousseau and other French writers, such as Félicité de Genlis, on educational methods in the English system was substantial. In these early tracts on education, there is no sharp distinction between the raising of small children at home and their education as young women, as most girls and young women were educated at home. Mrs. Cartwright, in her *Letters on Female Education, addressed to a Married Lady* (1777) – a work dedicated to Elizabeth Montagu – begins with religious instructions as the basis for an education, after which she provides moral lessons and pays extensive attention to the handling of money. Mary Wollstonecraft's *Thoughts on the Education of Daughters* (1787), her first book, also provides educational instructions covering a girl's life up to early matrimony.

Instructions about how to teach children to deal with money and not spend it extravagantly is a common point of attention shared by these authors. With her father Robert Lovell Edgeworth, Maria Edgeworth wrote two books on raising children and their education: *The Parent's Assistant* (1796) and *Practical Education* (1798). Hester Mulso Chapone (1695–1730), daughter-in-law of Sarah Chapone, who became a member of the Bluestocking Society, wrote in her *Letters on the Improvement of the Mind. Addressed to a Young Lady* (1773) about the importance of economy in a woman's education, arguing:

> Economy is so important a part of woman's character, so necessary to her own happiness, and so essential to her performing properly the duties of a wife and a mother, that it ought to have the precedence of all other accomplishments, and its rank next to the first duties of life. It is, moreover, an art as well as a virtue; and many well-meaning persons, from ignorance, or from inconsideration, are strangely deficient in it. (1773: 121)

Hester Chapone considered economy understood as an attitude to be a crucial part of good household management, as did many of her contemporaries.

There is, however, a long trend of arguments to be found in the debates on women's education that state that "study" or a serious education would damage women's femininity, if not their female reproductive organs. Overall, the training of most young eighteenth-century British women from the aristocracy, the gentry, and the upper-middle classes lacked intellectual content. Lessons would be focused merely on preparing the young woman for marriage within the class she was born into, or, preferably, for marriage into a higher class. English, French, geography, history, writing, ciphering, drawing, and dancing were the pursuits that filled most of these students' days (see e.g. Miller, 1972). This education for girls, however, left them helpless when widowed or when they did not marry at all. At best, these skills may have helped some of these women to become a governess themselves, but such jobs were scarce, the wages low, and most governesses earned only food and shelter.

Political economists were not heavily invested in improving the education of girls. Daniel Defoe, economic historian and author of *Robinson Crusoe*, who also wrote "On the Education of Women" (1719), is an exception. He made a strong case for women's access to learning, stating: "We reproach the sex every day with folly and impertinence; while I am confident, had they the advantages of education equal to us, they would be guilty of less than ourselves." Defoe also argues for the education (and employment) of impoverished children to train them for their future working life. It would take much more, however, to bring about a publicly funded educational system. By 1770, public education for both boys and girls was a broadly and intensely debated topic in Scottish society. Adam Smith weighed in, including one paragraph in his *Wealth of Nations* in which he addressed the economic position of girls and women directly. In that paragraph, though, he dismissed straight out the necessity for girls to learn anything more than the skills they need when they get married and have to run a household, stating:

> There are no public institutions for the education of women, and there is accordingly nothing useless, absurd, or fantastical in the common course of their education. They are taught what their parents or guardians judge necessary or useful for them to learn; and they are taught nothing else. Every part of their education tends evidently to some useful purpose; either to improve the natural attractions of their person, or to form their mind to reserve, to modesty, to chastity, and to œconomy: to render them both likely to become the mistresses of the family, and to behave properly when they have become such. (1976 [1776]: 781)

Smith's view of education follows Locke, in that he perceived the difference between a professor and a porter to be based on education and daily experience. He perceived training on the job to be crucial, as he considered the increase in workers' skills to be an important effect of the division of labor and a cause of economic growth. He saw women, however, as almost a different species; a species that does not figure in his description and analysis of factories and the economy. Smith's take on the matter thus went against what was argued in most French salons and against what his friends and acquaintances, including David Hume, Elizabeth Montagu, and Thérèse de Lambert believed: that girls should be educated, perhaps not in the same way as boys, but they must learn how to read, write, and do algebra, and learn about history and obtain skills.

Until halfway through the nineteenth century, there was hardly any training provided for the professions that women did have access to: teaching, nursing, doing needlework, midwifery, and the profession of governess. Women and girls who had lived in France were assumed to make suitable governesses due to their ability to teach French and other subjects. As these women had not received a decent education themselves, they generally could not offer more than some knowledge of the French language, let alone on other topics. Feminist tracts on the topic, like Hester Chapone's *Letters on the Improvement of the Mind* (1773), Mary Wollstonecraft's *Thoughts on the Education of Daughters* (1787) and Clara Reeve's *A Plan for Education* (1792), all criticize the devastating impact of either the wrong-headed education of young middle-class and gentry girls or their total lack of any education at all.

Wollstonecraft's text on the education of girls also reflects a distinct class awareness. The first things, according to Wollstonecraft, that children should "be encouraged to observe, are a strict adherence to the truth; a proper submission to superiors; and condescension to inferiors" (1787: 21). There is a general and consistent concern that over-educating girls would "raise their hopes" to a life above their ranks and would therefore set them up for disappointment. In her *Reflections* (1798) Priscilla Wakefield takes ample room to explain that education for the four classes of girls should prepare them for their later station in life, and nothing more.

It was the early socialist Robert Owen who gave education a central place in his economic reasoning. Owen applied his ideas in practice through his design and running of the utopian community – New Lanark in Scotland. In addition, other early socialist thinkers, like Charles Fourier and, later, John Stuart Mill, perceived education as a goal in itself and as a means to train and enlighten both the workers and the upper classes in society to move beyond mere self-interested behavior and bring society to a higher level of civilization.

In *The Subjection of Women*, Mill, together with Harriet Taylor, considered education as a central feature in economic growth. Education also played a central role in Mill's *Principles of Political Economy* (1848), especially during what he describes as "the stationary state." The stationary state describes the phase in the economy when economic growth no longer takes place and is no longer needed, and during which investment can focus on human development, with lifelong education taking center stage. Mill and Taylor did not heed women's unpaid contribution to the education of young children, though. Mill's focus on the economic role of education gets lost in the "marginalist revolution," the emergence of a coherent neoclassical theory, and the later shift from political economy to economics (Pujol, 1992). Unlike Mill, Alfred Marshall and Joseph Schumpeter argued that technology and entrepreneurship were the strong forces behind the growth in productivity, much more so than education of the working population and the general public more broadly.

As the full process of education transgressed the boundary between private and public, its particular goal being to train young people and to introduce them into society, and increase the abilities and skills of workers, these aspects are hard to capture in the binary concepts of production and consumption. Nevertheless, the education of young children has generally been conceptualized as consumption by the parents (of durable goods) and the education of older children and young adults as investment in their (human) capital. Since, historically, the government has carried most of the attendant costs, education has been largely considered a public good. The costs of early education in the home, however, have remained invisible and those costs have been shifted onto the caregiver (Folbre, 2008).

Over the course of the nineteenth century in the UK, as well as in the rest of Europe and the US more generally, individual initiatives involving starting schools, the school movement, and the increase in the demand for educated workers resulted in a system of general public education, co-ed universities, private colleges, and polytechnics, most of which also admitted women and people of color. The increasing access to higher education among women, however, met with resistance every step of the way. Even for families who supported the education of their daughters, the education of the boys in the family still had priority, and, when funds ran out, the girls would miss out on their opportunities (Pott-Buter, 1992). In the US, the segregation of education based on race would stay in place well into the twentieth century before being – officially – undone.

During the second half of the nineteenth century, the state of girls' education was reported on in conferences of the National Association for the Promotion of Social Science in the UK and its then newly founded sister body, the American Association for the Promotion of Social Science. The London-based Langham Place group led by Barbara Bodichon argued for better access and pay for women in professions, better rights for women, and changes in the marriage laws, and extensively reported on the lack of and low quality of girls' education.

Whereas boys' schools were generally well-funded and able to hire quality teachers, the conditions, teaching materials, and either voluntary or low-paid teachers in girls' schools made them essentially defunct. The point made by Bodichon, for instance, in her paper on "Middle-Class Schools for Girls," is that these schools for girls should be better held to a higher national standard, and that "the attention of the wealthy and charitable should likewise be drawn to the importance of endowing a certain number of day-schools for girls, to correspond to the grammar schools so richly endowed for boys" (1860: 79). The American economic writer Caroline Healy Dall (1822–1912), who was strongly influenced by the writers from the Langham Place group, makes a similar point for the US in her book *The College, the Market, and the Court; or Women's Relation to Education, Labor, and Law* (1867). This book is based on a set of lectures, among them "Women's Claim to Education," delivered in 1858 (1972 [1867]: x). Dall accounts in the preface of her book how she found similarly minded spirits in Barbara Bodichon and Bessie Rayner Parkes.

Although women began to gain access to higher education in the industrialized countries during the last decades of the nineteenth century, access to obtaining a full PhD degree would take longer. Mary Paley (1850–1944) and eight other women were initially supported by Alfred Marshall and Henry Sidgwick to work on their PhDs in political economy at Newnham College, Cambridge, a college that provided an exam specifically tailored to women. Mary Paley was working on *The Economics of Industry*, which she published in 1879 together with her tutor and, by then, husband Alfred Marshall. After her marriage in 1877, she stepped back from a career in political economy and would support her husband for the rest of his life. She wrote one short article, "Conference of Women Workers" (1896), published in *The Economic Journal*, in which she comments on a conference and describes favorably a speech made by Beatrice Potter Webb demanding more factory regulations that would include men and a minimum wage. Paley Marshall's attempts to change the rules at the University of Cambridge around women's access to a full PhD led her husband to effectively bar a proposal along these lines. He argued that "things can go too far," and for keeping "the old system" in place (Groenewegen, 1995; Paley Marshall, 1947). Later in life Paley Marshall would publish again, but *What I Remember* (1947) is little more than a description of her life with Alfred.

By the end of the nineteenth century, the education of women in the US had improved as well, including the education of black women. Access to higher education had been achieved and women's colleges opened their doors for women students at, for instance, Barnard College (Columbia University), Pembroke College (Brown

University), and Radcliffe College (Harvard University), in addition to a group of separate women's colleges, such as Mount Holyoke College, Wellesley College, and Spelman College. Anna Julia Cooper stressed the importance of education for the individual and for the country as a whole, distinguishing between those who give and those who consume more than they give or produce: "The man who consumes more than he produces is a destroyer of wealth and should be estimated precisely as the housekeeper estimates moths and mice" (2016 [1892]: 128). On the worth of black people, Cooper argues that the worth of a person is determined by this difference between production and consumption by the individual. Education in her view is an important tool to improve the value of production but she makes a poignant remark about the quality of the education provided: "I care not even for the reasonableness and unimpeachable fairness of your social ethics, – if it does not turn out better, nobler, truer men and women, – if it does not add to the world's stock of valuable souls" (2016 [1892]: 138).

In the early twentieth century, academic societies started opening their doors to women, with the French Académie des Sciences being one of the last to do so in 1942. In the following decades, women's education kept improving. By the 2020s, more women than men are graduating from college. Most of them, however, do so in fields other than science, technology, engineering, and mathematics (STEM), thus missing out on the better paid jobs and careers.

The importance of an educated workforce for a country's economy has long been neglected in economic theorizing. It is not clear whether the fact that education had been associated with women and that women wrote about this topic extensively had anything to do with that, but this herstory of economic thought certainly leaves that impression. Besides John Stuart Mill and Harriet Taylor Mill, few political economists addressed the impact of the absence of women's education for the labor market and economic growth more generally. This lack of concern did not change with the shift in economic theory that caused the name of the field to change from political economy to economics. It was only much later, when Gary Becker's standard economic model was applied to a range of traditionally non-economics topics that education became again a topic of attention, now as part of "human capital" – the education, skills, and experience of workers. In his *Human Capital* (1964) Becker derives the value of education, skills, and years of experience from empirical data on wages, while only including formal and on-the-job training. The experience that comes with spending hours and money on training toddlers and older children are neither acknowledged nor included by Becker and labor economists. This means, however, that a large part of women's management skills are neglected and that differences in educational achievements of children are, at least in part, mistakenly assessed as "talent" and "merit."

This lack of attention to the impacts and differences in early child education – at least to some extent – also meant that it took until 1990 for the World Bank to realize and report that when mothers receive an education fertility rates fall, children are better fed, and child mortality rates decrease. This brings back the older argument that the better educated mothers are, the better they will educate their children and the fewer children they will decide to have. In the last decade of the twentieth century, partially based on the growing critique on the GDP index as the main measurement tool of economic growth, Amartya Sen, winner of the Nobel Memorial Prize in Economics (1998), and others developed the Human Development Index (HDI). In addition to income, the index includes health and a country's level of literacy (education). The HDI gets used as a correction on the GDP ranking (see UNDP, 1995), and it encourages policymakers all over the world to pay more attention to the health and literacy of their population.

Get your own education – start a school!

The situation in the early years of industrial development, in which boys of wealthy parents were educated by private tutors and workhouses kept poor children off the streets, was very unsatisfactory to many women economic writers. As there were few schools that taught children skills, the solution that these eighteenth-century women often propagated and practiced was: "Start your own school!"

Mary Astell's friends, Lady Mary Wortley Montagu, Elizabeth Elstob, Lady Catherine Jones, and Lady Elizabeth Hastings, decided to carry out the plan Astell had laid out in her two volumes, *A Serious Proposal to the Ladies*: they started a Charity School toward the end of Astell's life, in 1729. When Elizabeth Montagu noticed that her workers had good incomes but were not educated enough to spend them well – other than on immediate satisfactions of men's pleasure, including booze – she also decided to start a school. She first founded one for boys and then another for girls. Montagu can be considered an early member of the Sunday School movement in England, the founder of which is generally claimed to be Robert Raikes (1735–1811) (Kuiper and Robles-García, 2012).

By the 1780s, many self-respecting, young, middle-class, and gentry women in Britain were starting schools. Sarah Trimmer (1741–1810) was a driving force of the movement. She herself gave birth to twelve children, ten of whom survived to adulthood. While bringing them up, she found the time to write a book series on raising children that was highly popular. Subsequently, she started teaching and developed a teaching method using the most modern insights, such as including images that showed not only biblical messages but also historical scenes. These activities and achievements finally culminated in *The Œconomy of Charity* (1787), which was written for an audience of women. The 600-page book comes close to being a manual of how to start a school, as it includes standard letters and descriptions of practical inventions that could be used in class. Sarah Trimmer was a force of nature; she worked with the poor, had direct contact with Queen Caroline, and edited a magazine commenting on the most recently published youth literature. Her work was educational as well as economic in kind and she was recognized as an authority in matters of children's education.

Hannah More of the Bluestocking Society also started a school, as did Mary Wollstonecraft. The school movement died out by the end of the century when the government took over this task and public schools started to appear. Becoming a teacher remained one of the few decent professions open to unmarried middle-class women. This field continued to be dominated by women, although men generally taught the higher-level classes and occupied the leading positions in the schools.

In the US, well-connected and wealthy women started women's colleges. Catharine Esther Beecher (1800–78) started Hartford Female Seminary in 1823 and recorded her concerns about the state of female education in *The True Remedy for the Wrongs of Woman* (1851). New educational institutions opened all over the country, funded by industrial capitalists such as the Rothschilds, the Rockefellers, and the Carnegies, as well as with the support of the government. Mary Lyon (1797–1849) founded Mount Holyoke Female Seminary in 1837; her documents and writings on why and how to start this seminary have now been collected and published (Hartley, 2008). Mount Holyoke would be the first of the Seven Sister Colleges (linked to male-only Ivy League schools) and would inspire others to found other women's colleges, like Hollins University and Smith College.

Society was changing, however, and during the 1860s and 1870s the demand for skilled labor increased throughout the Western world. At this time, the Ivy League schools – Harvard and Yale in the US, and, in England, Oxford and Cambridge – were still the powerhouses that educated the next generation of the elite while remaining closed to women. So again, in order to provide women with a much-needed education, Barbara Bodichon, together with Emily Davies, started Girton College and Sidgwick and Marshall founded Newnham College, both at the University of Cambridge. At Oxford, Lady Margaret Hall and Somerville College were founded for women students in the late 1870s. Beatrice Potter Webb and her husband Sidney Webb founded the London School of Economics in 1896; the school's doors were open to young women from the very beginning.

In response to the segregation of schools in the US, the black community started their own schools and colleges; Mary Church Terrell (1863–1954) was able to give a speech on "The Progress of Colored Women" before a meeting of the National American Woman Suffrage Association (NAWSA) in 1898. She reported about how far black women had come and how they had caught up with white women in terms of educational achievements. She started her talk by stating:

> Fifty years ago a meeting such as this, planned, conducted, and addressed by women would have been an impossibility. Less than forty years ago, few sane men would have predicted that either a slave or one of his descendants would in this century at least, address such an audience in the Nation's Capital at the invitation of women representing the highest, broadest, best type of womanhood, that can be found anywhere in the world. (1898: 113)

Terrell recounted the achievements of women of color in terms of starting and running child centers, schools, and clubs, as well as schools for nurses. She named the charitable institutions being supported by the black community, such as orphanages, hospitals, homes for the elderly, and praised those who excelled in literary ability, entrepreneurship, and educational achievement. Black women, according to Terrell, were "seeking no favors because of our color, nor patronage because of our needs, we knock at the bar of justice, asking an equal chance" (1898: 119).

Spreading the word: Teaching political economy and economics

The first books in political economy were not readily accessible to the larger public or suitable for teaching the subject to laymen. Both

Adam Smith's *Theory of Moral Sentiments* and his *Wealth of Nations* were big books that assumed the reader to be well-read and able to comprehend long and abstract sentences. In addition, few people had the time to read these extended treatises. Thomas Malthus's *An Essay on the Principle of Population* (1798) is a shorter book, but it is not that easy to read without knowledge of other economic publications. David Ricardo's *Principles of Political Economy and Taxation* (1817) is rather abstract, addressing concepts like wages, interest rates, profits, investments, and economic growth.

As we saw in Chapter 1, Maria Edgeworth wrote some easier introductory texts supporting parents in the economic education of their children. Other women economic writers, like Jane Haldimand Marcet (1769–1858), who had access to the required education and also the background and support to read the works by the early political economists, discussed these and found a way to reach a larger audience. Later women economic writers – for example, Harriet Martineau and Millicent Garrett Fawcett – developed this idea and established a tradition of popularizing the ideas of political economists such as Smith, Ricardo, and Malthus.

Marcet was the first woman economic writer to publish a book with the aim of explaining basic economic concepts. She appropriated the French and Swiss traditions of women organizing dinners and invited a wide array of interesting people to dinner. Living in London and well connected even with some of the economists she wrote about, she welcomed to her home people such as Mary Somerville – the first woman, along with Caroline Herschel, to be elected an honorary fellow of the Royal Astronomical Society – Harriet Martineau, Maria Edgeworth, and David Ricardo. Dorothy Lampen Thomson (1973) suggests that Marcet had probably been influenced by Mary Wollstonecraft's *Thoughts on the Education of Daughters* (1787), among others. It is the format of a conversation between a teacher and her pupil that Marcet used to explain the basic notions of a range of scientific fields. First, she applied this format in the field of her husband: chemistry and, ten years later, she published *Conversations on Political Economy, in which the Elements of that Science are Familiarly Explained* (1816). The conversation between Mrs. B. (the instructor) and Caroline (the student) in Marcet's book is easy to relate to and thus to follow. It starts with Caroline admitting that she feels some antipathy to political economy. This attitude is then addressed and dissected by her teacher, showing that the student is already engaged in political economy as it is so much part of her daily life. The content of these teachings did not move beyond the explanation of the concepts, principles, and theories of Smith,

Malthus, and Ricardo. Marcet, according to Thomson, "accepted their ideas, quoted their words uncritically, and displayed a general complacency with the *status quo* of economic society" (1973: 19). Nevertheless, Marcet's *Conversations* became very popular and even turned political economy into a suitable topic for ladies, as Maria Edgeworth described at the breakfast table of David Ricardo (Thomson, 1973: 24). Marcet published further books explaining a variety of other topics using a similar format. *John Hopkins's Notions of Political Economy* (1833) consists of a set of nine fairytales through which the author explores and explains wealth and income inequalities, and some non-fiction short essays on the population principle, emigration, the poverty rate, machinery, foreign trade, and the corn trade. *Rich and Poor* (1851) provides an explanation, or as James and Julianne Cicarelli put it, "a well-reasoned rationalization of the prevailing social and economic stratification of society" (2003: 110).

Twenty years later, Harriet Martineau (1802–76), the prolific economic writer who we met earlier traveling in the US, decided to revive Marcet's approach of telling short stories to teach young girls the main principles of political economy. Martineau, who grew up in a well-to-do family, where she and her brothers and sisters received a good education, showed a specific interest in political economy from early on in her life. Due to the economic crisis of 1825, however, the family lost their business and Harriet's father died in 1826. Dependent on her own resources, Harriet decided to earn a living by her pen. Her *Illustrations of Political Economy* (1834) were first published as a series of short stories or small novels that explained the economic ideas of Smith and Malthus by applying them to the daily lives of common people. Her stories bring the principles of political economy to life, and she puts flesh on the bare bones of the abstract economic notions. Smith's and Malthus's principle of population growth, for example, became a story about the effects on the food supply of having numerous children on a small island at the West of Scotland. In the story "Weal and Woe in Garveloch: A Tale," the reader learns about these effects and about the importance of investing time and money in the means of future generations. While workers remained abstract in Malthus's *Essay*, Martineau provides her characters with the agency to make good or bad decisions and shows the consequences of their behavior.

Where Jane Haldimand Marcet took the status quo as a given and focused on explaining Smith's, Malthus's, and Ricardo's economic concepts, Harriet Martineau showed the workings of the principles of political economy and applied them in a more thought-provoking manner. The influence of Martineau's short stories can hardly be understated. The income she earned with these stories enabled her to travel to the US and to address other topics. *How to Observe Morals and Manners* (1838), for instance, is an early book on the methodology of the social sciences, in which Martineau applied the positivist philosophy of science of August Comte to the social sciences.

Not all economists were pleased, however, with this popularizing and pedagogical branch of their academic field. Initially, Adam Smith's *Wealth of Nations* (1776), Ricardo's *Principles of Political Economy and Taxation* (1817), and John Stuart Mill's *Principles of Political Economy* (1848) had defined the field; Alfred Marshall's *Principles of Economics* (1890) was next in line as the central textbook in economics. Marshall (1897) dismissed Martineau's work and that of other women economic writers by stating: "Never again will a Mrs. Trimmer, a Mrs. Marcet or a Miss Martineau earn a reputation by throwing economic principles into the form of catechism or of simple tales, by aid of which any intelligent governess might make it clear to the children nestling around her where lies economic truth" (see also Groenewegen, 1995: 445). After John Maynard Keynes reproduced this statement in his *Essays in Biography* (1933), the references by economists to the work of these women indeed stopped (Henderson, 1995: 64).

The tradition of teaching economics to a broader public, however, is further developed by Millicent Garrett Fawcett (1847–1929), one of the central figures in the women's movement during the late nineteenth century. She was president of the National Union of Women's Suffrage Societies and married to the political economist Henry Fawcett. Fourteen years her senior, Henry Fawcett was a professor of political economy at the University of Cambridge. Millicent worked with him on his economic publications and enabled him to continue his studies after he lost his sight (Thomson, 1973). Besides her work as a well-known political activist for women's suffrage, Fawcett enlarged the audience of political economy by explaining concepts, theories, and ideas of the current economic doctrine. In 1870, she published *Political Economy for Beginners* to great acclaim. The book is a textbook that mostly presents Mill's political economic notions, although Fawcett included the wage fund doctrine, which Mill had stepped away from in 1869. With "a word of apology to Miss Martineau for my plagiarism of the idea," Millicent Fawcett also published *Tales in Political Economy* (1874), a narrative similar in structure to Defoe's *Robinson Crusoe* (1719), which centers on a shipwrecked sailor on an island. Most of her other political economic writings were published together with her husband (Thomson, 1973). Fawcett lived to see the passage of the Representation of the People (Equal Franchise) Act that passed in Parliament in 1928 and that gave all women over the age of 21 in Britain equal voting rights to those of men.

Most of the endeavors to popularize political economy mentioned thus far were successful and made their authors rich. None of them, however, were as successful as the publications of Ayn Rand (1905-82). Rather than focusing on mainstream economic notions, Rand's publications aimed to popularize specific economic notions, notions with which she addressed a specifically rightwing crowd. At the age of 21, Rand fled St. Petersburg in the USSR. She started her career in the US writing screenplays. As this proved unsuccessful, she attempted novel writing. *The Fountainhead* (1943) signified Rand's breakthrough. The economic content is explicit in that it propagates an extreme version of Austrian economic theory and worldview. Rand placed the entrepreneur at the center of the economy; an entrepreneur who is strong, talented, and active, and the driving force behind innovation and economic development. The male entrepreneurs in her books are hampered by incompetent government officials who aim to control them by rules and regulations. Rand's libertarian main characters take on the functioning of the current economic system and propagate a new more extreme capitalist morality: that of the man who pursues his self-interest and does not engage in altruism and sacrifice.

Rand's *Atlas Shrugged* (1957) was even more successful and influential, especially among young people. The narrative revolves around the protagonist and her evolving relationship with the central male character: a hero, described as an *Übermensch*. He is portrayed as an unacknowledged genius who fights for economic freedom against those who are putting constraints on him: his family, rules, and reality. The book contains a more than fifty-page-long political manifesto in the format of a talk on the radio by the hero and the hidden hand behind the events in the book: John Galt. Rand's books are written to appeal to young people; with a sugar coating of sexual language, she constructs an artificial world in which the individual is under threat and suppressed, providing radical solutions of change that provide confirmation for the ego.

Rand's books were foundational for the rise of the US political movement, the Tea Party, in the 2000s and they still sell in huge numbers. With the notable exception of Alan Greenspan, Chair of the Federal Reserve from 1987 to 2006 and an outspoken supporter of Rand's views, her work did not make it into the academic economic discourse. For more left-leaning economists, the fact that she was an outspoken rightwing ideologue was generally enough to exclude her from the discourse, and for the Austrians her lack of economic theorizing, in addition to her gender, may have relegated her to the fringes. The impact of her work on American politics and on the economic thinking of a large part of the US population would have been legitimate reasons, however, for economists, including historians of economic thought, to pay attention to her ideas.

Instruction books in political economy, written for and by women, contributed extensively to the propagation of political economy and later economics, although the original contribution these books contained was limited. The writings of Jane Haldimand Marcet and Millicent Fawcett were predominantly based on their studies of available documents, on debates, and on their perspectives as white middle-class women. The critical work and interpretation by Harriet Martineau, on the other hand, which addressed sensitive topics like family planning and women's daily life experiences, moved beyond a mere application and explanation of ideas. So did Ayn Rand's novels, as she created an imaginary universe in which she explored and outlined her economic and moral ideas, without, however, addressing women's issues in any way, shape, or form.

Over the twentieth century, the popularization of economics concepts and theories would be taken over by the teaching of a standardized body of thought in textbooks taught to an increasing number of economics students at universities all over the world. Paul Samuelson (1915–2009), who synthesized neoclassical economics and Keynesian economic theory in his textbook *Economics: An Introductory Analysis* (1948), gave mathematics a central place. His book became the most popular economics textbook over the second half of the twentieth century, followed more recently by, for example, Olivier Blanchard (1996) on macroeconomics and Gregory Mankiw (1997) on microeconomics. Samuelson stood firmly in the tradition of Adam Smith in the sense that women do not occur or play any substantive role in his book; the same was the case in later economics textbooks. In 1990, Susan Feiner and Bruce Roberts analyzed, for the first time, modern economic textbooks and reported on the extent to which they mentioned and addressed women and women's issues – such as the gender wage gap, occupational segregation based on sex and race, the impact of childcare on female labor participation, discrimination, etc. The outcome was: not a lot, if at all. Things have changed since then and most textbooks apply the established neoclassical and Keynesian economic theory in the analysis of the gender wage gap, the labor market, time use, and family behavior.

The abstract character of economics as a science strengthened over the 1980s and 1990s. Shifting away from economic policy-making, academic economists became more and more oriented toward producing scientific work or "pure theory." The mathematization of economics reached an all-time high as a new generation of PhD students, among whom there were by that time quite a few young women, showed their skills and proficiency in mathematical modeling. David Colander and Arjo Klamer (1987) reported that PhD students in economics did not consider knowledge of the real world highly relevant for becoming a successful economist; being good in mathematics was instead considered the crucial factor. In response, feminist economists thought it was time to publish their own textbooks. Francine Blau and Marianne Ferber, for instance, published *The Economics of Women, Men, and Work* (1986) on feminist economic theory covering household behavior and labor market issues; and Drucilla Barker and Susan F. Feiner compiled *Liberating Economics* (2004), which provided a feminist perspective on the economy more generally.

4

Women's Relation to Wealth: Capital, Money, and Finance

Introduction

Thus far, we have explored early women's economic writings and the gender context of Adam Smith's *Wealth of Nations* and other seminal texts in political economy. We turn in this chapter to women's economic writings on wealth, capital, money, and finance. We have seen that political economy raised broad questions about nations' overall wealth and economic growth, taking the exploitation of workers and enslaved people, the marital transfer of wealth, and the control and exploitation of natural resources as a given. While political economists aimed at explaining the real value of goods, or "the real price of everything, what everything really costs to the man who wants to acquire it" by "the toil and trouble of acquiring it," and "which it can impose upon other people" (Smith, 1976 [1776]: 47), more and more daylight was put between women and *their* possessions – the capital they inherited, their handling of money, and their control over financial assets. In this chapter, we will explore women's response to the economic changes in these three areas using various genres: novels, pamphlets, poems, and essays, and, later, papers, articles, and books.

Women's loss of control over their capital

Sarah Chapone (1735) mentioned the change in attitude due to the decline in Christian norms and values ruling behavior that made married women more and more vulnerable in their full dependence on their husband. In England, common law protected to some extent women's control over land-ownership, but gave men control over personal property, which he could invest, spend, or dispose of in any way he wanted. Any capital in the hands of women before marriage or inherited during the marriage would come under the direct control of their husbands. Before lending money became acceptable on a larger scale and banking became more general in Europe, most capital was accumulated and transferred through marriage and inheritance (Erickson, 2005). English marriage laws, in addition to the practice of primogeniture, in which the whole estate is inherited by the eldest son, contributed to the concentration and accumulation of capital in an exclusive group of men. The inheritance that some newlywed women thus lost to their husbands could be considerable. The availability of this capital to aristocratic, gentry, and middle-class men often enabled them to invest in industrial and risky endeavors. Married women might see their husband squander their capital on frivolous useless endeavors; others might see it being spent on productive investments and successful enterprises. The exact extent of the capital formerly controlled by women but lost by marriage, and its role in the foundation of the wool industry (which formed the basis for England's industrialization) and other factories, has yet to be documented. Although the use and investment of their wife's inheritance may have been perceived by the men involved as mainly an economic issue, these issues were described and discussed mostly in moral terms where these women were concerned.

For women of means, loss of control over their capital had a profound impact on their lives. Anxieties about their economic futures were profound and brought about a whole literature that emerged around their dependency on the men in their lives. These novels explored the terrors of the insecurities around marriage, trust funds, gold diggers, and destitution among women. British women stood at the cradle of these novels, in which an imaginary world was inhabited by "characters" who told a story that generally contained a moral or a message for the reader about right and wrong. Women dominated this genre, especially that of the so-called "Gothic novel."

Gothic novels that appeared during the second half of the eighteenth century built on nostalgic and romantic longings for the past, injected with contemporary anxieties about economic uncertainty, thus providing a thrill of suspense for middle- and upper-class women. The feebleness of a man's heart was for many women of fortune their main hope and basis for a comfortable future. This makes it easy to understand that the horrors of seduction, out-of-wedlock pregnancies, and confidence men who acted as lovers but ultimately ruined a naive woman's name were effectively turned into exciting themes and fine ingredients for such stories. Women's full dependency on men, who were supposed to protect them and provide and secure their fortune and future, enabled Gothic novelists to explore the limits of trust, honesty, right, and wrong, and juxtapose love and self-interest, all while imagining the gruesome consequences of a young women's naivety or plain bad luck. Edward Copeland states that "the Gothic terror in women's fiction is unremittingly economic" (1995: 36). He refers here to Ann Radcliffe's *The Romance of the Forest* (1791), which opens with the phrase: "When once sordid interest seizes on the heart, it freezes up the source of every warm and liberal feeling; it is an enemy alike to virtue and to taste – this it perverts, and that it annihilates" (Radcliffe, 1999 [1791]: 1). *The Castles of Athlin and Dunbayne* (1789) and *The Mysteries of Udolpho* (1794) are two other well-known economic horror stories by Ann Radcliffe (1764–1823) that made tangible these financial and emotional concerns of women. The accounts of the emotional responses in these novels played out in dramatic contexts of loss of fortune, love, and social status. On one of the very first pages of *The Romance of the Forest*, Radcliffe lays out such a context:

> As Madame de la Motte leaned from the coach window, and gave a last look at the walls of Paris ... the scene of her former happiness, and the residence of many dear friends – the fortitude, which had till now supported her, yielded to the force of grief. "Farewell all!" sighed she, "this last look and we are separated for ever!" Tears followed her words, and sinking back, she resigned herself to the stillness of sorrow. The recollection of her former times pressed heavily upon her heart: a few months before and she was surrounded by friends, fortune, and consequence; now she was deprived of all, a miserable exile from her native place, without home, without comfort [and] almost without hope. (1999 [1791]: 2)

Mary Hays, who we know from her *Appeal to the Men of Great Britain*, also wrote the novel *Memoirs of Emma Courtney* (1796). While the narrative recounts the coming of age of an heiress who is concerned about independence when her inheritance proved too small, the novel deals with topics such as suicide, gender, and social inequality. Comical but at the same time telling is the story of *Cecilia; or, Memoirs of an Heiress* (1782) by Frances (Fanny) Burney (1752–1840). Cecilia gains access to a considerable fortune on condition that she marries a man who will take her name rather than she his. By showing how a seemingly minor condition appears as such an insurmountable obstacle for marriage, Burney lays out the importance of rank and family in the upper classes of British society. Burney's three novels – *Evelina, or A Young Lady's Entrance into the World* (1778), *Cecilia* (1791), and *Camila; or, a Picture of Youth* (1796) – all portray complicated and developing characters to a large extent captured by a social and economic world that leaves them limited choices and uproots the traditional notions of right and wrong. Although this literature is obviously too vast to be covered in this chapter, relevant here is that these novels are clearly organized around the impacts and implications of the social and economic changes in this period in which the old landowning class and its attendant norms and virtues were being replaced by the new order of the rich middle class and their own norms and notions of virtue, in which money and self-interest played a major role.

The Gothic genre was highly influenced by French literature and philosophical ideas like those of Jean-Jacques Rousseau. The French Revolution of 1789 and the political upheaval in the following years had invoked in England a response of anxiety, repression, and romantic nostalgia (Wright, 2013). In a concluding remark, Copeland states: "Women writers of the 1790s look about their rapaciously, money-oriented society to find their worst nightmare realized, that theirs was indeed a society in which a woman without access to cash might have no place at all" (1995: 37).

It is against this background that political economy developed as an academic field of study. Focusing on self-interested behavior, the production of wealth, and economic growth, it reflected the male interests of the rising middle class. Political economists still defined capital at this point in time, to use Adam Smith's description, as "stock." Stock could only be enlarged by savings, mostly out of profits. Marrying a rich widow, though in practice a source of capital, is not mentioned by Smith. Women economic writers, on the other hand, described the loss of control over their fortunes, their legal agency, and the increased dependence on men in a world where money was becoming increasingly important, and thus brought to light underlying maelstroms and anxieties invoked by these shifts in values and institutions.

Jane Austen (1775–1817) is probably the most famous and familiar author to the reader from this group of authors, as are her books *Sense and Sensibility* (1811) and *Pride and Prejudice* (1813). Austen's books feature a wealth of economic content, while lacking the horror aspect of the Gothic novels. In *Sense and Sensibility*, for instance, there are good men and also villains who lie about their fortune. Putting trust in the wrong man threatens to ruin the reputations and the future of one of the main characters, Marianne. She is, however, saved by marriage to the friend of the house, Colonel Brandon, who truly loves her. The damage done is revealed mainly in terms of broken trust, sickness, and the crushing of feelings. The sugary coating of the happy ending prevents any confrontation with real-life consequences that would have been in store had Colonel Brandon not stepped in. These real-life consequences of single womanhood or financial destitution are merely hinted at as a faraway threat. Austen weaves romantic and intriguing characterizations of the privileged gentry and higher classes, exploring the new middle-class moral codes and behavior.

During the first decades of the nineteenth century, conservatism dominated in the UK, in the sense that there was little intellectual space for public feminist debate. Mary Wollstonecraft had been unwittingly disgraced by her husband William Godwin's candid biography of her (1798), and many women writers, such as Hannah More and, later, Charlotte Elizabeth Tonna, expressed themselves first and foremost within a religious frame of thought. When economic crises hit the UK and the US in the 1850s alike, women economic writers picked up their pens again. Ann Stephens (1810–86), for instance, wrote serial novels in the US over a period of thirty years, with titles such as *Fashion and Famine* (1854), *Mary Derwent* (1858), and *Married in Haste* (1870). These can be called American Gothic novels, serial style, in that they tell the stories of women's ruin brought about by men who ruthlessly pursue their self-interest, and the episodes about the pain inflicted on women are repeated over and over again (Bauer, 2020). Other authors who are part of this wave include Mary Jane Holmes (1825–1907) and E.D.E.N. Southworth (1819–99). Southworth's serial novels often include prison life as a particularly horrible setting, exploring gruesome experiences that went with proposals for positive change. Dale Bauer (2020) lays out the wide variety of topics and emotions that were addressed, including a shift from the family as the natural place to return to toward "honest and hard work" as a means to cleanse the soul. Over the generations the cultural judgment of these authors of US society increased in harshness (2020: 130).

As women lost control over any capital they might have inherited, "capital" became a central concept in political economy in the nineteenth century. Karl Marx (1818–83) defined capital as a social and economic relation rather than as a relation between men and things; he distinguished between constant and variable capital, where variable capital is that portion of capital that is invested in labor and resources, and constant capital that which consists of machines and land. The definition and conceptualization of capital shifts when the marginalist economists take over the field. In neoclassical economic theory, as proposed by William Stanley Jevons (1835–82), capital is defined as "*the aggregate of those commodities which are required for sustaining labourers of any kind or class engaged in work*" (1965 [1871]: 223; emphasis in original). While Jevons elsewhere places women in the household, which he considers to be the moral realm, when he speaks about capital, he perceives paid and unpaid household work as capital by implication:

> Housekeeping is an occupation involving wages, capital and interest, like any other business, except that the owner consumes the whole result. ... Now if we allow to what is invested in hotels, hired furnished houses, lodgings, and the like, the nature of capital, I do not see how we can refuse it to common houses. We should thus be led into all kinds of absurdities. (1965 [1871]: 263)

Whereas Jevons reduces the unpaid work of the housewife to either the commodities it produces or to activities in the moral realm, Alfred Marshall (1842–1924) perceived this labor as investment in human capital. He defines capital as "all stored-up provision for the production of material goods, and for the attainment of those benefits which are commonly reckoned as part of income" (1890: 138). Concerning women's contribution by raising children, Marshall wrote: "The most valuable of all capital is that invested in human beings; and of that capital *the most precious part is the result* of the care and influence of the mother" (1890: 564; emphasis added). Thus stated, the work of the mother has no value in itself; it only becomes concrete, visible, and valuable in the human capital of her sons. Marshall acknowledges the importance of women's unpaid work in a footnote, but does not bring it into his economic theorizing. So, on the one hand, he acknowledges the fundamental importance of women's unpaid work as resulting in a form of capital, yet this "most valuable of all capital" is immediately made invisible when its value is located in the human capital of the son instead (see also Kuiper, 2001).

The role of capital accumulation, the measurement of its value, and its contribution to the emergence of economic crises shifted center stage over the next decades of the twentieth century. Economic theorists such as Carl Menger, John Bates Clark, and Eugen von Böhm-Bawerk considered capital to have, if not a similarly productive, then a comparable role in the production process as labor, and they measured its value in terms of its marginal production. Thus, its value becomes determined by its contribution to the production of a product, which price is determined at the market and ultimately by the utility this product provided to the consumer. It remained difficult, however, to actually measure the value of capital. In the 1970s a debate on the topic got rather heated, when Cambridge economists in the UK criticized the assumption that capital could be considered as "putty clay" – meaning fluid in its concrete form. Hyman Minsky (1982, 1992) assigned an independent role to the growth of capital – through the shift of economic borrowing relations from being fully backed up to Ponzi scheme-like banking relations based on empty promises about profitability that would bring along the next financial crisis. It would take years before another attempt was made to measure capital's value. This time the research was conducted on an historical empirical basis. Thomas Piketty visited the centers of the industrial world before and after publishing *Capital in the Twenty-First Century* (2014), in which he defended his thesis that, when the rate of return on capital grows at a larger pace than the rate of growth of output and income, the increase in concentration of wealth threatens, and may eventually end, democracy. The participation of women in wealth accumulation came late in the industrialization process. In general, women's control over capital increased from around 5 percent in the US and UK in 1860 to about 25 percent in 1900 and about 40 percent in 1953 (Deere and Doss, 2006: 1). Black women, however, were still not able to build up many financial reserves at all. When women joined the decision-making process with respect to investment and economic decision-making in the financial industry, the institutions were already fully developed and black women had yet to obtain access to the theorization of finance.

Women's attitude toward money

Women not only lost control over their capital during the 1700s and 1800s; the new bourgeois morality also held that, for middle- and upper-class women, the handling of money was "unfeminine" and vulgar, since only lower-class women engaged in buying and selling. Against the background of early industrial transference of productive activities for household sustenance toward workshops and factories that had been an integral part of the industrialization process, money and monetary values became increasingly important in Western society, and middle-class women were taught to maintain a double standard toward money and finances.

The gendered morality around money both reflected and strengthened the idea that middle- and upper-class women would be better off not dealing with money matters or getting a paid job, let alone earning their own living. Doing so would be perceived as likely impacting their femininity in a negative manner and leaving them defeated, even suffering a possible moral downfall. Taking up a nursing position was more acceptable and morally defendable when the woman concerned was not paid, but worked voluntarily. On the other hand, women needed to run their household, and the values that were basic to the new industrial society – prudence, efficiency, propriety, and honesty – did not come naturally. These values and behaviors, fundamental to a well-functioning capitalist system, needed to be instilled in children. Hannah More (1745–1833), the most religious and prolific member of the Bluestocking Society, wrote *Cheap Repository Tracts* (1795–8), little booklets that instructed children about money handling, prudence, and honesty in business. These short tales cost just a penny apiece and were meant for the general public to read. A characteristic example is the "Apprentice Turned Master." It tells the story of a shoemaker's apprentice's career in business. The apprentice's master is sloppy, dishonest, and prone to drinking; he ends up in the gutter while "his faithful apprentice, by his honest and upright behaviour, so gained the love and respect of his late master's creditors, that they set him up in business" (n.d.: 3). The moral of the story is clear: to be a successful businessman, you need to be honest so you can acquire the trust of your investors and customers.

Maria Edgeworth and Robert Lovell Edgeworth addressed the economic behavior in the household in "Prudence and Economy," a chapter in *Practical Education* (1798). Their instructions, addressed to parents, inform them that girls had to be taught with more "caution" than boys for various reasons. "Economy," in the authors' words, "is in women an essential domestic virtue" (1815 [1798]: 701). Furthermore:

> Economy may be exercised in taking care of whatever belongs to us; children should have the care of their own clothes, and if they are negligent of what is in their charge, this negligence should not be repaired by servants or friends, they should feel the real natural consequences of their own neglect, but no other punishment should be indicted. (1815 [1798]: 702)

Economy in the context of the household, according to the Edgeworths, consisted of prudence, experience, skill in the use of goods and resources, and minimization of waste. Their commitment to teaching children the value of money made them fervent protagonists of pocket money for children. Moreover, "young women should be accustomed to keep the family accounts [and] they should learn the price of all necessaries, and of all luxuries" (1815 [1798]: 704). This awareness of prices, "exactness about property," and "a respect for the rights of others, rather than a tenacious anxiety about their own" should protect young women and men from spending money that they did not have once they left their parents' house. This double attitude toward money made handling capital and earning an income dirty and incompatible with women's feminine character, while at the same time characterizing spending money sparingly – not one's own after all – as an important virtue for women and girls.

The set of norms and values that kept women separate from money and that supported them in not even asking to be paid for their labor had, by the second half of the nineteenth century, become a common notion. Barbara Leigh Smith Bodichon (1827–91) considered this notion as lacking any legitimacy. In *Women and Work*, she mentions that "it seems hardly worth-while to say that there is a prejudice against women accepting money for their work. But there is one, therefore it is as well to say a few words upon it" (1857: 61). She goes on to make the point that, in general, work must be done for money and that paid work for women should be made honorable. These norms and values around gender and money that devalued the work and the woman who took it on, *because* it was paid, kept women from earning their own income, even when it was legal. Harriet Hanson Robinson (1825–1911), one of the first Lowell factory girls (see Chapter 6), lets us know that in the US too "a woman was not supposed or capable of spending her own or of using other people's money. In Massachusetts, before 1840, a woman could not legally be a treasurer of her own sewing-society, unless some man were responsible for her" (Robinson, 2021 [1898]: 68).

The relation of women with money remains of interest even into the twentieth century. In her famous book, *A Room of One's Own* (1929), Virginia Woolf (1882–1941) describes the feeling of having self-earned money in her wallet for the first time. Her description of this experience, and of the feeling of power that appears to accompany it, speaks to the impact on women's agency of earning an income and handling one's own money. The phenomenon of economic dependency combined with a lack of control over one's economic life resurfaced in the form of the suburban housewife, the image and existence of which was attacked by Germaine Greer (*The Female Eunuch*, 1970), Shulamite Firestone (*The Dialectic of Sex*,

1970), Susan Brownmiller (*Against Our Will*, 1975), and Angela Davis (*Women, Race, and Class*, 1981), to mention only a few. These books gave a voice to a movement of newly empowered women who wanted to take back control of their lives and destinies.

Even today, for young heterosexual women, starting a discussion with their future life partner about the division of work, time, and income is still pretty much taboo, as it is perceived incompatible with the romance and assumed trust between the lovers. The more practical take on this, however, would be to not enter into a long-term relationship without first discussing and agreeing on these matters. The romantic take that denies the importance of the future control over capital and money still mostly works out to the detriment of women, who tend to end up with the short end of the stick.

The financialization of the economy

In the meantime, the world of credit, banking, investment, and stock markets developed separately from the household and from what had been defined as the woman's realm. The world of money and finance, at least where financial decision-making was concerned, became and remained fully male-dominated. Abigail Adams (1744–1818), wife of the first American President, who was an investor in government bonds and made a firm profit, was an exception, and there were a few more like her. Priscilla Wakefield, whom we met in Chapter 2 as the author of *Reflections on the Present Condition of the Female Sex* (1798), and who, due to her husband's fruitless investments, needed to earn her own income, not only started to write for a living, but also founded a savings bank for women and children. She took in and lent out small amounts of money and, as such, can be considered one of the first micro credit bankers. In 1870, Victoria Woodhull (1838–1927) became the first female stockbroker on Wall Street and she started a brokerage firm with her sister. Hetty Green (1834–1916) was an investor who gathered significant capital by working the New York stock market. Such women bankers were not necessarily feminists. Hetty Green certainly wasn't. They did, however, counter the narrative that women could not be trusted with financial decisions and control over large capital accounts. Although interesting, we are here particularly interested in those who wrote about their experiences and analyzed the practices they were involved in.

Judith Sargent Murray (1751–1820), an upper-class woman from New England, for instance, was one such. She took part in and to some extent molded the discussion on gender relations at the time (Skemp, 1998). She came from a merchant family and read widely but eclectically, including the works of Rousseau, Voltaire, Wollstonecraft, and Catharine Macaulay. Murray was twenty-five when the American Revolution broke out, and, even though women were kept out of political decision-making, the war did strengthen their position in society. After the death of her husband, she was able to live independently due to her writing. She married a second time in 1788, and became more involved in financial matters such as investments, banking, and stocks. Her husband's handling of money was not particularly fruitful, which informed her, sometimes quite painfully, about the limited rights of women to engage in business by themselves. The goal of becoming economically independent remained a driving focus throughout her life. In a collection of her contributions to the *Massachusetts Magazine*, published under the title *The Gleaner* (1798), Murray made the case for women's education and showed her knowledge of running a business, keeping accounts, and banking practices.

The financial role played by enslaved people both in lending money and by functioning as collateral for loans for their owners is described by Harriet Jacobs (1813–97) in *Incidents in the Life of a Slave Girl* (1861). She gives an account of her life as an enslaved person, the work, the practices at the plantations, and the emotional and financial impacts of being considered property without any rights. She also mentions her mother, who saved many hundreds of dollars over her lifetime doing some business on the side, some of which she planned to use to buy back her children. Slaveowners, however, often "borrowed" money from their slaves, promising to pay it back, which would never happen. Jacobs wrote:

> While my grandmother was thus helping to support me from her hard earnings, the three hundred dollar she had lent her mistress were never repaid. When her mistress died, her son-in-law, Dr. Flint, was appointed executor. When grandmother applied to him for payment, he said the estate was insolvent, and the law prohibited payment. (2001 [1861]: 13)

As such, enslaved people provided their owners with more than only the fruits of their labor, which were substantial. They also played a considerable role as assets in the capital accumulation in the South as well as elsewhere in the US, and provided the slaveowners with collateral for loans that were used to buy slaves and to invest and back-up risk-taking (Martin, 2016).

With respect to the nineteenth-century financial industry, women had no access to positions that involved financial decision-making. Caroline Healy Dall, an American economic writer and also an activist in both the women's and the abolitionist movements, was part of the circle of intellectuals in Boston that included Ralph Waldo Emerson, Elizabeth Peabody, and Margaret Fuller. Dall, who provided an overview of the debates on education, women's suffrage, and women's labor, tells us – with some sarcasm – that women were not considered to be financial decision-makers:

> When Freeman Clarke was Comptroller of the United States Currency, he decided that a woman, not being a *citizen*, could not be a bank director. I consider this logical and satisfactory. I wish more decisions of this kind could be made. If the position was that woman is not a citizen were pushed to the extreme, it would become untenable, her property could not be taxed, and the necessary remedy would be applied. (1972 [1867]: 472)

The exclusion of women from finance and the emerging world of international finance was in part linked to the fact that women were almost entirely absent at the higher levels of banks, governments, and the international financial institutions, and that the fields of international relations and international political economy focused exclusively on the relations between the state and the financial industry (Assassi, 2009).

It was not until the early 1990s that there was a marked increase in the number of well-educated women choosing jobs on Wall Street. Most of these women, however, faced an uphill battle that many lost due to intimidation, sexual harassment, and lack of support at home and/or at work. Those who stayed faced an extreme kind of pushback in the form of sexual harassment, which remained hidden for many years due to the signing of non-disclosure agreements (NDAs) that concealed payouts of millions of dollars (Antilla, 2003).

In terms of historical analyses and theory development with respect to the world of finance, feminist economics and women economic writers more generally come in late. Setting aside exceptions like Marie Dessauer-Meinhardt (1901–86), who wrote about the functioning of the English and German banking systems in the 1930s (Trautwein, 2000), it was not until the international debt crisis of the 1980s that Susan George published her blistering report on the devastating impacts of the structural adjustment policies of the World Bank (George, 1988).

In her wake, Noreena Hertz (2004) articulated a critique on the international financial structure and the process through which loans were provided to countries in the South that were thus set up to fail. Two of her books, *The Silent Take Over* (2001) and *IOU. The Debt Threat and Why We Must Defuse It* (2004), contained original and accessible contributions to the discussion on topics that, at the time, were largely neglected by the economics discipline.

From then on, feminist economists started to bring gender concerns into analytical frameworks on the international financial system. Gary A. Dymski and Maria Floro (2000) developed a theoretical economic framework analyzing the relationship between gender, power, and economic crises. In their framework they link an increase in the participation of women in the labor force to a larger access to loans, which leads to growing household debts and, when the economic crisis hits, impacts women more severely than men. Nahid Aslanbeigui and Gale Summerfield (2000) provide an account of the Asian economic crisis and the role of international financial institutions such as the International Monetary Fund (IMF), introducing into the debate gender concerns and considerations. Irene van Staveren (2002) subsequently explores the link between global finance and gender, and the various forms and impacts that gender inequality has in this respect. She brings together gender segregation in the financial industry, gender inequality in property rights, and the discriminatory norms in financial markets, and assesses the effects of women's under-representation in economic decision-making in these markets and the industry. She argues for more transparency in (international) financial institutions and improved representation of women at all levels, and suggests that, as well as more attention for microcredits and gender audits, the women's movement should engage more at the macro level of international financial and economic policy-making (see also Elson, 2002).

It is the financial crisis, or Great Recession, of 2008/9 that would finally provoke feminist economists to start analyzing and writing in larger numbers about gender and (international) finance. Assassi (2009) analyzed the role of gender in the historical emergence of financial markets, the development of complex financial tools, and the processes through which finance and credit are used to control the poorest sectors of society. Assessing the gender impact of the financial crisis, Brigitta Young (2013, 2018) argued that women and minorities had been disproportionally sold subprime loans and mortgages, which led to an enormous loss of wealth among women and in the black community.

The trade floors in the banks that were considered too big to fail, on the other hand, were predominantly populated by young men. These men worked with complicated and nontransparent mathematical models and were under huge pressure to make short-term profits, earning extremely high bonuses. Iceland, the only country that went bankrupt during this crisis, was also the only country to imprison a large subset of its bankers afterwards. As banks run by women survived, the country elected its first female prime minister in the person of Jóhanna Sigurðardóttir (PM from 2009 to 2013).

Overall, however, the financial industry maintained its white, male character. The power struggle over access to economic and financial decision-making took various forms. The replacement of IMF president Dominique Strauss-Kahn (DSK), ousted as a sexual predator, by Christine Lagarde led to a major shift in the IMF's stance on gender issues. The IMF published findings on gender equality and – albeit to a limited extent – took into account the impact of the gender wage gap on economic growth. At the same time, Janet Yellen became director of the US central bank, the Federal Reserve, where she shifted the focus toward strengthening the Fed's role in countering unemployment. At the time of writing, under the Biden administration, Yellen is Secretary of the US Treasury Department. With Ngozi Okonjo-Iweala becoming President of the World Trade Organization (WTO), the idea that women cannot and should not handle money has largely disappeared in the Western world. This does not mean, however, that women yet have equal access to the table where the decisions are being made – far from it.

Over the past few decades, the financial industry has become increasingly dominant in a number of national economies, especially those of formerly manufacturing industrialized countries like the US, the UK, and other countries in Europe and Asia. Feminist economists articulated critiques on the international financial system and its institutions, developing policies for changes and alternatives (see, e.g., Elson, 2002; Mellor, 2010; van Staveren, 2002).

The field of economics has shifted accordingly in the sense that finance-based language is now used in economic theorizing and modeling. Concepts like "risk-seeking" and "risk-averse behavior" come up in explanations of income differences, and insurance terminology is being applied to conceptualize and design social and economic policies concerning pensions, social benefits, and healthcare. The idea that women and men would have different attitudes toward risk-taking emerged at the same time. It was Julie

Nelson (2014) who deconstructed this research and characterized the results as a construction and as directed by confirmation bias. This criticism, of course, did not stop the current tendency to use financial language in economic analyses to coin concepts and direct questions, and to design economic policies.

5

Production

Introduction

The shift of production from inside the self-sufficient agrarian household to outside the household, into workshops, factories, and, later, international corporations – a shift here referred to as the monetization and marketization of production – increased the efficient use of (some) resources. On the other hand, it externalized a large part of the production costs while business owners made profits. This led to, among other things, goods and services and their modified versions being sold over the market at a price too high for those who had produced them themselves before to purchase them. This meant that some of these goods and services became unaffordable for those who had themselves earlier produced those same goods and services. This process of industrialization required women, especially, to adapt as they saw productive activities leaving the household and economic dependency on their husband taking its place (Pinchbeck, 1930; see also Horrell and Humphries, 1995).

Although women and the household were consistently excluded from political economic theorizing, in reality the role of women in the production, distribution, and consumption of goods and services was both substantial and subject to change. Women's economic writing about the production process focused not only on their work in the household (see Chapter 1), but also – and this is the topic of this chapter – on their paid work in the agricultural sector, in domestic service, in manufacturing workshops and factories, and eventually in predominantly the service industry. This chapter will start with an overview of women's economic writings containing descriptions and explanations of the increase of women's participation in paid work, and will then move to women's writing on the gender segregation in industrial sectors and jobs. It ends with a discussion on women's writing on female entrepreneurship, the setting up and running of a business.

Women's participation in monetized and marketized production

Working-class women as well as those in rural areas have always worked for pay. During early industrialization in the UK and on into the nineteenth century, working-class women constituted around 25 percent of the labor force, which is defined as anyone over the age of fifteen who has, or is looking for, a job. In the early 1700s most women who worked for pay worked in agriculture either as farmers or as day workers. One of the first-known texts that makes the strong claim that women worked and contributed as much to production as men is *The Woman's Labour* by Mary Collier (*c.*1688–1762). Collier was an English washerwoman who had learned to read and write from her mother, and who had developed the habit of reading everything she could lay her hands on. As soon as her mistress heard about the poem Mary had written, she supported its publication (Ferguson, 1985).

In *The Woman's Labour* (1739), Collier criticizes Stephen Duck, another working-class poet, for his misogynistic take on women and their work, as can be read in his poem *The Thresher's Labour* (1736). Duck's poem shone a spotlight on the burdens of a thresher and the drudgery in a working man's life. In response to Duck's poem, Collier described her work during the harvest in summer and fall and at the big estate during the winter, and claimed that female farm laborers worked as hard as the threshers described by Duck, if not harder. Collier (1739) made her point by describing her daily activities in detail. She compared the man coming home and getting his dinner served, with the woman who has another shift waiting for her and needs to work until she goes to sleep:

> WHEN Ev'ning does approach, we homeward hie,
> And our domeftic Toils Inceffant ply:
> Againft your coming Home prepare to get
> Our Work all done, our Houfe in order fet;
> *Bacon* and *Dumpling* in the Pot we boil,

Our Beds we make, our Swine we feed the while;
Then wait at Door to fee you coming Home,
And fet the Table out againſt you come:
Early next Morning we on you attend;
Our Children dreſs and feed, their Cloaths we mend;
And in the Field our daily Task renew,
Soon as the riſing Sun has dry'd the Dew.[1]

(Emphasis in original)

The issue that Collier describes here – men may have to work hard, but most women have a second shift that includes their household and caring tasks – is still with us today (see, e.g., Hochschild and Machung, 1989). Implicitly referring to Bernard Mandeville's "Honest Hive" in her last and moralizing phrase that starts: "SO, the induſstries Bees do hourly strive, To bring their Loads of Honey to the Hive," Collier joins Duck in his critique of "Their sordid Owners [who] always reap the Gains, and poorly recompenſe their Toils and Pains." Collier published a collection of poems later in her life, but *The Woman's Labour* stands out as it fully focuses on women's productive contribution from the perspective of a working-class woman, for the humor it contains and the strengths of the images it presents to us. In England's class-structured society, working-class poets were a rare phenomenon, since working-class people hardly received enough education to read and write, let alone become poets. This was even more the case for female working-class poets (Ferguson, 1985). More work of such women has been retrieved over the past decades, like that by Mary Masters (1694?–1759?) and Ann Yearsley (1753–1806), the working-class poet whom Hannah Moore took under her wing (Landry, 1990).

A fascinating and early story from the US is the one about Martha Moore Ballard (1785–1812), whose diary has been analyzed and published under the title *The Midwife's Tale* by Laurel Thatcher Ulrich (1990). The book gives us access to the diary of a midwife during the period of the first settlers in the US. As Ballard was the midwife and dealt with life and death on a daily basis, she was a central, trusted, and respected figure in the small economy of Hallowell, Maine. She was also the one who, once a year, closed the books and made sure that people evened out their mutual debts.

Other diaries by working-class people in the US, including those of enslaved people, started to appear during the second half of the nineteenth century. These diaries provide us with accounts of the

---

[1] ſ = s. Reading the poem out loud will help with understanding its content.

work done in the fields, their productive contributions to the harvest, and the circumstances under which this work took place. The earliest enslaved woman to escape and who was able to put pen to paper to describe her experience was Mary Prince (1788–after 1833). She gives an account of her situation, work, escape, and provides her reflections. The focus of her and other enslaved women's writings is not so much on the heaviness of the work they did throughout their lives, since that, to some extent, seems to be taken for granted. The narrative is more about explaining the horrors of a life as an enslaved person, the circumstances and main events of their lives, including the relations with and separation of their loved ones. When Prince tells the reader about her work, the phrase is immediately followed by a description of the way she is treated by her mistress, clearly of more importance than the tasks at hand:

> The next morning my mistress set about instructing me in my tasks. She taught me to do all sorts of household work; to wash and bake, pick cotton and wool, and wash floors and cook. And she taught me (how can I ever forget it!) more things than these; she caused me to know the exact difference between the smart of the rope, the cart-whip, and the cow-skin, when applied to my naked body by her own cruel hand. (1997 [1831]: 66)

This production that Mary would engage in was not actually paid, though food and shelter were provided. As the enslaved people themselves were marketized, they were considered to be without rights and available for exploitation and abuse.

Back in England, Elizabeth Montagu's letters explicitly mentioned the importance of the farm work of women and girls in the fields. This insight, however, gets lost in the theorizing of political economists such as David Ricardo, who stressed the division of work between men and their specialization in more and more specific tasks as some of the main causes of economic growth. While French physiocrats perceived agriculture as the only sector that produced "value," in Ricardo's view value was created and added when resources were turned into goods by the utilization of labor. He, and most other political economists, perceived "surplus value" as the value produced by the workers minus the cost for their subsistence. For political economists, whether a worker is a woman or a man seemed of little relevance, even though we have seen that gender severely structured the lives, rights, and behaviors of both women and men in industrial society. It is in this context that Ricardo only refers to male workers, and explains that "the natural price of labour, therefore, depends on the price of the food, necessaries, and conveniences required for the support of the labourer and his family" (1911 [1817]: 52). In this perception of society, women engaged in unpaid production did not create or add value by their work; those with jobs in workshops and factories were considered as workers, the only difference from men being that they were paid less.

Fights, strikes, struggles, and critiques of unmitigated capitalism increased in the first decades of the nineteenth century; the abolitionist movement saw its numbers grow, while political economy provided the rationale for the exploitative industrial practices. Political pressure increased in the 1820s and 1830s in the form of strikes and riots. Many female activists fighting for women's rights were at the time doing so as members of the abolitionist movement. When, in the early 1840s, the UK government published a report about the situation in the mines – where girls and boys as young as ten years of age were working, ruining their health for life – the general public demanded interventions to protect the workers. It is against this background that Charlotte Elizabeth Tonna (1790–1846) wrote a collection of children's religious novels, in one of which she directly referred to Adam Smith's famous pin factory.

In "The Little Pin-Headers" (1843), Tonna leads the reader by the hand to a room at the back of the pin factory to see what lies behind the closed doors of the factory in Smith's famous example about the gains produced by the division of labor. This example concerned "a very trifling manufactory; but one in which the division of labour has been very often taken notice of, the trade of the pin-maker; ... I have seen a small manufactory of this kind where ten men only were employed, and where some of them consequently performed two or three operations" (Smith, 1976 [1776]: 14–15). Tonna uses Smith's example as she describes how one would enter the pin factory and find the men in the first room. Walking on, however, one would find young women and children in terrible circumstances doing their work, practically in the dark, in the back of the building:

> We enter at once a new scene – the interior of a pin manufactory. It is winter, the chilliness of a November day ... We proceed through several departments of busy employment: in one there are children winding slender wire, which, being passed through a machine by steam-power, is drawn out by men. Here, the boys work, generally under their fathers; and whatever we may think of their close, protracted confinement, the labour itself is not severe. In the next room we find many little fellows, more fatiguingly employed, being perpetually on foot, walking to and fro, assisting their seniors by the operation of straightening the coiled wire furnished by the drawers,

which the men cut into length and point. ... Hitherto, we found no girls, nor very little children; but enter the next department, and the scene will change. Here is a room, if we can call it by that name ... and here, seated before machines unlike any that we have yet surveyed, are about fifty children, of whom the eldest maybe thirteen, but the general age is less, much less – they are mere babes. (1843: 63–4)

This scene is followed by Tonna's account of the work these young children are engaged in. By describing this as vividly as she did, she successfully drew in her readers and made them identify with those working in these horrid circumstances. The public outrage and the shared interests of male-dominated trade unions and employers led the government to accept what came to be referred to as "factory laws," which would initially protect children and women against long working hours and dangerous working circumstances, before they were extended and applied more widely. This did not prevent, however, revolutions from breaking out all over Europe in 1848.

The political economic theory of labor relations that spoke about the employer and the worker as equal partners in the labor market did not capture the ruthless struggles and conflicts between employers and workers. Early socialist thinkers like Charles Fourier, Saint-Simon, Simonde de Sismondi, and Robert Owen, and later Karl Marx and Friedrich Engels, brought the conflict between the employer (the capitalist, or the owner of the means of production) and the worker (the laborer who produces the surplus value) to the center of attention. Although early socialist economic writers did write about the exploitation of women, enslaved people, and the abuse of Native Americans, scientific Marxist theory focused on the class conflict between the capitalist and the workers in particular. It was Engels who indicated that the male wage-earner household was inherent to nineteenth-century capitalism. It was this household model that became naturalized as the most civilized and that Alfred Marshall would have liked to have seen spread to the working classes as well (Groenewegen, 1995). This household model may have worked out for those middle-class women who had a good marriage and a husband who earned a decent income, but for the rest of the women in Britain, Europe, and later the US, it had serious negative consequences.

The Langham Place group in London, the women artists, poets, educators, and economic writers around Barbara Leigh Smith Bodichon and Bessie Rayner Parkes (1829–1925), argued and made policy proposals for the improvement of women's education and rights to vote, and a substantial part of their work concerned women's paid work. Bodichon's *A Brief Summary, in Plain Language, of the Most Important Laws Concerning Women* (1854) and *Women and Work* (1857) contained materials that backed-up the claims brought forward by her and the Married Women's Property Committee she started. After the unsuccessful attempt to get the Married Women Property Act accepted, the Committee decided to start the *English Women's Journal*, which was published monthly from 1858 to 1864, and would become a central forum for feminist discussions in Britain and abroad (Lacey, 1987). Change would come and the social pressure they organized resulted in the acceptance of the Divorce Act in 1857 and the Married Women's Property Act in 1870 (Sockwell, 2000: 53; Holcombe, 1983).

In *Women and Work*, Bodichon advocates opening up more professions for middle-class women so they could engage in decent work and earn a decent income; work that would enable them to be useful in society and provide them with an income they could call their own. "There is nothing in the world so sad, so pitiful to see, as a young woman, who has been handsome, full of youthful joy, animal-spirits and good nature, fading at thirty or thirty-five" (1857: 39). The idea that most middle- and upper-class women were destined to live a frivolous life, void of meaning except for the raising of sons, was strongly contested by the Langham Place group. Bodichon and her fellow feminists used data from the census and local statistical bureaus to point out that there were simply not enough men in general and, moreover, not enough who could afford to single-handedly provide for a wife and children. This limited the number of eligible men for all the young women who were on the marriage market. The Langham Place group made the point that at least those women who remained unmarried should be allowed to earn their own living.

Bessie Rayner Parkes wrote about women's working conditions in workshops and factories. She criticized the state of the available data on unmarried women's labor force participation in Britain, which she estimated to be about 1.2 million out of a total labor force of 7 million people, domestic workers not included (1860: 175). She also recognized that, although she did not consider industrial society a natural state of affairs, the public sphere had increasingly become home to women as well (Parkes, 1862). It was not that she wanted to see all women earn their own livelihood, but since the male wage-earner household model did not work out for so many women, for those who needed an income, appropriate training and professions should be open to them.

Jessie Boucherett (1825–1905), also a member of the Langham Place group, who founded the Society for Promoting the Employment of Women, also pointed out that the lack of jobs and professions open to women made it difficult for them to maintain themselves. This leds, according to Boucherett, in turn to "the number of adult women inhabiting workhouses in England and Wales in March, 1861, [to be] 39,073, yet this does not represent the number of those requiring relief, for as we see, many are excluded who would be glad to get in" (1864: 270). Frances Power Cobbe (1822–1904) computed that, in addition to the natural excess of females over males of about 4–5 percent, about 30 percent of women in England would "never, marry, leaving one-fourth of both sexes in a state of celibacy" (1862: 355). Cobbe discussed the barriers that prevented old maids and widows from living happy and healthy lives. She also suggested some solutions, such as more marriages and the proposal "to dispose of the matter by observing ... the transportation of 440,000 women to the colonies, [which would] at least *relieve the market* for those who remain" (1862: 363; emphasis in original). It would be this group of middle- and higher-class women, with sufficient time and energy, who would form the groundswell of those who would constitute the women's movement, standing up against this arrangement, and fighting for women's suffrage and economic independence.

In the US, Caroline Healey Dall (1822–1912), who was inspired and encouraged by the work of the Langham Place group, was a faithful reader of the *English Women's Journal*. In her book *The College, The Market, and the Court*, Dall addressed issues related to education, labor, wages, and the legal position of women. In the chapter "Death or Dishonor," she based women's claims to labor in "the absolute necessity of bread," women's physical and psychical ability, and their natural drive to work, which she referred to as "an attraction inherent in the ability" (1972 [1867]: 135). In addition, she provided numbers and examples of women who, while facing devastating economic circumstances, saw no other option than to engage in prostitution. Dall's argument here was that women needed work and sufficient pay to earn a living for themselves and their dependents.

Dall, like Bodichon, Parkes, and others, argued for women to be trained and to have the opportunity to work, and thus expressed the desire to actively engage in labor as a way to improve one's skills and apply one's energy in a useful manner. This was in contrast to most political economists of the time, who perceived most workers as predominantly lazy and as people who needed to be incentivized by poverty, hunger, and pay to get the work done. Except for the early and Marxist socialists, who acknowledged the inherent value and meaning of (decent) work for a person's well-being, marginalists like William Stanley Jevons (1965 [1871]) perceived workers as machines orientated toward weighing pleasure and pain – maximizing utility – which meant working as little as possible. Jevons, one of the founders of marginalist economic theory, argued, in response to the high mortality rates in British larger cities, for "the ultimate complete exclusion of mothers of children under the age of three years from factories and workshops" (1883: 172). This kind of reasoning worked out detrimentally for working-class mothers of young children who needed an income to survive. Helen McCarthy (2020) indicates that, according to the dominant moral framework within which motherhood was understood by the end of the nineteenth century, married female wage earners were considered to be a problem in the UK. This would, however, change over the course of the twentieth century.

Edith Abbott (1876–1957), an American economic historian, who was also a statistician, a social worker, and an educator, a not uncommon combination of skills shared by women economists at the time, identified an important difference between the UK and the US where the labor force participation of women was concerned. Abbott (1910) mentioned that whereas in the UK land was scarce and the population abundant, in the US male settlers were working the land and there were concerns about the idleness of women and girls. While, in the UK, men were available to work in the factories, there was a push for women and children to stay at home. In the US, however, young women and girls were pushed out of the home to populate the mills and factories, which was looked upon positively, as it would keep them occupied.

Elizabeth Leigh Hutchins (1858–1935) was a British economic historian who wrote, with James Mallon, *Women in Modern Industry* (1915). Hutchins reported on, among other things, the fact that it was young women in particular who worked in the factories, and, to a lesser extent, single and widowed women. According to Hutchins, women's labor force participation rate was 35.5 percent and she stressed that this number mostly included (young) girls. As soon as these young women married, they would leave their job, only to return if necessity forced them to. Hutchins estimated that there were about 250,000 single women between the age of 35 and 44 working for pay as domestic servants, professional women, and textile workers (1915: 169–70).

Hutchins was a member of the Fabian Society, which was founded in 1884 and consisted of a group of left-leaning, socialist intellectuals including Bernard Shaw, H. G. Wells, Beatrice Potter Webb, and Sidney Webb. The Fabian Women's Group (FWG) organized gatherings and published tracts on women's economic independence, women and trade unions, and other issues related to the "woman question." This group was a power house of feminist activists and economists who aimed at transforming the capitalist system into a (democratic) socialist system through the political process. Of particular interest in the context of this herstory of economics is work by Barbara Hutchins, Mabel Atkinson, Eleanor Rathbone, Barbara Drake, Emma Brooke, and Beatrice Potter Webb. The work of some of these women will be discussed here in more detail.

At one of the FWG meetings, Hutchins presented "The Working Life of Women" (1911), in which she describes women heading into the labor market as moving from one level ("plane") of social development to another; from the pre-capitalist household to a higher level of social development, which is capitalist society. From the world of value-in-use, which is the household where work has only use-value, women move, according to Hutchins, into the world of value-in-exchange, which is the labor market, where work obtains an exchange or market value. Hutchins argued that value-in-use cannot sustain a family because, in a capitalist society, the value-in-use is lower than the value-in-exchange, or, in other words, the opportunity costs of staying home are higher than the benefits of women's time at home. A household will, therefore, be better off with a mother who has a paid job than a mother who is exclusively at home. Hutchins continues: "In the face of such facts it is absurd to tell women that their work as mothers is of the highest importance to the State" (2020 [1911]: 176). We see here an early version of Barbara Bergmann's (1986) argument that, when the opportunity costs of staying at home are higher than the benefits of raising children, women will decide to take a paid job.

Mabel Atkinson (1876–1958) considered and analyzed, after an overview of the shifts in women's work and household models from agriculture to industrial society, the difference in class interests within the women's movement. Discussing the various sets of circumstances and interests, Atkinson (1987 [1914]) clearly outlined why, for working-class women, class interests dominate feminist interests: working-class women are exploited like their male counterparts. Middle-class women, on the other hand, are forced into parasitic behavior and a life of economic dependency and uselessness. When inequality and circumstances change, the conflicts in the women's movement may be resolved with them, is Atkinson's hope.

Not a member of the FWG, but thinking and writing along similar lines was Olive Schreiner (1855–1920), a novelist from South Africa, who worked for many years on the research for her book, to be called

"Woman." However, she lost the final manuscript and her notes to fire after an attack on her house during the Boer War. Schreiner was only able to restore part of the manuscript, which she then published under the title *Woman and Labor* (1911). Schreiner argues that the focus on the "sex relation" and the cult around motherhood that developed by the end of the nineteenth century should be seen as a sign of decline of Western civilization. The system in which a large part of the population – both married and single women – is not permitted to train and work their bodies and minds, but instead are forced into indulgence and "parasitism," weakens not only the women concerned, but their children as well and corrupts the relations between women and men. In similar vein to Charlotte Perkins Gilman (1998 [1898]), Schreiner states: "The debilitating effect of unlabored-for-wealth lies, then, not in the nature of any material adjunct to life in itself, but in the power it may possess of robbing the individual of all incentive to exertion, thus destroying the intellectual, the physical, and finally, the moral fiber" (1911: 101). Her solution is to support women in becoming economically independent. Her demand is *"Give us labor and the training which fits for labor!"* (1911: 27; emphasis in original).

Women economic writers and economists also analyzed the general structure of production, going beyond the focus on women's role and contribution. Ida Minerva Tarbell (1857–1944) is a good example. Tarbell was an American journalist and the author of *The History of the Standard Oil Company* (1904), a book that made quite an impression. It was based on investigative journalism and aimed, according to Tarbell, to "just bring out the facts." It showed the dark side of Rockefeller's oil company, and contributed to the US Department of Justice suing Standard Oil and a few years later the splitting up of this corporation into tens of smaller companies by an order of the Supreme Court in 1911. In 1906, Tarbell and other progressive journalists – referred to as "muckrakers" by many – started their own outlet, *The American Magazine*, in which Tarbell would publish most of her articles. After her work on Standard Oil, she shifted her focus to the "woman question" and focused on women's work in particular.

In Europe, the socialist movement was growing stronger, and Rosa Luxemburg (1871–1919) contributed substantially to Marxist analysis. She was a social activist and socialist thinker who studied law and political economy and was part of a humanist and democratic Marxist movement. In *The Accumulation of Capital* (1913), which contains her main economic analysis, she explains the expansion of the capitalist system abroad as being partly due to lack of demand, on the one hand, and to misguided demand, on the other. Distinguishing between those industries that produce capital goods – machines, pipes, boilers, drills, etc. – and those that produce consumption goods – clothing, tables, shoes, carpets, etc. – Luxemburg indicated that, as capital goods have a longer lifespan, the markets for capital goods would tend to be satisfied sooner than those for consumer goods. Thus, there would be a surplus of capital goods, or rather an under-demand for these goods. The way this is solved in the capitalist system is by expanding the markets for these goods, by making sure that not-yet-industrialized countries start to buy capital goods to set up their industry of consumer goods. As this would herald an exportation of the capitalist system and these new factories would, at least initially, be owned or controlled by the traditionally capitalist countries (to enable "developing countries" to accommodate capitalist production), the culture and domestic institutions of the developing countries would have to change with it.

Luxemburg had to pay dearly for her views and was imprisoned several times in her life. After the German, or November, Revolution freed her in November 1918, she went back to work but soon died at the hands of a German paramilitary group in 1919 (Nettl, 1969 [1966]). Imperialism as described by Luxemburg not only implied the expansion of capitalism to other cultures, but also meant the growth of the markets within industrialized nations, increasingly commodifying unpaid household production, and the monetization of services formerly provided for free within the household – a development that has surfaced in this book as well.

It was World War I, or the Great War, that cut through the myth that middle-class women simply could not take up and function successfully in male-dominated professions. Women in the UK had answered the call to contribute to the war effort, making women's paid work in the labor market visible and respected. Women proved to be essential to the war effort, and as Eleanor Rathbone (1872–1946) claimed, they would not leave their new and well-paid jobs willingly. In the middle of London, Waterloo Bridge (also called "the Ladies' Bridge") still bears witness to the fact that women were able to produce munitions, guns, and whole bridges, if given the opportunity to do so. Women economic writers like Atkinson (1987 [1914]) and Rathbone (1917) recognized the fundamental change in the perception of women's abilities and its (potential) implications. Atkinson's historical overview of the changes in household models – for both the working and the middle class – identified the problem of the future for women as being the combination of work, if not a career, with their ability to have a family.

Nevertheless, as soon as the war was over, women were pushed out of the labor market as the returning soldiers took over their jobs. This exclusion from their workplaces was further exacerbated by the Great Depression in the late 1920s and 1930s (Scharf, 1980). Laws that prohibited married women from holding a job were put into place all over Europe and in the US. At the same time, technologically advanced tools such as the washing machine, the refrigerator, and the vacuum cleaner meant that fewer servants were needed. These technological developments alongside the rise in (male) wages made it possible for housewives to spend more time raising their own children, ornamenting their house, and doing the cooking themselves. Women's magazines developed imagery and expectations around these tasks that made them much more time-demanding than they had been, for instance, during the war. The domestic industry thus took a big hit as the average number of servants per household went down to one or zero in the 1950s, after which, for most middle-class households, only incidental help remained. The further marketization and monetization of household production, the opening up of administrative jobs, and an increase in women's wages over the course of the twentieth century would, however, lead to a continued growth in women's paid labor participation. This, in turn, furthered the ongoing outsourcing of unpaid household activities, a decrease in the number of children, and a further increase in household technology.

The social and economic impact of the increase of female labor participation over the twentieth century meant that most women moved from being engaged in unpaid household production to taking a paid job. Women became more and more both care and financial providers for their household. In Sweden, Alva Myrdal (1902–86) wrote about changes in the modern family and claimed that "workers are entitled to have a family" instead of the more commonplace claim that mothers should have the right to work. This approach in Sweden appeared successful (see, e.g., Ekerwald, 2016). Together with Viola Klein, Myrdal published *Women's Two Roles: Home and Work* (1956) in which they argued that women had to choose between a career and raising a family, which was unfair and unnecessary. In agreement with Charlotte Perkins Gilman (1998 [1898]), who had claimed earlier that women were easily able to work both as young women *and* as older women after their children had left the home, Myrdal and Klein argued that women could still build a career as soon as their children were old enough. Their book provides a set of adjustments that women themselves had to make (in planning their professional life, choice of vocation, keeping improving vocational skills, and, of course, obtaining the support of their partner) and various ways the government and employers could accommodate women's return to the labor market (by providing part-time work, extended paid maternity leave, training for those over forty for re-employment, etc.) (1968 [1956]: 154–65). In 1938, Myrdal and her husband Gunnar moved to the US and Alva received the Nobel Peace Prize in 1982 for her work on nuclear disarmament.

Together with stagnating male wages in the US from the 1970s onward, the increase of female labor force participation continued and the transitional household model became prevalent in industrial societies. "The transitional model of the household," in which both husband and wife are financial providers but the wife remains the main care provider, hampered women considerably in their careers, especially for leadership positions in corporations, in which working 60–80 hours per week along with permanent availability remained the norm. Arli Hochschild and Anne Machung referred to this phenomenon as *The Second Shift* (1989): the situation in which women have a full-time paid job, but remained primarily responsible for raising the children and running the household. As we saw early on in this chapter, this resonates with Mary Collier's observations already made in 1739 in *The Woman's Labour* with respect to working-class women.

Between the 1960s and 1990s, the labor force participation rate increased for married women from 34 percent to 66 percent in the US, from 35 percent to 69 percent in the UK, and, for comparison, from 7 percent to 47 percent in the Netherlands and from 41 percent to 87 percent in Sweden (Sainsbury, 1996: 105). Barbara Bergmann (1925–2015), an outspoken and widely respected feminist economist, described the strong increase in the female labor force participation rate in most post-World War II Western economies in *The Economic Emergence of Women* (1986). Bergmann mentions as explanations the technological innovation and investments leading to productivity increases and raising wages over the twentieth century, the innovations in household technology, and the decline of the number of children per household, which together decreased the benefits and increased the opportunity costs of women's time spent at home. Claudia Goldin (1990) mentions the improved education of women, the growth of sectors accessible for women, and the shorter workday – and, in addition, the decline in fertility and innovations in household technology. All in all, the monetization and marketization of women's productive labor contributed substantially to economic growth in terms of GDP. These developments impacted the South to some extent similarly, but also differently.

After political dominance of the West over their colonies ended and was replaced by economic dominance, economic policies enacted by the IMF and the World Bank impacted many countries in the South. Ricardo's concept of comparative advantage through bilateral trade was further developed by Eli Heckscher and Bertil Ohlin (1991) into a model in which trade between two countries was perceived as increasing the economic growth of them both; certain countries would specialize in producing high-level technology and capital goods using the resources with relative low opportunity costs, while other countries would import these capital goods and export those goods the production of which used the resources that were relatively cheap for them: primary resources and cheap labor. Critiquing this mainstream take on international trade from a women's perspective, Ester Boserup (1910–99), a Danish economist by training, developed economic models on subsistence economies that differed from the static and ahistorical models of most of her colleagues. In 1965 she published *The Conditions of Agricultural Growth* in which she developed a theory of development that related technological development to the level of population. Thomas Malthus had claimed that population growth was exponential where the food supply would only grow at best at an arithmetic or linear rate, which eventually would cause disease, famines, and wars to restore the balance between the two. Boserup argued that agricultural methods and technology induced by population growth would cause the food supply to increase at a sufficient level. Speaking from a strong position in the emerging field of developing economics, Boserup also published *Woman's Role in Economic Development* (1970), showing that in many cases economic growth in a development country like India, while having a positive impact on the income of men, could have negative consequences for women. This revolutionary analysis meant the start of a literature on the topic that would become referred to as "Women in Development" (WID).

Subsequently, feminists, including economists, started to question the neoliberal economic system more generally and renamed the field as gender and development (GAD). Throughout the 1980s, 1990s, and 2000s, millions of women globally moved into the labor market to get a paid job; most of them, however, ended up doing informal and precarious work. Their production, however, now monetized and marketized, became increasingly visible (see e.g., Elson, 1991). The gendered character and impacts of the neoliberal economic regime were outlined by women authors such as Lourdes Benería (2003), V. Spike Peterson (2003), and Suzanne Bergeron (2004).

In the 2000s, Barbara Ehrenreich and Arli Hochschild (2002) and Rhacel Parreñas (2001) brought to light that, with the increase of economic migration in the 1990s, more and more women were traveling to the US and Western Europe to sell their care labor and to nurse the children of Americans and Europeans, thus enabling Western women to participate in the labor market. Countries like the Philippines literally export care labor and mother love to the West, leaving children in their home countries without the nursing and love of their own mothers. The payments that migrants sent home, including those involved in the Global Care Chain, were good for millions and millions in remittances each year, and now equal, if not exceed, other major international money flows. Dealing in care work, set off by the global inequality between the North and the South, has become a trade in itself, which often occurs in the form of trafficking. Linda Lucas's edited volume *Unpacking Globalization* (2007) is a work in which women from the South relate their experiences with the impacts of structural adjustment policies and increasing immigration, and their involvement in supplying domestic work abroad.

Gender segregation in industry

In the West, and in the US in particular, women, people of color, and immigrants worked in the lower echelons of the labor market. Some could improve themselves, or make their children go to college; a select few could even become millionaires – in other words, live the American Dream. Overall, however, horizontal segregation (the overrepresentation of a specific group in a job or profession) and vertical segregation (the overrepresentation of members of certain groups in higher and lower positions within an industry or sector) developed alongside industrial society. Jobs open to women, paid or unpaid, tended to be similar to the work they had been doing in the home – for example, jobs in the food and hospitality industry, nursing, and teaching. Black and Hispanic men and women generally worked in agriculture, domestic work, restaurants, and cleaning services, and held the lowest paid jobs in industry. Chinese workers tended to have jobs building the railroads, while Hispanic people worked in sweatshops. It is good to note here that, while the American Dream always consisted of opportunities to make it or to enable your children to create a better life for themselves, over the past few decades social mobility has decreased in the US and is now one of the lowest of the industrialized countries. This structuring of the labor market, occupational segregation by gender or race, is a main explanation of the gender and racial wage gaps that will be discussed in more detail in Chapter 6, "Distribution."

Like Mary Hays (1798), who demanded access for women to more jobs and professions, Priscilla Wakefield (1751–1832), in her pamphlet *Reflections on the Present Conditions of the Female Sex* (1798), made the same point, demanding better access to jobs and productive activities for women of all classes. Midwifery is an example of a profession over which a fierce fight took place regarding whether it should be a woman's or a man's job. Wakefield made the argument that this profession should remain a woman's job since it concerned a service to women; having a male midwife assisting women in giving birth would simply not be decent. Wakefield proposed opening up professions at all levels of society that serve women in particular, like hairdressers, midwives, undertakers, etc., while respecting society's class structure. Laying out what should be done for girls and women in each of the four classes in society, she argued for keeping class boundaries in place and training the girls accordingly. By arguing for economic equality between women and men in considerable detail, however, her pamphlet is radical in its implications.

Soon after the emergence of workshops and factories early on in the industrialization process, women and men were separated into various jobs with the argument that this segregation was required to protect women's decency. This job segregation process seldom went off without a hitch though, as it meant that women were excluded from the better paid jobs. Joan W. Scott stresses the role of language and the masculine representation of class in defining workers' problems, in which women were not "seen as appropriate political actors on behalf of the class," but were instead perceived as to be represented by men (1988: 64). Scott gives a detailed account of the struggles of seamstresses in early nineteenth-century France and the role played by contemporary debates in political economy in providing the narrative that enabled employers to settle these debates and riots.

Caroline Healey Dall (1860) attacks the lack of access to professions in the US, France, and the UK, and the overrepresentation in some fields, which would make the wages in those industries go down. She discusses, among other things, women's (hard) work in a broad range of professions and critiques the fact that women's labor participation in many fields remained unreported. Around 1845, there were in the US, according to Dall, 75,710 women and 55,828 men working in the textile industry as workers: "as *employers*, they are very few." To give an impression of the kind of work women were engaged in, this is her list:

Makers of gloves	Physicians
Makers of glue	Pickers and preservers
Workers in gold and silver leaf	Saddle & harness makers
Hair-weavers	Shoemakers
Hat and cap makers	Soda-room keepers
Hose-weavers	Snuff and cigars makers
Workers in India-rubber	Stock & suspender makers
Lamp-makers	Truss-makers
Laundresses	Typers and stereotypers
Leechers	Umbrella-makers
Milleners	Upholsterers
Morocco-workers	Card-makers
Nurses	Grinder of watch crystal.
Paper-handers	

Dall criticized the census, among others the one from 1845 in the city of Boston, for leaving out job categories (she mentions "washer woman," "char woman," and "servant," together good for about 5,000 workers) and for thus estimating the number of women engaged in paid employments as too low (1860: 97–100).

Dall also discussed the slow shift in occupational segregation and women entering various male-dominated fields such as medicine, woodcarving, and jobs such as ministers and prison guards, to mention a few. In the chapter "Death or Dishonor," Dall calls out the practices in the cotton, silk, and wool industry, and shows that the especially dirty work of carding is mostly done by women, who are paid "half-wages" (1860: 43). Such wages were too low to live on, especially when one had a family to provide for. Dall also describes the work done by children, including girls, working in the mines, mills, and pin-factories, where from the age of five, "in spite of the delicacy of their sex" (1860: 50), girls slaved for sixteen hours per day, with detrimental impacts on their health. Many women, due to the low wages, would fall to their "moral death" – in other words, end up in the sex industry and on the streets.

Virginia Penny (1826–1913), a Kentucky-born middle-class woman, did her own empirical research during 1858–62 that formed the basis for her book *The Employments of Women: A Cyclopaedia of Women's Work* (1862) in which she describes in detail the occupations in which women were active in the US. Discussing each occupation in alphabetical order, she provides the wages, the first woman in this position, and characteristics such as where and how many women do this work (Gensemer, 2000).

Women's representation in various sectors changed over the centuries. Economic historians like Elizabeth Hutchins and Ivy

Pinchbeck in the UK, as well as Dall and Edith Abbott in the US, have provided data on women's representation in a range of fields and industries.

The Great Depression and, later, World War II led to a substantial backlash against women's economic progress. Most women and people of color were excluded from the 1930s New Deal social programs. Women were pushed out of their jobs and careers, while welfare programs for men were put into place. Unemployed males entered jobs and professions formerly dominated by women, and women were passed over for promotions. The diminishing of career prospects demotivated women and girls in their fight for higher education, which reinforced this development (Scharf, 1980). Those women who were more highly educated moved into social work and policymaking. While there was over the twentieth century a general increase in female labor force participation of mothers and women in general, women were pushed out of the well-paid jobs and careers, and the progress made in academic jobs was undone and would take decades to be restored. For economics science, all this meant that there was a significant dip in the number of women economists between 1930 and 1970.

Besides legislation that prevented married women from working as civil servants, there were social expectations and institutional policies and practices such as school hours, lack of transportation, and childcare that put limitations on women's labor force participation and that remained in place over the decades that followed. It was not until 1963 that the Equal Pay Act was put in place that prohibited discrimination between men and women who work in the same workplace doing similar work. The Civil Rights Act of 1964 prohibited discrimination on the basis of race, origin, religion, or sex. This legislation put an end to explicit discrimination and prohibited job advertisements including statements such as "we are looking for a male janitor."

Neoclassical economists, increasingly influential after World War II, came to fully dominate the field of economic science in the 1980s and 1990s. They focused less on the production process as their attention had shifted to the consumption process and the functioning of markets, which is, in their view, the location where the value of goods and services is established and the prices and quantities of the produced goods and services are determined.

As Rosa Luxemburg had indicated, imperialism caused the boundaries of commodification to move and the marketization and monetization of formerly unpaid production to increase. As unpaid household production, including care work, had long been taken for granted, when women moved into the labor market in large numbers, the need for, the value of, and the contribution of this kind of labor became visible as these services had now to be provided for by the market and thus had to be paid for. Feminist economists engaged in a lively debate on the topic in the 2000s. These debates centered around the definition and the theorization of care work. What made this issue particularly complex was that, until then, care work had only been defined in the negative, as "not-work," and as "not-productive." Feminist economists such as Susan Himmelweit, Jean Gardener, Maren Jochimsen, and Nancy Folbre, among others, took up the challenge to coin new concepts and conceptualize the moral, emotional, and practical dimensions of caring for sick family members, friends, and neighbors, the raising of children, and care of the elderly. Although paid care work in hospitals and homes for the elderly was part of the monetized economy and was generally addressed as a marketized activity, care work in general was – or at least was perceived to be – less motivated by self-interested behavior, which made its conceptualization incompatible with a framework based on self-interested behavior. Nancy Folbre (1994) developed a framework that combines notions of Marxist and neoclassical theory to explain care behavior; she considers agents who choose rationally but in a context of group norms and values and in the presence of constraints that limit behavior in various ways.

All in all, women have always worked. Motivated by pull factors such as a higher income, good ideas for (new) products and services and connections, and/or by push factors such as sexual harassment and discrimination at their current workplace, feeling useless and undervalued – one way or another, women have always been starting and running their own businesses. The economic writing on that topic is what we turn to in the next section.

Women minding their own business

Susan Lewis (2009) wrote a history of women entrepreneurs, making the point that such an investigation brings its own difficulties given that such work transgresses the public domain, which is generally understood as politics/government and business, while the private domain refers to the home and private life. For many women, being active as a businesswoman often meant that, while running a self-employed one-person business or a business that hired more than one person, they worked from home. This, however, also ensured their invisibility. Although the literature about how to run a business well is still largely dominated by men, let me mention a selection of women writers who were themselves entrepreneurs or who addressed women as managers and entrepreneurs. The genres used by these women entrepreneurs varied, as did the function of their writings.

One early female entrepreneur, Glückel von Hameln (1646–1724), wrote a diary, which was meant for her children, who would be taking over the business empire she built. In her diary (1920 [1715–17]), she describes the jewelry business that she took over from her husband, and she accounts for various decisions she made. In expanding her business from Germany to all over Europe, her children played an important role, and Glückel was instrumental in arranging their marriages in such a way that it would profit her business. In Chapter 1, we met Elizabeth Montagu, who was also an entrepreneur and whose letters contained reflections on her experiences as a coalmine owner and her relations with her colleagues. In her view, running a coalmine and managing workers was being a part of a community. She fiercely disagreed with her colleagues about the practice that forced workers into contracts that, in reality, would make them slaves to the owner of the mine. Montagu valued – at least according to her – her involvement with her workers more than the pecuniary benefits her position brought her. In Chapter 2, we met Eliza Lucas Pinckney, who was well known for having started the indigo trade in the Carolinas. Another example out of many was Kezia Folger Coffin (1723–98), of Nantucket, the island off the coast of Massachusetts, where many women were running businesses, due to the men being engaged in the whale hunt (Mitchell, 2020).

There have been countless more women who ran smaller and larger businesses (see, e.g., Alice Clark, 1919), and there are many more texts of a similar character to be found that may inform us about women's experience in running a business, their contribution to the industrialization process, the impact of their gender on their experiences, and their approach to running their business (see also Davidoff and Hall, 1987). Research has been coming out only relatively recently, due to women's businesses generally being small – and thus less spectacular – and because most of those activities took place inside the home and have thus been invisible. Women entrepreneurs, or in Lewis's terms "proprietors," were overrepresented in "petty retailing," in producing food and clothes, and in running inns, boarding houses, and hotels. As Lewis (2009) argues, however, this research on the history of women in business may well have a substantial impact on how the role of small businesses in the economy is perceived and it may change the perception of women's productive contribution to the economy more generally.

6

Distribution

Introduction

Over the herstory of economics, the basis of the distribution of income and wealth has always been at the core of the debates; what work is valued, how much, and why? Political economists perceived the distribution of income as a crucial determinant of economic growth, in both the shorter and the longer run. To them, it made a crucial difference which class – the landowners, the owners of capital goods, or the workers – was able to appropriate most of the surplus produced. After all, this would decide how this income was used: for consumption goods (landowning class and working class) or for investments and accumulation of capital (capitalists). When workers and the landowning class were the predominant spenders, this would lead to economic decline, but when the capitalists obtained enough profits, this would mean growth of the economy and increasing wealth for everybody.

With the shift to neoclassical economics, the distribution of wealth was taken as given and the income of the various classes became perceived as a mere derivative of economic growth; each production factor (land, capital, and labor) would receive an income based on its marginal productivity. Where political economists had considered labor as that which produced value, William Stanley Jevons (1965 [1871]) and Alfred Marshall (1890), among others, determined that the decision about the value of a good takes place on the demand side by consumers, who rank goods and services according to the utility these provide, and express their demands on the markets accordingly.

The market mechanism, constituted by numerous interconnected (and generally assumed to be perfect) competitive markets, would then, through the working of demand and supply, determine the price for each good and the quantity that would be produced and supplied. The American economist John Bates Clark (1847–1938) completed this picture by developing a marginalist theory of income distribution. According to Clark (1899), each factor of production – capital, land, and labor – would be rewarded according to their contribution to production, or their marginal productivity, and the entire income produced would be completely distributed over the various production factors. Thus, the distribution of income changed place in economic theorizing from a central determinant of economic growth to a derivative of economic growth. For workers, this meant that their pay was no longer based on the costs of subsistence but, rather, on the basis of the (marginal) productivity of the worker, at least according to the theory.

For women, we see a shift during early industrialization from a household model based on patriarchal power toward one based on the economic dependence of the wife and the "generosity," "charity," or "chivalry" of the husband: the male wage-earner model. As women gained access to the labor market in larger numbers and took up the role of secondary wage earner in the household over the twentieth century, the transitional household model (Hochschild and Machung, 1989; Barker and Feiner, 2004) emerged and, over time, became dominant and, at least in the US, women held more jobs than men in December 2019 (Bureau of Labor Statistics), while the single parent household also increased in numbers.

This chapter will discuss various approaches of women economic writers and economists to these household models as specific arrangements for control and distribution of resources between men, women, and dependents. In the third and the final section, the discussion focuses on the debates and explanations of the gender and racial wage gaps.

Shifting patterns of distribution

Over the course of the nineteenth century, people, including political economists, came to realize that industrial society was a system that was here to stay. At the same time, with the level of wealth and inequality increasing, the idea of equality between men was on the rise, importantly due to the abolitionist movement and the early socialist movement. *The Declaration of Sentiments* (1848), which was accepted at the first women's conference in Seneca Falls, New York, turned America's Declaration of Independence into a radical feminist document by just adding "and women" wherever "men" were mentioned, and is generally perceived as the start of the organized US women's movement. Until then, the basis for gender relations had generally been based on power, strength, political, and legal exclusion, and the norms and values to support this. Race relations in US would long be marked by the system of slavery in the South and, to a limited extent, in the North.

Adam Smith had proposed to dissolve slavery, making the argument that the practice was not efficient:

> The wear and tear of a slave, it has been said, is at the expence of his master; but that of a free servant is at his own expence. ... It appears, accordingly, from the experience of all ages and nations, I believe, that the work done by freemen comes cheaper in the end than that performed by slaves. (1976 [1776]: 98–9)

In response to many strikes and slave riots in the 1820s and 1830s, the economist Nassau Senior (1790–1864), who stated the status quo and the current income and wealth distribution as "natural," followed up on Smith's remark, talking about how "freemen" take care of themselves and their families. Over the course of the nineteenth century, the system of slavery in the US would be replaced by the system of wage labor, and the male wage-earner household model that supported the exclusion of married women from the labor market would become, at least for middle- and higher-class households, the standard, guaranteeing for men a stable supply of unpaid household products and services. The Thirteenth Amendment to the US Constitution put an end to slavery in 1865, but retained the option to treat incarcerated people as slaves. The practice of "convict leasing" became widespread in the South, and to some extent is still with us today due to the longstanding practices around incarceration.

In industrial society up until quite recently, there were women's wages and men's wages. Women's wages were about 40–60 percent lower than those of men; women of color earned even less, if they earned anything at all. Women workers experiencing these low wages did not consider their income fair or "natural," not by a long shot. Factory girls and women, who received particularly low wages as well as having to run their households, were deeply involved in food riots in early nineteenth-century Britain, and also riots, strikes, and walk-outs against mechanization within the agriculture and textile industries (Pinchbeck, 1930; Thompson, 1966 [1963]). Harriet Hanson Robinson (1825–1911) was one of the first girls to be put to work in the Lowell textile mills in Massachusetts. Starting out as an experiment in which child labor was replaced by the work of educated young women, who would work until they got married, the circumstances deteriorated over the years. Robinson (2021 [1898]) provides an economic history of the mills and a detailed eye-witness account of the process in which these young women, not having the time and energy left to socialize, remained unmarried and became "degraded" by the work and circumstances in the mills. Robinson, however, remained positive about the economic experiment of Francis Cabot Lowell, who had had the vision to open factories in the village that would be named after him (Lowell was also called "the Manchester of America"). Robinson ascribes the success of the Lowell Mills to its management "by men who were wise enough to consider the physical, moral, and mental needs of those who were the source of their wealth" (2021 [1898]: 18). In 1836, however, the wages went down by 25 percent and "the girls turned out," of which Robinson gives a first-hand account, claiming the event as "one of the first strikes of cotton-factory operatives that ever took place in this country" (2021 [1898]: 83). Later in life, she became involved in the abolitionist movement and the women's suffrage movement.

In the US the first labor unions were formed in the 1830s and 1840s. Women played a substantial role in the formation and running of these early unions. The appreciation of the interests of women was a radical aspect of the early socialist movement. In this movement, labor was central and almost considered sacred; the distribution of income should be based fully on work performed and its contribution to value and economic growth, in contrast to established political economic notions. In 1840 the female textile workers started *The Lowell Offering*, a magazine for and written by themselves (Robinson, 2021 [1898]). Sarah Bagley (1806–89) and four others started the Lowell Female Labor Reform Association in their fight for a ten-hour working day (Maupin, 1964: 2). Bagley would later become a central figure in the textile workers' unions in New England.

Working-class women who worked for pay, and were exploited in the same way as their fathers, brothers, friends, and husbands, shared the class interests of the men. Where enslaved people were concerned, the situation was even more dire. As the abolitionist and socialist movements gained strength, the latter were backed-up by Karl Marx's purportedly scientific economic analysis of capitalist development. Much later, around the time of the 1917

Russian Revolution, the German Marxist Clara Zetkin (1857–1933) addressed the contribution and role of working women in the socialist movement in her speeches "Women's Work and the Trade Unions" (1893), "Women of the Working People" (1915), and "Fascism Must Be Defeated" (1932). In these talks, Zetkin laid out the way that the social economic base – huge income and wealth inequalities in particular – had led to the emergence of fascism. She contrasts this to the socialist movement and makes a plea (in vain) for women to be recognized and included in the movement. Based on her experience with the socialist movement that put feminist demands consistently on the back burner, she would later make the case for an independent feminist movement.

In line with Engels (1972 [1884]), Alexandra Kollontai (1872–1952), a Russian Communist, was one of the women economic writers who considered feminism to be a bourgeois endeavor and, as such, disruptive for the socialist movement. Kollontai criticized Western feminism again and again for its neglect of the interests and concerns of working women and girls. The first woman in the Bolshevik government after the 1917 Revolution, Kollontai founded the Women's Department, and argued for equal rights between working-class women and men (1920; 1971 [1926]). Kollontai lost this battle. Her insistence on the economic independence of women, the need to enable them to choose their partners freely, and to reduce unpaid household work were not supported broadly enough (Holt, 1977). The USSR would turn into an authoritarian state that killed millions of its own citizens. Over time, however, women workers came close to obtaining the same rights as their male counterparts, taking up positions and taking over in fields that were not accessible to women in the West, and were provided with an extensive system of childcare, cutting back their household duties substantially.

Economic chivalry and the wage labor system

There is a shift in laws, policies, institutions, norms, and values in the dominant ideological and economic gender arrangement over the course of the nineteenth century. Harriet Taylor Mill and John Stuart Mill, arguing for the full equality of married persons before the law, stated that "we have had the morality of submission, and the morality of chivalry and generosity; the time is now come for the morality of justice" (1997 [1869]: 259). They were, however, way ahead of their time, as the high days of economic chivalry were yet to come. The concept of chivalry went back to medieval times and over the centuries resurfaced over and over again in debates about civilized relations between the sexes (see, e.g., O'Brien, 2009; Taylor, 2005). It provided a notion of masculinity that recognized the agency and even the equality of women and men, while still maintaining men's supremacy. Alfred Marshall, who was in his private life a convinced adherent of chivalry-based gender relations (Groenewegen, 1995), used the term "economic chivalry" in an article in *The Economic Journal* in 1907 to advocate for an attitude of altruism and generosity of employers and other people with means to use their wealth in a socially responsible manner. Marshall proposed this as an alternative to socialism and the cooperative movement. Economic chivalry, in feminist economic scholarship (see, e.g., Pujol, 1989, 1992) referred to the perceived attitude of generosity of the husband toward his wife and children, whom he protects and provides for. This concept mirrors "the cult of motherhood" that referred to late nineteenth-century notions of femininity in which the wife devoted her life to her husband and children, while acting as moral guardian of the household. This moral underpinning of the male wage-earner household would reach its zenith in the last decades of the nineteenth century to return in the aftermath of World War II.

This situation in which middle-class women were excluded from the labor market and lived a life of forced economic dependence was referred to by Charlotte Perkins Gilman (1998 [1898]), Olive Schreiner (1911), and Mabel Atkinson (1987 [1914]) as "parasitism." Women economic writers had criticized the patriarchal perception of gender relations for centuries and fought economic chivalry. Gilman called this gender economic arrangement out as "unnatural." "We are," she states in Chapter I of *Women and Economics*, "the only animal species in which the female depends on the male for food, the only animal species in which the sex-relation is also an economic relation" (1998 [1898]: 3). Her attack on this gender arrangement is to the point, merciless, and enlightening. Using biological and evolutionary metaphors and reasoning based on the Darwinian notions of competition and natural selection, she points out that the forces of natural selection and sexual selection are out of balance. By making the female economically dependent on the male, "man, in supporting woman, has become her economic environment." Gilman perceives this as both damaging to women and to "the race." Eleanor Rathbone would later criticize this same model of redistributing the income between the sexes, based on economic chivalry as "the indirect and extraordinary clumsy method of financing the male parent and trusting to him somehow to see the thing through. It does not even finance him directly, but leaves it to what it is fond of calling 'blind economic forces' to bring it about that the wages of men shall be sufficient for the purpose of bringing up families" (1917: 61).

Ada Heather Bigg (1855–1944), in her article "The Wife's Contribution to Family Income" (1894), claims that women had contributed substantially to production before industrialization, and she described the transition to industrial production in which a lot of the work still took place in the home and was done by the entire family. She wrote: "In face of all this evidence, it is simply absurd to denounce their [women's] increased employment in the present or to seek to saddle nineteenth century civilization with the onus of having evolved the working woman and set up competition between the sexes" (1894: 54). Bigg stated that more than objecting to the work being done by women, the issue seemed to be particularly about married women earning a wage. It should be left to women, she argued, how to run her family and make it work.

At the end of World War I, during which there was an increase in women's labor participation, and based on their contribution to the war effort, the critiques of the gendered system of income distribution became louder. Rathbone characterized the economic chivalry gender arrangement as an outdated and ineffective redistribution mechanism to support women and children. She wrote, about the husband who is expected, according to the system, to engage in economic chivalry:

> Whether he expends the wages so received upon his family or upon his own "menus plaisirs" depends, of course, entirely upon his goodwill, since the State, though it recognises in theory the rights of wife and children to maintenance, does practically nothing to enforce it; such laws as do embody this right being so imperfect and so badly carried out, that they are next door to valueless as a protection. (1917: 61–2)

Rathbone subsequently argued for government, businesses, and unions to step in and change the gender arrangement so that women could earn their own wages and contribute financially to the household, while the government would contribute to the costs of raising children by paying families allowances.

At the same time, most economists were wedded to the gender arrangement based on economic chivalry. Herbert Spencer (1820–1903), an influential sociologist and philosopher during the second half of the nineteenth century, was also popular among progressives like Beatrice Potter Webb and Sidney Webb, who were staunch believers in progress and Darwin's notions of evolution. As a Social Darwinist, Spencer coined the term "survival of the fittest" and argued in *Social Statics* (1851) that man's happiness is firmly based in natural laws. In a later work (1900 [1862]), he ranked cultures based on evolutionary notions and his own racially based views. In his view, English culture topped the ranking based on the dominance of economic chivalry in the sense that economic wealth had made it possible to "free" the wives from paid work, enabling them to devote their lives to the raising of children.

In the US, during the Progressive Era (1896–1932), American institutionalists like Sophonisba Breckinridge, Edith Abbott, Hazel Kyrk, and others analyzed institutional practices such as the dual labor markets that prevented women from accessing higher paid jobs. Their involvement and experience in social work (Breckinridge) and research on the history of wages in the US (Abbott), provided them with intricate knowledge of the workings of the system and its impact on the less privileged in society.

As women were entering higher education in larger numbers and were starting to build careers, Joseph Schumpeter (1883–1950), the Austrian economist, articulated concerns about the moral foundation of marriage. Schumpeter perceived these changes as part of capitalist development. He described the unavoidable decline of capitalism that was linked to men and women applying the "utilitarian lesson and refus[ing] to take for granted the traditional arrangements that their social environment makes for them, as soon as they acquire the habit of weighing the individual advantages and disadvantages of any prospective course of action" (2008 [1942]: 157). In other words, as soon as women and men realized the sacrifice that parenthood demanded, of women in particular, fewer and fewer parents would be willing to make those sacrifices. In a similar vein, men would lose the capitalist ethics that "enjoins working for the future irrespective of whether or not one is going to harvest the crop oneself" (2008 [1942]: 160). Schumpeter seems here to be making a plea for the traditional notions of male virtue, sacrifice, and chivalry as an important part of the culture of capitalism.

As the twentieth century progressed and women's participation in the labor force increased, the new gender economic arrangement that had emerged during World War I became more widely spread and, over their lifetime, women's connection to the labor market grew stronger. In the transitional household model, women were recognized as able to take on jobs and become professionals, and they were increasingly expected to earn an income independently of their husbands. At the same time, however, women remained overall responsible for care work in the household.

As women in the West finally entered higher education in large numbers, many of them studying and working in economics departments in the 1970s and 1980s, they not only asked questions like "Where are the women?"; they also asked "What work do women (of color) do?"; "What do they earn?"; "Why so little?"; and "Why is it always women who do most of the domestic work?" In early research on this topic, women economic writers and economists applied Marxist, neoclassical, institutional, and Keynesian theories, while also criticizing these theories for their male bias and limitations in conceptualizing, explaining, and providing satisfying answers to these questions. While socialist feminists applied mainly Marxist economic theory (Benería and Sen, 1981; Elson and Pearson, 1981; Folbre, 1982; Hartmann, 1979), liberal economists predominantly applied neoclassical economic theory and models (Bergmann, 1986; Blau and Ferber, 1986). Economists such as Jacob Mincer (1962), who worked in the neoclassical tradition, which by then became increasingly established as the mainstream in economics, explained the increase in labor participation of married women by the idea that the choice between the supply of work hours versus the demand for leisure should for women be replaced with the choice between the supply of work hours, the demand for leisure, and the demand for hours to spend on "work at home" (1962: 65). Mincer came to the conclusion that married women's behavior in the labor market was largely determined by the income and employment of "the head of the family" and when there was a decline of that income, in particular, married women emerged on the labor market as "added workers."

In his *A Treatise on the Family* (1981), Becker conceptualized household behavior in the economic chivalry tradition, naming the male head of the household as "the Altruist" and the wife as "the Beneficiary." Becker starts out with two identical individuals who decide to start a family and enter into an exchange relationship, conceptualizing this in terms of comparative advantage. In later chapters of the book, the agency of the wife disappears and her utility is expressed as part of the utility function of the husband. Becker considered the "Altruist Family" as the most efficient family model. In this model, the wife and children – all dependent on the husband and his appreciation of their utility – have an interest in making sure that the Altruist is well taken care of. The assumption that the marriage will last and thus that the wife has no other options or threat-points is an important part of the model. In addition to Marilyn Manser and Murray Brown (1979) and Marjorie McElroy and Mary Horney (1981), who applied game theory to explain intra-household decision-making, Shoshana Grossbard-Shechtman (1984) analyzed marriage as an exchange of labor. Later, Notburga Ott (1992, 1995) applied bargaining theory, arguing that, for the wife in the Beckerian model to be fully specialized in household labor, the exclusion of the possibility of divorce is a crucial one.

Although over the twentieth century the transitional household model became increasingly dominant in Europe and the US, mainstream economists clung to what economists considered the standard household model: Becker's approach to the family. Game theoretical approaches were applied to analyze intrafamily conflicts about labor supply and the spending of income, among other things, on (male or female) children. Feminist economic analyses in development economics were particularly fruitful in assessing the impacts of this gendered notion of distribution of income on economic growth, and were eventually joined by the World Bank in arguing that gender equality would increase economic growth (World Bank, 2001). The increase in the number of single mothers and the feminization of poverty that went along with it, particularly in the US, however, was a clear and poignant example of the profound and extended institutionalization of the male wage-earner family. The lack of an updated narrative both in mainstream economics and in American politics, one that acknowledged the change in household models in the US, prevented a thorough understanding of the causes of the gender wage gap, and hampered the effective implementation of policies to finance and support women's productive activities in the home, and protect and facilitate the raising of the next generation.

The debate on equal pay for equal work

To explain why women's wages were so much lower than men's, Priscilla Wakefield (1798) had decried the lack of "decent professions" open to women and she brought up the crowding argument – namely, that the high number of applicants for the jobs in the few professions open to women would bring down the wages in those professions, sometimes to almost nothing. Caroline Healey Dall (1860) referred to examples from various countries and continents, arguing that women were often employed in the same jobs as men, but in those cases earned only 30–50 percent of what men were paid and therefore could not earn a living for themselves and their dependents. Barbara Bodichon (1857), Olive Schreiner (1911), and others had made the point that women's low wages made it impossible for single women to live independently. Similar debates about equal wages for equal work had been taking place in most industrialized countries in Europe over many decades. Economic historians like Elizabeth Hutchins (1915) and Edith Abbott (1910) addressed gender wage gaps and factory regulations that protected women from long hours and working conditions. Many feminists considered these laws as paternalistic and as limiting women's choices, while others argued for the expansion of these labor laws to also include men.

In 1891 political economist Sidney Webb was invited to present a paper to the newly established British Economic Association on the wage differences between women and men, which was subsequently published in a very early edition of *The Economic Journal*. Webb had started this project without much prior knowledge of the topic (1891: 635), and without taking the historical background into account. He argued that when women and men were engaged in similar work, they were paid more or less the same, but that overall they were doing different kinds of work and working in different industries. The value of the products women produced and the services they supplied, according to Webb, were of lesser value than the goods and services produced in male-dominated sectors. This difference in the value produced, exceptions aside, explained the differences in wages. All in all, the main conclusion was that the markets did their work as they should.

Webb's article set off a debate in the pages of *The Economic Journal* about the existence and extent of gender wage inequality. Millicent Garrett Fawcett (1892) responded, and later others, like Eleanor Rathbone (1917), Beatrice Potter Webb (1919), and Maria Edgeworth's nephew Francis Y. Edgeworth (1922, 1923), joined the debate (see Pujol, 1992; Chassonery-Zaïgouche, 2019). Millicent Fawcett (1892) initially agreed with Webb and, restating the non-competing groups of labor argument, she stressed that women worked in different sectors from men, sectors that produced less wealth. This would make it "an error, both in principle and in tactics" for women to demand equal pay with men, according to Fawcett, as this would lead to their being competed out of the market. Over the coming decade she would change her mind and come to the opposite conclusion (Fawcett, 1918).

Eleanor Rathbone (1917) discussed the wage differences between women and men in great detail. She reflected on how women's services in the household and in paid work should be rewarded, looking ahead to the period after the war. Rathbone started her argument by agreeing (to some extent) with Webb, stating that "women earn less than men, first, because they do, or till lately have done, chiefly the less valuable kinds of work" (1917: 60). She here repeats the occupational segregation argument: women earn less because they work in those sectors that pay less, and these sectors pay less because they produce goods and services of lesser value. Directly following on from this, she claims that even with the difference of the value of the goods and services produced taken into account, women still make less than they deserve. Rathbone argues that

> [Women] are also paid less in proportion to the value of the work they do, and that is the part of the problem which concerns us here. The reasons for the inferiority may be roughly scheduled as four:
> 1. Lack of trades organization.
> 2. Pocket-money or supplementary wage earning.
> 3. A low standard of comfort.
> 4. A wage requirement based on individual subsistence. (1917: 60)

Rathbone analyzes the last point in greater detail, criticizing the idea and practice of paying men a "family wage." A man's wage would increase when he married or when his first child was born. Women would not receive such a wage increase once they started a family; rather, they would run the risk of being fired. Rathbone perceived the demand for "equal pay for equal work" as "vague and ill-defined," and expressed concerns that, when granted, it would price women out of the labor market. Since she believed that the option of paying less according to the ratio of women's lower productivity was not practically feasible, her solution was that the government should pay a family allowance to mothers with children.

Based, among other things, on her work as the President of the National Union of Women's Suffragettes Societies and the experiences during World War I, Millicent Fawcett (1918) revisited her position with respect to whether women should demand equal pay for equal work. She acknowledged the discrimination that made the sex of a worker an important determinant of their income, the exclusionary practices occurring at the work place, the lack of female representation in the labor unions, and the lack of training of women on the job. She takes over Rathbone's definition of equal pay for equal work, as the "claim to secure for women a fair field of competition with men, their work being accepted or rejected, on its merits, recognizing that any permanent disadvantage that adheres to women workers as such should be allowed *pro rata* reduction in their standard rates" (1918: 3–4). There is, according to Fawcett, nothing vague or ill-defined where this demand is concerned. Given that women's wages did not reflect their (potential) productive contribution and they deserved more training and access to the better paying jobs and professions, the demand for equal pay for equal work, Fawcett concluded, was justified.

Beatrice Potter Webb (1858–1943), a member of the Fabian Society and a socialist economist, who was married to Sidney Webb, also took part in this debate. Potter Webb was appointed as a Member of the Royal Commission on the Poor Laws that ran an investigation from 1905 to 1909. Although she was for a long time opposed to feminism, Potter Webb changed her mind in 1906 (Pujol, 1992: 85). She decided to write (the extensive) *Minority Report of the Poor Laws Commission* (1909), in which she argues for some form of minimum for mothers "having the charge of young children, by themselves or their husbands, of any form of Public Assistance, should receive enough for the full maintenance of the family" (1909: 342). In her view, "parasitic industries" that could not survive paying their workers a decent wage are industries that had lost their right to exist. Based on these findings, Potter Webb argued (1919) that separate wages for men and women existed because, overall, wages were largely based on the sex of the worker.

Pujol (1992) reports that Francis Edgeworth's contributions to the discussion in his "Equal Pay to Men and Women for Equal Work" (1922) and "Women's Wages in Relation to Economic Welfare" (1923), both published in *The Economic Journal*, were the last in this debate. Starting out as an exercise in marginalist theory, Edgeworth ends with a partial and ideologically laden argument in favor of the patriarchal status quo. His articles more or less settled the debate for economists, taking the topic off the table until it returned in the 1960s.

Explaining gender and racial wage gaps

In the last decades of the twentieth century, Western Europe and particularly the US experienced an increase in income inequality. The gender wage gap decreased but remained persistent, especially for white people, whereas for people of color it was rather the racial wage gap that remained large (30–50 percent), and for Black Americans the racial wealth disparity increased.

For neoclassical economists, labor had become a commodity to be used in the production of goods and services, meaning that all labor was perceived as essentially identical – homogeneous – and only differed in the level of human capital (i.e., education, skills, and experience) it contained. The idea that workers should be paid a subsistence wage, as the political economists had reasoned, was left behind, and, in the new frame of thought, it was reckoned that workers should be paid according to their – marginal – productivity. The historical analysis of gender and race differences in wages, based on long-time historical economic oppression and exclusion, were now understood by neoclassical economists in an ahistorical manner and reduced to differences in productivity of these workers and the level of demand for their labor. This resonated with Webb's and Edgeworth's view that low wages must mean low productivity or a low value of the goods and services provided. That the causation could also go the other way was hardly discussed.

Feminist economic analysis will make exactly that point. The fact that women and people of color had been excluded from (well-)paid jobs over a long period of time and had been overrepresented in agriculture (paid or unpaid), in domestic work, and in sectors that had monetized and marketized the jobs that women used to perform in the household (childcare, cleaning, nursing, teaching, hospitality industry, etc.) was considered to be the main cause of gender and racial income gaps in addition to other reasons such as (motherhood) discrimination and the lack of training and opportunities (see, e.g., Bergmann 1974; Hartman, 1976; Davis, 1981; Amott and Matthaei, 1991).

When gender and racial wage gaps re-emerged as an economic anomaly for standard economic theory in the 1960s and 1970s, socialist feminists understood women workers as part of the labor reserve army, although married women's position outside the class system hampered the combination of feminist analysis of patriarchy with the Marxist analysis of capitalism (see, e.g., Sargent, 1981). Institutionalists like Ann Jennings (1990), and Deborah Figart, Ellen Mutuari, and Marilyn Power (2001) reported and analyzed the wage setting processes and the role of racist and sexist norms and values. Neoclassical economists, applying methodological individualism in their research, focused on the individual as the basic unit of analysis. The explanation of gender and racial wage gaps was theorized as an issue that only concerned the labor market and the research focused almost exclusively on the supply side of the labor market. Conceptualizing labor relations as negotiations between individual employers and individual workers, differences in average wages and in wages for the same work were thus explained either by individual preferences of the employer (Becker, 1957) and/or by the differences in the worker's characteristics. This latter research took off in the 1980s.

Claudia Goldin, who in 1973 became the first woman to obtain a position in the Economics Department of Harvard University, conducted historical and empirical economic research on women's labor force participation and the gender wage gap in the US. She argued (1990) that the gender wage gap appeared to decrease during the Industrial Revolution, and again during the first decades of the twentieth century, and she expected (correctly) this to happen again in the 1990 and 2000s. Overall, however, Goldin concluded that the gender wage gap is persistent and that the lower increase of human capital for mothers due to their stepping away from the labor markets while raising children cost them their promotions and often their jobs.

Gary Becker (1957) had argued that discrimination meant the employer's preference to work (or not work) with certain groups of workers or customers, that this preference was costly, and that competition would therefore drive discriminating employers out of business. As that did not happen, some feminist economists used the door that Becker opened by narrowing neoclassical economic theory down to merely a *method* of analysis. They applied this method to the study of economic behavior in the household, women's labor market participation, and gender and racial wage gaps. Francine Blau and Lawrence Kahn, in one of their first articles in a long series on the gender wage gap, reported a decrease over the period 1971–88 in the gender gap to 30.4 percent, mainly due to increasing inequality and declining male wages and an increase in female wages (1992: 28). Siv Gustafsson and Danièle Meulders (2000) initiated and collected work on female labor participation, gender wage gaps, and gendered employment patterns.

Explaining the gender wage gap now focused mainly on the human capital of the worker. As we read in Chapter 3, a worker's human capital consists mainly of education. This education is considered an investment that will be paid back later in life by higher earnings. In addition, economists identified the level of skills (due to additional training) and experience (due to years on the job) as additional explanations of wage differences between women and men and between racial/ethnic groups.

With the improvement of education levels of women and people of color, the gender wage gap between the median income of men and women did narrow from 40–60% percent to 30 percent in the 1980s to 20 percent in the 2000s. The racial wage gap decreased as well, but remained large in the US, except for Asian American women. Over the period 1980–2015 white women saw their gender wage gap decrease from 40 percent to 18 percent, black women from 44 percent to 35 percent, Latina women from 46 percent to 42 percent, and Asian women had a difference in median income compared to white men of 13 percent in 2015, down from 21 percent in 2016 (Patten, 2016). Economists working within the neoclassical economic theoretical framework focused their attention on improving their explanation of the gender wage gap by bringing in variables such as the number of children, the presence of childcare, etc. The remaining gender wage difference of 7–12 percent that could not be explained this way was then relegated to sociological research under the label "discrimination," thus leaving more detailed research on discrimination to the sociologists. Recently, there has been an emerging realization that institutional factors, such as corporate culture, discriminatory policies, lack of support and accommodations for women workers, and the segregation of certain populations in certain segments of the labor market (occupational segregation, dual labor markets), may need to be taken into account to fully understand the gender and racial wage gaps (see Blau and Kahn, 2017).

Encountering the norms and regulations around work, many women economic writers, feminist economists, and especially women of color claimed that their wages and salaries were directly and indirectly determined by their gender, race, and class through power mechanisms, exploitation, discrimination, and occupational segregation. Paula England (1982), for instance, criticized neoclassical economists for their limited ability to take occupational segregation into account. Feminists like Angela Davis (e.g., 1981) have focused on gender, race, and class as basic and related economic categories and the way these have structured economic behavior and the economy. Teresa Amott and Julie Matthaei (1991) provided an overview of the economic histories of the perspectives of white, African American, Latina, and Native American women, thus contextualizing "white history" that is taught at high schools throughout the US (see also Browne, 1999). Marlene Kim (2007) showed, using standard economic tools, that the intersectionality of discrimination against women, who are also facing discrimination based on the color of their skin, results in an economic set-back for these women that is larger than the loss based on an addition of the economic impact of gender discrimination and race discrimination taken together.

Folbre (1994) aimed to theorize the distribution of care, the impact on women's wages, and the costs of care. Later (2020), she presents a more comprehensive theory that explicitly aims at doing justice to the intersectionality of the categories of race, gender, and class, and the groups, group behavior, and group dynamics that also impact and to some extent determine the development of patriarchal systems, particularly capitalism. The way Folbre creates a place for care work, and the rise and decline of support from welfare states for these kinds of activities, represents a firm step away from traditional economic theorizing and toward a feminist economic theoretical framework that includes and does justice to a lot of women's interests and concerns that were historically neglected in economic research.

7

Consumption

Introduction

The perception that consumption, and the consumption of luxury goods in particular, corrupted the soul changed with the emergence of industrial society. Although important as the aim of production, consumption had played a minor role in political economic theory and consumption of luxury goods long remained a contested issue for political economists. Adam Smith had argued that "consumption is the sole end and purpose of all production; and the interest of the producer ought to be attended to, only in so far as it may be necessary for promoting that of the consumer" (1976 [1776]: 660). Demand was assumed, however, to just exist. Or, as Jean-Baptiste Say notoriously claimed, "supply creates its own demand" – in a barter economy that is. Say's perspective on this issue was that people would supply their labor *in order* to buy what they wanted; demand for the goods was therefore guaranteed. Thomas Malthus, however, was concerned about the fact that the landowning class could become too small, and that, even though they might be very rich, their consumption would be too limited to carry economic growth over a long period of time. One can, after all, consume only so much food and so many luxury goods. As the rest of the population would be too poor to buy the consumer goods produced, "a glut," or an economic crisis, or worse, long-term economic decline, would thus ensue. As value, according to political economists, was constituted by the use of labor in the production process, consumption was in turn assumed to take place within the household and to not create value.

On the contrary, the more that was spent on consumption, the less could be spent on profits and capital accumulation. All consumption by the working class beyond the reproduction of the worker and his family was, therefore, basically misspent.

While in the agrarian society it was mostly women who went to the market to sell and buy, in industrial society the market became, for political economists, more and more an abstract notion and one that was perceived as dominated by men representing their households. In practice, however, women remained the predominant daily consumers as they were the ones who either directed their servants to go to the shops or did the shopping themselves. Women also constituted the expanding markets for the luxury goods that were obtained in the colonies: clothing, trinkets, furniture, ornaments, kitchen tools, tea, coffee, spices, and so on. In her economic historical study, Maxine Berg (2005) describes the development of various trades of luxury goods and their markets. With regard to the emerging class of consumers, she not only provides us with insights concerning how goods were designed and manufactured for the middle classes, she also describes the process through which the customers and shoppers themselves were "made." "Consumption was learned in response to the expansion of goods, the multiplication of choice, new and more specialized shops, and advertising and fashion codes" (2005: 195).

Women economic writers wrote extensively about the emerging culture of consumption. The growing importance of shopping, fashion, and the meaning of clothes was widely discussed in nineteenth-century novels. Jane Austen is, of course, well known for her detailed descriptions of not only the looks and behavior of her characters, but also (and not least) their financial positions, including their status of potential heiress, the value of their estate, and their prospects (see also Clery, 2017). These and many other aspects of the emerging consumption culture were taken up by Elizabeth Cleghorn Gaskell (1810–65). Gaskell wrote for Charles Dickens's magazine *Household Words* and provided her readers with an impression of middle-class and gentry life in nineteenth-century British society in novels such as *North and South* (1855), *Sylvia's Lovers* (1863), and *Wives and Daughters* (1864–6). One of the very first chapters in *Sylvia's Lovers*, for instance, "Buying a New Cloak," describes in great detail the visiting of a shop, the checking-out of the merchandise, the feel of the materials, comparing and negotiating as being all part of the buying process, which places the shop at the very center of the events occurring in the chapter. These novels provide a subtle and analytical description of the increasing role that consumption played for the social status, distinction, and identity of middle-class women. By the end of the nineteenth century, the Victorian ideology around motherhood and economic chivalry being at its height, even feminist writers like Charlotte Perkins Gilman did not shun this aspect of femininity for middle- and upper-class women. At the same time, we see a new ideal of womanhood that came to the fore in her day, which was in part determined by her consumption pattern: the New Woman. This was an educated, professional woman, who was independent as a result of her education and fashion, and, assisted by her bicycle, by her increased ability to move around freely.

This chapter focuses on women's economic writing on the process of consumption and its contribution to economic theorizing of consumption behavior. The chapter ends with the work of women economic writers and economists on the over-consumption of natural resources and its impact of the environment.

Women economists theorizing consumption

So instead of the distribution of surplus over the three main classes and its impact on the economy, economists now focused on the most efficient use of resources in situations of scarcity. While accepting the current income and wealth distribution as the status quo and rational self-interested behavior as "natural" or "normal," neoclassical economists turned to analyzing economic problems in terms of marginal changes in quantities, leaving out economic history and population growth. They addressed the economy basically as a static and ahistorical phenomenon and focused their attention on quantitative and technical market relations: the determination of prices and quantities and the impacts of external changes on market equilibria.

With marginalist economists increasingly taking over the field, consumption moved center stage as the location of the determination of value. It is in the process of providing utility, by satisfying the needs and wants for goods and services, that, according to the neoclassical economists, these goods and services create value, and it is through the price mechanism at the markets that prices and quantities are determined. Whereas economists had considered the household merely as an ahistorical and unchanging realm outside the economy, value for neoclassical economists was now determined by consumers in the household, in that part of daily life that men, including the economists among them, did not have much experience with. At the same time, this gave the decision by the individual, which was perceived as "purely" determined by his preference and choice, the flavor of objectivity, and assigned to individual choice the authority of moral judgment.

At more or less the same place and moment in time – during the first decades of the twentieth century that is – more women were getting into higher education and moving into a wider set of professions, and female economic writers and economists stepped forward. In the UK, such women were mostly active as members of the suffragist movement, the cooperative movement, and the labor movement. A few increased their impact as wives of economists, and still others as journalists and independent researchers and authors, but women had not yet gained access to jobs in economic departments. Instead, women economic writers presented their work at conferences, conventions, and clubs (both women's and men's). For instance, Emma Brooke (1844–1926), who was a member of the Fabian Society, explored the debates around feminism, socialism, and sexuality in her *A Superfluous Woman* (1894) and *Transition* (1895). Other women active in the Fabian Women's Group were Annie Besant (1847–1933) and Maud Pember Reeves (1865–1953). Annie Besant was an activist for family planning and the propagation of birth control, who founded and edited the journal *Our Corner*. Reeves (1912) explored the spending patterns of low-income families and laid out various budgets for different incomes. Showing that low incomes could hardly cover the costs of a healthy living, Reeves asked: "How then is the man on a pound a week to house his children decently and feed them sufficiently? How is his wife to care for them properly? The answer is that, in London at least, be they never so hardworking and sober and thrifty, the task is impossible" (1912: 218). This kind of close attention of the spending patterns in a household, making a distinction between costs of basic needs and more "luxury" spending, showed the hardship facing these families. In contrast, neoclassical economists spoke about these situations in a much more abstract manner in terms of income restraints, preferences, indifference curves, and optimization of utility.

In the US, the American institutionalist approach to economics and its eclectic methodological approach enabled women economic writers to conduct their research and be heard. Based on knowledge generated in the academic fields of anthropology, psychology, sociology, and economics, economists like Thorstein Veblen (1857–1929) had fewer scruples about analyzing the process of consumption and women's role in it in depth. Veblen's *The Theory of the Leisure Class* (1899) characterizes part of the consumption of the richer classes as "conspicuous consumption," or the consumption of expensive but useless goods to showcase one's wealth. "Vicarious leisure and consumption," on the other hand, referred to the showing off of one's wealth by the consumption of somebody else, mostly the wife or a child (1899: 81).

Applying a similar wide range of methodologies, most women economists directed their attention to the other end of the social economic spectrum and many of them became active in the field of social work. Sophonisba P. Breckinridge (1866–1948), who had a PhD in political science and economics (1901, University of Chicago), became a professor of social economics, co-founded the journal *Social Service Review*, and became President of the American Association of Schools of Social Work. Breckinridge pressed the government to engage with the increasing economic inequality in the US by implementing social programs. Discussions by women economists at the University of Chicago focused on the process of economic decision-making, the measuring and theorizing of consumption, and the development of advertising, basic and standard budgets, and price indices (Hammond, 2000b). Between 1905 and 1923, Breckinridge wrote a set of articles, some with Edith Abbott, in the *Journal of Political Economy* on, for instance, labor unions and legislation, housing, and equal wages.

Marion Talbot (1858–1948), who had set up a department for household administration at the University of Chicago, and Breckinridge published *The Modern Household* (1912). In this small book, they built on the active role and responsibilities of the housewife. They make the point that "it is ... of supreme importance that for women of that group [who were administering incomes between two and ten thousand dollars, and who were not professionals] the dignity and responsibility of their tasks should be made clear, and ideas of efficiency and utility substituted for those of waste and social competition" (1912: 3). The focus here was clearly on efficient spending or allocating income earned by the husband. This part of the process of household management can be compared to the process described by economists such as Carl Menger (1840–1921), who theorized that a consumer allocates his income in such a way that the marginal utility of the spending on each good is equal. Talbot and Breckinridge, however, directly linked consumption and household work, discussing in detail the matter of whether to buy something or to make it themselves. They argued that "we know for today, that the newly assumed function of spending is as important as the old function of making" (1912: 6).

During these first decades of the twentieth century, when women were hired in economics departments, it was in the fields of household administration, home economics, and marketing, which were considered "feminine fields" within the discipline. Home economics, like household administration, built on the long tradition of household management (see Chapter 1). Pathbreaking theoretical and empirical research on consumption was conducted by Hazel Kyrk (1886–1957), an American institutionalist, also from the University of Chicago. Besides restructuring the home economics department at the University of Chicago, shifting the focus away from the traditional household management approach to a more analytical and scientific approach, Kyrk conceptualized consumption as a separate field of economic study. In her book *A Theory of Consumption* (1923), Kyrk outlined her research program on consumer behavior. Mapping the field, she identified three modes of study that come together in the theorization of consumer behavior: neoclassical economic theory, business economics, and the field of household management. She mentioned the neglect of consumption by classical political economists and she is even more critical of the marginal utility school, particularly of William Stanley Jevons, one of the founders of this school. In Kyrk's view "the theory of economics must begin with the correct theory of consumption," whereas, among other things, "the marginal [economic theory] is, and was intended to be, primarily a theory of exchange value or prices" (1923: 16).

The theory of consumption, according to Kyrk, required an interdisciplinary approach. To complicate things further, she noted, "the consumer" is not a specific class of people, since everybody consumes; what defines consumers as a group is their interests "as consumers." According to Kyrk, "the interests of the individuals as consumers are definite, distinct realities, which may be differentiated from the interests of individuals in their other capacities" (1923: 2). She perceived consumption as a process through which the consumer has three distinct problems to solve: choice and budget making, marketing or buying, and using concrete commodities. For Kyrk, the consumer economist is interested in the relation between income, wealth, and happiness. The economist who aims to understand, analyze, and theorize consumer behavior therefore has to pay attention to (a) the larger context in which the consumption process takes place, (b) the way the consumption process is controlled and guided, (c) on what basis, in terms of norms and values, choices are being made, and (d) to what extent and how human welfare is a function of human wealth. Kyrk addressed these questions in her book in a comprehensive and systematic manner in which the role of norms, values, and advertising in the process of decision-making also comes to the fore.

At the very beginning of her book, Kyrk mentions how the conceptualization of consumption changed over time from a passive role to a more active one in the economy. After having referred to consumers as men using the pronouns he/him throughout the book, Kyrk states on the very last page:

> The consuming unit is originally not an individual but a household, just as the standard of living is a concept of proper family life, not that of an isolated individual. The expenditure, the purchasing, the direction of the consumption of this unit is usually the function of the woman at its head. The nature of the service she is rendering and its importance have not been completely realized either by women themselves or by others. The assumption has frequently been that with the departure of the household arts women lost their economic function; and if they remained within the household became parasites upon the economic order. While the extension of the ideal of ladyhood as the proper status of women has tended in this direction, what has really happened in the main is a new division of labor between men and women. The welfare of the household depends upon the efficiency of both in their respective fields. A clear recognition of the nature and importance of the task at present assigned to women should have marked results upon their practical training. (1923: 292)

Kyrk perceived the role of the consumer as entailing more than just ranking preferences and making a choice between goods and services offered taking prices into account. Considering consumption an active process, she perceived consumers as playing a substantial role in determining the direction of the economy as much as those involved in production. In contrast to Say's law stating that supply creates its own demand, Kyrk argued that it is, rather, or at least as much, demand that creates supply.

In addition, Kyrk conducted ground-breaking research for the Bureau of Home Economics of the US Department of Agriculture. She made a considerable contribution to a large survey on household expenditures (Kyrk et al., 1941), which provided the base-year prices for the official consumer price index (Lobdell, 2000: 253), and developed standards for what could be considered as the minimum requirements for a "decent living" (van Velzen, 2003: 42). In *The Family in the American Economy* (1953), Kyrk looked at a wide range of economic aspects of the household, such as provision for the future through saving and insurance, and she discussed social security and the economic position of stay-at-home moms, or, in her words "homekeeping women." In the last two chapters she lays out her work on the cost and standard of living, its measurement, and its changes over time.

Margaret G. Reid (1896–1991) was a student of Hazel Kyrk and earned her PhD in 1931. Furthering Kyrk's research program, which perceived the household as an active, productive, and integral part of the economy, Reid published her thesis under the title *The Economics of Household Production* in 1934 (earlier discussed in Chapter 1). Reid distinguished between consumption and household production, and distinguished four methods to value household production: opportunity cost, retail price, hired workers cost, and boarding service costs. She was hired at Iowa State University where she taught consumer economics and met Elizabeth Hoyt (1893–1980). Reid became a full professor in 1940 and during World War II she worked at the Division of Statistical Standards in the Executive Office of the President; after the war she led the Family Economics Division of the Department of Agriculture for three years (Forget, 2000). In 1951 she joined the Economics Department of the University of Chicago as a full professor. Together with Kyrk and Hoyt, Reid was committed to improving consumer education in America and the field that we today call economic literacy. In Reid's view, the consumer had to be educated in matters of personal financial planning, assessing the information provided in advertisements, making household budgets, and choosing between producing goods at home or buying them. This part of the old study of household management got lost in the neoclassical reduction of women's household activities to the allocation and spending of income. Reid's work would later receive much more recognition by economists than that of most of her female colleagues. For instance, economists Milton Friedman and Franco Modigliani recognized her work and, after some pressure, Gary Becker did so as well, after he had adopted her distinction between household production and consumption, and the so-called "third person criterion" (Forget, 2000).

Elizabeth Ellis Hoyt based her PhD, titled *Primitive Trade: Its Psychology and Economics*, on a collection of worldwide field reports about the development of economic market trade from gifts and other exchanges (Thorne, 2000: 216). Appointed a full professor in economics at Iowa State University at the age of thirty-five, she published *The Consumption of Wealth* in 1928. A substantial part of her research, conducted together with Hazel Kyrk and others, is on cost-of-living indices, which later resulted in the consumer price indices (Parsons and Tadajewski, 2013). Hoyt's approach to consumption is more anthropological than that of her colleagues, but no less interesting. For example, she analyzes the "creation of demand" and argued that "[m]an is not a bundle of unsatisfied interests; on the contrary, he has to learn his interests, and usually he learns hard; but if he has a teacher he learns more readily than he learns by himself" (1928: 101). Hoyt thus accepted the monetization and marketization of formerly household production as an unavoidable effect of the industrialization process. It was the consumer who faced a process of adaptation of behavior.

The advertising industry, according to Hoyt, was crucially important in teaching consumers about their interests, wants, and demands. To the question to what extent "aggressive sales methods" were effective, she answered: "In fact nobody knows. There are other influences beside selling efforts affecting demand: general social tendencies, changes in demand for complementary goods, frequently an improvement in the good itself. There is no doubt, however, that in some cases the speeding-up process due to advertising is huge" (1928: 102). Hoyt subsequently discussed the impact of culture on consumption, the changes in the standard of living and population growth; she ended her book with a discussion on measuring standards of living and some guidelines for budget building.

Hoyt developed an extended argument against the amounts spent on advertising, because of the billions of costs involved, about which she states that "of course, the consumer pays it." Hoyt also made the point that economists are familiar with "class prices," which she defined as "the setting of various prices to appeal to different classes on what is essentially the same product" (1928: 106). Joan Robinson (1903–83) discussed price discrimination – a term first coined by Vilfredo Pigou – extensively in two chapters of her *The Economics of Imperfect Competition* (1933). Her analysis of price discrimination is considered one of her most important contributions to economic theory. She pointed out that price discrimination depends on a difference between the elasticity of demand (how the demand for a good responds to a change in its price) in the markets in which the good is sold (1933: 185). This makes price discrimination in Robinson's view a matter of the shape of demand curves; when the demand curves of all the customers for a particular good are identical, price discrimination does not occur.

Robinson was able to obtain a position as a lecturer in the Economics Department at Cambridge, England, which was headed by Pigou and later by John Maynard Keynes, with whom she would work closely. She was critical toward neoclassical economics and is considered one of the founders of post-Keynesian economic theory. Although she barely discussed gender or feminist issues, she explained the gender wage gap as a case of price discrimination in the labor market (1933: 302), again as a matter of demand. For Robinson, the cause of the gender wage gap, here discussed in Chapter 6, thus lies not on the supply side of the labor market – the behavior and characteristics of the worker – but on the side of the employer. Over the years Robinson became more and more radical in her critiques on neoclassical economics, some of which she brought together in the booklet *Economic Philosophy* (1962).

More recently, the problem of price discrimination based on the gender of the customer has become considered to be problematic as producers and retailers ask different prices for essentially the same goods to women and men and to boys and girls. Women who buy products, some of which are designed as "feminine," are paying a higher price for things such as deodorants, shoes, t-shirts, and secondhand cars. Most women and girls are not aware of this, nor are they being informed about this, as they would otherwise probably adjust their demand for the "feminine" products. To counter this development, New York State outlawed this practice of pricing based on gender, referred to as "the Pink Tax," in 2020.

Most students will consider marketing to be part of business economics. In the 1920s, however, marketing was an emerging field that that was relatively open to women, investigated women's behavior with respect to the way they spent money, and developed advertising and writing as a link between the emerging markets of consumer goods and the women who desired these goods and bought them. The *Journal of Historical Research in Marketing* published a special issue in 2013 to bring attention to a selection of women founders of the field of marketing. One of them was Helen Woodward (1882–1960), who argued that marketing is part of consumer behavior. Woodward explored and developed the field of marketing theory and advertising practice in the 1920s (Tadajewski, 2013). Coming from a poor family and traveling upstream as a woman, a Jew, a radical, and a pacifist, she pursued economic security throughout her life, and built herself a successful career in teaching consumers how to spend their money efficiently. Woodward was one of the first to develop writing for advertisements. She rejected the one-sided approach in the emerging sales marketing branch, referred to above as "aggressive sales methods," and was convinced that this approach of providing one-sided if not false information about products could not last. She became one of the first copywriters in the field, but, as a woman, she had to fight hard for her accounts and each job that was "given" to her. In addition, she wrote a line of books, among which *Through Many Windows* (1926) is the most autobiographical. This book gives a personal account of her career, including her experiences with what makes a good worker and, in particular, a good sales person.

As the traditional field of household management developed an academic approach and was taken up in areas of household administration, home economics, and marketing, the remaining aspects, such as early child development, housekeeping, and "household bacteriology," were still practiced and taught in high schools, colleges, and universities. To modernize its image, in 1994 major professional associations in the field renamed it "family and consumer sciences" (Stage and Vincenti, 1997).

While economists like Marshall and Keynes moved toward conceptualizing consumption as the buying of goods and services, utility was eventually perceived as rooted in the goods and services purchased, and as a result the value of goods and services were considered to correspond to their prices. In microeconomics, the short-term and longer-term level of income, the level of inflation, and interest rates were all considered in terms of their impact on individual economic decisions over how much income to spend on consumer goods and services and what to purchase in response to changes in price. The process of economic decision-making in the household thus became neglected and was eventually only perceived as being of interest to businesses selling their products.

The boundary between unpaid work in the household and personal care, on the one hand, and monetized and marketized activities, on the other, continued to shift. What was formerly household production either moved out of the household or became seen as consumption or as personal care. Spending (quality) time with the children, for example, by helping the kids with their homework, was either outsourced or perceived and experienced as part of the consumption process (the reference of Becker to children as durable consumption goods is enlightening in this respect). Arlie Russell Hochschild (2012) has described this shifting of the commodification of personal care. For those working for a minimum wage, without social networks to provide the required childcare, affording children became increasingly hard, and economic hardship could easily make them lose control over their children to child protective services. In 1975, this lack of support for working mothers and career women led to a national women's strike in Iceland, and in the 1990s to a so-called "birth-strike" in Italy; in Japan in 2017, the fertility rate hit a low of 1.4 (an average of 2.1 children per woman in the childbearing age keeps a population at the same level) (Brown, 2019: 16). In the US, the process has been similar, but it is new immigrants who have always upheld the fertility numbers over 2.1, thus guaranteeing the replacement and growth of the population over time.

In economics, this hyper-individualized approach is reflected in an increased focus on individual decision-making with respect to economic – mostly consumer – choices. In neuro economics, economists focus on processes taking place in the brain in response to controlled input from the outside. Behavioral Economics, the study of economic decision-making by consumers applying psychology and neurological studies, emphasizes preference formation, the role of mistakes and illusions, the impact of advertising and the framing of the economic choice at hand. These theoretical models and tools can all be applied in very useful and innovative ways, and that is done, while addressing highly relevant issues. It is, however, the direction of the development of what is considered economics that interests us here. Gender differences, in these fields, have been constructed as part of humans' hard wiring or seen as self-evidently impacting behavior, using an ahistorical approach. Feminist scholars have contested and disproven these claims (see, e.g., Fine, 2010; Rippon, 2019). At the same time, it is clear that these approaches, with their strong focus on individual behavior, lose sight of the rest of the economy, its structure, its institutions, its communities, its social relations, and its history.

Consumption and environmental concerns

The conceptualization of consumption as the antithesis of production has done more than declare the household as predominantly the site of emotional and social support, shelter, and the provision of needs and the satisfaction of wants. It contributed to turning the economic process into an ahistorical and linear one, and changed the perception of the household into a place where goods are mainly "consumed" – i.e., turned into waste. Taking out its productive features unlinked the household to future generations. Moreover, it made the reproduction of workers and the production of the next generation of workers invisible and took the maintenance of goods, the reduction of waste, its role as part of the community, and the conservation of the environment out of the equation. The idea that, because there is no time or opportunity to have goods fixed, buying new goods is more efficient cannot be defended in any way as a more efficient way of using resources, of course. Instead, this kind of reasoning is mainly based on the externalization of the costs of goods and a lack of information available to the customer.

In the decades after World War II, as consumption became increasingly central in US society, it was predominantly women who did the shopping. Betty Friedan's (1921–2006) *The Feminine Mystique* (1963) gave voice to "the problem with no name" that afflicted women in the suburbs who had chosen marriage and children over a career and faced both isolation and competition with other house-wives in a life centered around shopping, cooking, and cleaning. Consumption became a way to express one's identity. Consumption became the Alpha and Omega, the beginning and end of the US economy.

As women did most of the shopping, food preparation, and other household work, they often experienced in a direct manner the impact of the environmental damage inflicted through industrialized food production; they noticed the decline in the quality of processed foods and directly faced the health impacts on their children of the toxic materials in products. Many became involved in environmental movements. Rachel Carson's book *Silent Spring* (1962) opened the eyes of many, as did *The Limits to Growth* (1972) based on research by the Club of Rome, by Donella H. Meadows et al. This was followed by the UN international women's conferences and conferences on the environment, the first being the 1972 Conference on Human Environment in Stockholm and the Earth Summit in Rio de Janeiro being the second (Pietilä, 2002). Gro Harlem Brundtland (1987) played an important role in the international discussion on environmental problems at the time.

Feminists or ecofeminists like Susan Griffin (1978) and Caroline Merchant (1980) argued that the psychological attitude toward women and toward nature was very similar. Ecofeminists, like Maria Mies (1986), Vandana Shiva (Mies and Shiva, 1988), Mary Mellor (1997), and Ellie Perkins (1997), stressed the parallels in the economic exploitation and oppression of women and nature, and their conceptualization as providing goods and services limitless and for free. Rejecting capitalism because of its exploitation of nature, women, and countries in the South, these authors stressed the impor-tance of cooperative behavior and the sustenance of the commons. Elinor Ostrom (1933–2012), who did not share the above-mentioned views on the capitalist system, developed an institutional approach to the governing of the commons. In 2009, Ostrom was the first woman to receive the Nobel Memorial Prize in Economic Sciences for her work on how to deal with what has been called "the tragedy of the commons" in the global economy; the tendency to destroy "common pool resources" like oceans, forests, the North Pole, by individual self-interested behavior (Ostrom, 1990).

The notion that women would "by their nature" be more closely connected to nature was considered problematic by many feminist economists, which brought a delay in the feminist economic theorizing of problems around global warming and climate change. Bina Agarwal addressed this ideological link between women and nature, using the experience of women in India as an example. She argued that although Indian women in rural households were victims of environmental degradation in gender-specific ways, they at the same time had been acting as agents actively contributing to environmental movements and forms of protection and regeneration (1992: 119).

Meanwhile, in mainstream economics the basic assumption that kept costs, in terms of unpaid household production and the exploitation of "nature," invisible, remained firmly in place. Since clean air was considered a "free good" because it was not scarce, and thus of no relevance for economists, the irreversible damage done by air pollution and irresponsible forest exploitation was considered to have no impact on the economy. The production of non-biodegradable plastics and other toxic waste was assumed not to impact the economy in a major way either – or, if it did, the assumption was that the price mechanism would take care of it, together with technological innovation driven by the higher prices for fossil fuels and the costs of goods and services. Clean air would be turned into a commodity was the idea. To address specific issues such as climate change, mainstream economic theory was extended and applied in the field of environmental economics.

Initiatives to develop broader and more innovative perspectives on the economy as social, moral, and sustainable in kind emerged and were presented initially at newly founded institutes, and networks that started out as social, political, and academic networks – e.g., the Institute for New Economic Theory (INET), the Green Economics Institute in Oxford, England, and the Community Economies Research Network (CERN). The 1972 edition of *Limits to Growth* was updated in 2004 and presented the Dynamic Systems Theory (DST). Instead of taking the individual as central unit of analysis, DST starts from a system as a whole, indicates the stocks and flows, positive and negative feedback loops, and then identifies the viability loops that have a balance of positive and negative feedback loops that signify a healthy system. Points of interference provide leverage points in the system where efficient policy measures can help restore viability loops.

More recently, economists, like Kate Raworth (2017), have provided entirely new base models of a sustainable economy. Raworth, who critiques the mechanical approach to science based on linear causality, proposes a circular model (a doughnut), which, for a specific locality, indicates the overshoot with respect to the use of resources (carbon dioxide, acidification of oceans, etc.) and the shortfall in terms of provision of social aspects (income, health, education, etc.). It is in the space between the shortfall and the overshoot that humanity can live in a sustainable manner. The work by Nazia Mintz-Habib is similarly innovative in the way her analysis starts from the sustainable development framework in which the economy, the social, and the environment are perceived as overlapping and integrated. Mintz-Habib (2016) applies behavioral and mainstream economic models and tools to carry out her design of sustainable economic policies. Neither of these two authors, however, brings in gender as an analytical category.

Although early work on environmental issues from a women's or feminist perspective made clear links between movements addressing class, race, and women's oppression and issues, work in feminist economics on sustainable development developed relatively late (see, e.g., Perkins, 1997; Perkins and Kuiper, 2005; Agarwal, 2010). Julie Nelson and Marilyn Power (2018) provide an overview of recent overlapping activities of the journals *Feminist Economics* and *Ecological Economics*. Their own work aims at reconceptualizing economics in terms of "provisioning" (Nelson, 1993; Power, 2004). The broader recognition of intersectionality by feminist scholars seems to be opening up feminist ecological economics to apply a wider set of theoretical approaches and associate with a broader set of political movements.

8

Government Policies

Introduction

With no direct representation until the early twentieth century, women in the UK and the US had a troubled relationship with the state. This started to improve when they obtained the right to vote and took their seats on local and national representative bodies. Until then, only under fierce pressure from the women's and workers' movements were they able to get laws changed, and to get new laws put in place that respected their interests. Political economists had provided arguments to push back the role of the state after the mercantilist era, in which the state controlled the economic process in detail, in favor of "the individual" whom political economists argued should be free in pursuing his interests and profitmaking.

This chapter focuses on women economic writers' and economists' ideas, concepts, and theories about the changing role and tasks of the state and the development of policy research on women's issues and interests. As such, the chapter addresses the shifts in perceptions of the responsibility of the state and its policies with respect to what is considered the standard household model in society. It also discusses the way women economic writers and economists would like to see social change made, paying specific attention to public policies on care work, the efficient use of resources, conservation of nature, and a less exploitative relation with the Global South.

The role of the state

Whether the newly monetized and marketed goods and services that had been formerly provided within the household should be provided by the private or the public sector was the topic of a major battle that emerged during the second half of the nineteenth century. This fight would continue throughout the twentieth and into the twenty-first century, going back and forth between those who argued for a strong state and those who favored a "free" market system. In this debate, economists were generally silent about the role of the household as provider of care for children, the elderly, and the sick, and emotional, social, and community support.

We saw in earlier chapters that women economic writers like Sarah Chapone, Mary Wollstonecraft, Barbara Bodichon, and Beatrice Potter Webb wrote pamphlets, pleas, and reports to politicians in the UK Parliament, and that Sophonisba Breckinridge, Elizabeth Hoyt, and others addressed the US Congress to change marriage laws, voting laws, and regulations that concerned working hours, a minimum wage, and wage equality, among other things. Over time, women economists continued to demonstrate considerable interest in policy analysis. In *A Biographical Dictionary of Women Economists*, Robert Dimand, Mary-Ann Dimand, and Evelyn Forget concluded that, overall, "women devoted more interest than did men to social policy and gender pay differentials" (2000: xxiii). Kirsten Madden, Janet Seiz, and Michèle Pujol argue that "a very large proportion of women focused on labor studies and the welfare of the working class, including gender-, age-, race-specific analyses, ... [and that] many devoted their energies to efforts to reduce gender inequality and rectify injustices associated with exploitation of the labor forces" (2004: xxviii–xxix). Madden's (2002) quantitative study on women economists' publications between 1900 and 1940 concluded along similar lines that labor economics, home economics, and gender equality had become the particular fields of interest of women economists in this period. Moreover, women economists, more than their male colleagues, used an interdisciplinary approach, often due to their backgrounds as civil servants, social workers, journalists, sociologists, or anthropologists.

Over the course of the nineteenth and early twentieth centuries, governments in the UK and the rest of Europe gradually became "welfare states," stepping in to implement regulations and adjustments designed in some cases to enable the market to function better, and in others to support entrepreneurs, and in still others to provide physical and economic security for their citizens. In the USSR and other socialist countries, the role of the state would be even more comprehensive in regulating and managing the economy through price controls, production plans, wage regulations, guaranteed employment, and childcare provisions. Some liberal women economic writers and economists were in favor of letting "the market mechanism do its work." Others favored a more extended role for the state. They argued that, besides pursuing its traditional tasks, the state should not only provide more public education, (high-quality) childcare, and factory regulation, but also take the lead in countering discrimination, supporting the redistribution of unpaid work in the household, and bringing about a more egalitarian household model.

The literature on social policies increased substantially over the twentieth century, both in scope and in volume. For women, state control over reproductive health and their economic position were closely intertwined. Limiting the number of children, for instance, often against the wishes of the Church, freed up women's time and enabled them to earn a better living. Whereas many of the European governments, and also the US government, were engaged in population control in (former) colonies – for example in Puerto Rico – family planning was promoted early on by economists such as Thomas Malthus and the young John Stuart Mill. In his adolescent years, Mill was arrested for distributing information about birth control, as was Annie Besant, a prolific writer, educator, and activist for the use of contraception. The authorities based these arrests on laws against obscenity, as talking let alone writing about sexual behavior was considered indecent and offensive. Among Besant's hundreds of publications is the pamphlet *The Law of Population* (1877), in which she brings to broader attention Malthus's law of population, backing up her arguments by reference to the work of John Stuart Mill, Harriet Martineau, Robert Owen, and John Ramsay McCulloch.

In the US, Margaret Higgins Sanger (1879–1966), who engaged in life-long activism and wrote several books on the impact of population control and birth control, faced arrest and was threatened with confinement in prison for going against the anti-obscenity laws of the day. After publication of the pamphlet *Family Limitation* (1914), which contains a simple but straightforward and illustrated explanation of how to prevent conception, Sanger was persecuted and she fled to Europe. Her husband, who stayed in the US, spent some months in jail. When Margaret returned to the US, public support for her cause had grown, which helped to prevent her from spending time in prison. In 1920, she published *Woman and the New Race*, in which she based her arguments for birth control on the overpopulation, poverty, lack of education, health problems, and mental disability that the lack of access to birth control caused. Reasoning in eugenic language, she stated that "every detail of this sordid situation means a problem that must be solved before we can even clear the way for a greater race in America" (1920: 13). Under the heading "Why not Birth-Control Clinics in America?" she referred to the founding of such clinics in the Netherlands, which, according to Sanger, had led to an increase in "the wealth, stamina, stature, and longevity of the people, as well as a gradual increase in the population" (1920: 61). Sanger became one of the founders of Planned Parenthood, an organization that still today provides reproductive healthcare in the US. Where Native American women were concerned, the US government often interfered with their rights to have and raise their own children, either in the form of forced sterilization or by taking children away from their families to be raised by white families or in educational institutions that repressed their culture. For Black Americans, who experienced the highest numbers of forced sterilization in the 1950s and 1960s (Stern, 2020), child protection services often interfered with similar consequences: the loss of bonding between parents and children and of control over their children's early education.

Social Darwinism, as articulated by Herbert Spencer (1820–1903), which applied Charles Darwin's ideas about evolution to human society, was, as we saw earlier, fairly common in intellectual circles. Spencer's *Social Statics* (1851) and *First Principles* (1862) also influenced Alfred Marshall's *Principles of Economics* (1890) on a fundamental level (Groenewegen, 1995). Progressive intellectuals, too, were concerned about the fact that the upper classes had substantially fewer offspring than the masses of workers and the poor, whom they saw as a threat to (their) civilization. Women economic writers like Charlotte Perkins Gilman and Beatrice Potter Webb applied these ideas and referred to concerns about the "improvement of the stock" (Webb) and the "improvements of the race" (Gilman). Eugenics and these more and sometimes less implicit white supremacist ideas about racial differences were also used to back up the Jim Crow system of racial segregation in the US.

Population (growth) as a relevant economic factor, which had been excluded from consideration in neoclassical economic theorizing, was taken up again as a topic by economists in the 1980s; this time as the applied field of population economics. Issues such as fertility rates, the timing and spacing of children, and the impact of the number of children on their mother's labor participation and wage level, etc. were researched using, predominantly, the neoclassical standard model and quantitative research methods. Women economists were relatively well represented in this field. Research of economists such as Francesca Bettio (2013), Claudia Goldin (1990), and Francine Blau and Marianne Ferber (1986) generated data, models, and empirical economic knowledge about the interrelation between household arrangements, economic policies, and fertility rates; this time, however, without the Social Darwinist language and assumptions.

Local and national governments in most European countries and in the US took responsibility for providing primary, secondary, and higher education over the course of the nineteenth and twentieth centuries. Increasing demand for skilled workers, women's struggle for both access to education and the provision of education for their children, discussed in Chapter 3, resulted over time in the increase of the age for mandatory schooling over the twentieth century – first until the age of twelve, then fourteen, and later until seventeen or eighteen in some countries. States professionalized and took over productive tasks not only from women in individual households, but also from men. Building bridges, railroads, ports, highways, and digging canals – all typically men's work – was undertaken by Western governments, enabling private enterprise to flourish.

The regulations that aimed to contain the forces of capitalism in Britain were referred to as the Factory Acts. Initially put in place to protect children, these laws were expanded to regulate working-class women's working hours and to prohibit them from doing jobs that were considered dangerous. Beatrice Potter Webb (1896) provided an overview of the main arguments in the debates about the usefulness of the Factory Laws. She argued that the new Factory Act of 1895, which aimed to regulate accommodations such as sanitary provisions and fire escapes, should be considered a good thing. She criticized Millicent Fawcett and Ada Heather Bigg, who opposed this Act and who viewed such legislation as

> something which, whether for men or for women, decreases personal freedom, diminishes productive capacity, and handicaps the worker in the struggle for existence. I [Beatrice Potter Webb] need not recall how firmly and conscientiously this view was held by men like Nassau Senior and John Bright in the generation gone by. Today there are evidently many ladies of education and position superstitiously clinging to the same belief. (1896: 18)

Another member of the Fabian Women's Group, Emma Brooke (1898), provided an overview of the factory laws in place in all European countries. Elizabeth Leigh Hutchins and Amy Harrison (1911) described the history of this legislation and mentioned the total lack of enforcement of the laws. As they show, the Factory Acts did counter some of the rough edges of industrial society, as they kept women and children from working in mine shafts, taking night shifts, doing heavy lifting, etc. The number of hours children were allowed to work, based on their age, was reduced from about fourteen to twelve hours per day, then to ten. In 1867, no children younger than eight years of age could be hired, and the Education Act of 1870, by making education mandatory, effectively ended child labor. In the US, the Fair Labor Standards Act of 1938 would put the forty-hour work week in place for all adults, together with a minimum wage and extra pay for working overtime.

Along with the increasing reach of the state, the production of data by statistical bureaus and the Census, separate from economic theoretical research, would become standard practice in economic science (on this topic, see, e.g., Poovey, 1998). The first British Census was conducted in 1801 and information on women's labor force participation was published for the first time in 1841. In the US, the first Census surveys were conducted in 1790. Early on in the development of the welfare state, both the French and the British governments undertook large-scale investigations. *La Statistique de l'Industrie à Paris* (1847–8) was published in France and the *Report of the Children's Employment Commission, on Mines and Collieries* appeared in 1842 in London (Scott, 1988; Hutchins and Harrison, 1911: 81). Women's economic writers made grateful use of these data and would later engage in several large-scale empirical research projects themselves. In France, for instance, Julie-Victoire Daubié (1824–74) conducted a large-scale research project financed by herself, for which she traveled around the entire country obtaining data for her prize-winning essay *La femme pauvre au XIXe siècle* (Poor women in the nineteenth century; 1866). She brought to light the extreme poverty of women in large parts of France. She showed the dire circumstances especially of single women, whose wages would not sustain them, and described many cases in which women had been pushed out of occupations. Daubié argued for reopening these occupations for women, especially the administrative positions they had lost access to after the 1848 Revolution (Ivory, 2000).

English social reformers, like Charles Booth, Seebohm Rowntree, and the team of Edward Cadbury, Cécile Matheson, and George Shann, conducted large-scale research projects in London and

Birmingham to measure the poverty rate and the work and living conditions at the end of the nineteenth and the beginning of the twentieth century. Social investigators went from door to door with questionnaires. Making use of both quantitative methods, including the Census outcomes of 1891, and qualitative methods, Booth (1903) and Rowntree (1901) found poverty rates of about 30 percent among the population of four million Londoners. Beatrice Potter Webb and Clara Collet both contributed to this endeavor; Webb (1979 [1926]) described Charles Booth's project, which stretched out over a period of seventeen years and resulted in a seventeen-volume final report, *Life and Labour of the People in London* (1903). It brought Beatrice Potter (not yet married to Sidney Webb) experience in research and insight in the living circumstances of the least privileged in London life. Later, she and her husband became active members of the so-called Cooperative Movement, which valued cooperation over competition as a guiding principle for economic behavior. These inquiries usually led to additional policies being put in place. Booth (1903), for example, according to Beatrice Potter Webb, contributed to the fact that "the Old Age Pension Act was passed in 1908, to be greatly enlarged and extended in 1911, 1919, and 1924" (1979 [1926]: 255).

Clara Collet (1860–1948), like Beatrice Potter, worked on the Charles Booth project, and contributed several sections on women's work in various sectors of industry in the final report. Collet, who had, as the first woman, obtained an MA in Political Economy from the University of London in 1886, would during her career focus on statistical research on women's work and women's wages, and would argue for a minimum wage (Collet, 1898, 1911). Her family background and later her active membership of several economics groups made her well connected with economists like Karl Marx, Francis Edgeworth, and Henry Higgs. Collet ended her career in an influential position as Senior Investigator for the Board of Trade, in which she was able to comment on and write parts of labor legislation (McDonald, 2004).

The large-scale empirical investigation undertaken by Edward Cadbury, Cécile M. Matheson, and George Shann (1906) focused on the working conditions of women in Birmingham. The report places women's wages in a social and historical context, rejecting a male wage-earner household approach to income distribution, as well as the related assumption that women earn only a secondary income and are therefore merely an appendage to a man. According to Cadbury et al., "it is imperative that, if possible, the economic status of women must be raised; for, while their economic inferiority is due to their past subjection, yet in turn the inferiority tends to perpetuate the subjection" (1906: 144; see also Pujol, 1992). The report was reviewed by Edith Abbott in the *Journal of Political Economy* as "interesting and suggestive, and if it has not furnished any new or valuable statistical evidence on the subject of the employment of women, it has succeeded where some of the more detailed studies have failed – in giving the public a thoroughly readable account of an important social problem" (1907: 564).

The same Edith Abbott and her colleague Sophonisba P. Breckinridge conducted similar large-scale research projects in the US, in Chicago to be precise. Like Breckinridge, Abbott had published a collection of articles in the *Journal of Political Economy* on women's work in several industries (e.g., cotton mills, cigar-making, boots, and shoes). Abbott included part of these materials in her *Women in Industry* (1910). Soon after, she started to work with Breckinridge. They conducted three large-scale empirical research projects. The first, *The Delinquent Child and the Home* (1912), focused on the causes and possible solutions for criminality in children; the second, *Truancy and Non-Attendance in the Chicago Schools* (1917), addressed urban school attendance in the Chicago area; the third resulted in *The Tenements of Chicago, 1908–1935* (1936). These studies indicated, Abbott and Breckinridge concluded, that poverty was a main source for many of the urban problems at hand, and they argued for a variety of government programs and interventions to solve these problems (Hammond, 2000a).

Sadie Tanner Mossell Alexander (1898–1989) was the first black woman to obtain a PhD in Economics (1921). Her thesis was titled "The Standard of Living Among One Hundred Negro Migrant Families in Philadelphia." At the job market for economists, Alexander experienced significant racial discrimination and could not find a job that fitted her level of education. After going to law school at the University of Pennsylvania, she worked for various governmental committees, including the Truman administration's Committee on Human Rights. She gave a range of speeches, including "Negro Women in Our Economic Life" (1930) and "The Economic Status of Negro Women: An Index of the Negro's Economic Status" (1934) about the labor participation and pay of black women, and provided an overview of the sectors that black women worked in. She showed that during the Great Depression blacks suffered a (relatively high) level of unemployment and at the same time a lack of support offered by relief programs.

Alexander spent her life investigating the economic situation of Black Americans and fighting for economic justice. During a time when eugenics was a common approach to racial inequality among economists, Alexander interviewed hundreds of immigrants who had moved to the North between World War I and the 1960s and assessed that poverty and the lack of education, training, and opportunity due to flagrant racial discrimination kept Black Americans stuck in low-paid jobs and poor neighborhoods (Banks, 2021). Inequality in the US economy, according to Alexander, had led to the Great Depression. She criticized the National Recovery Administration (NRA) for their implicit racism by not protecting the jobs of Black Americans. To deal with this and similar issues, Alexander later proposed installing affirmative action programs and government-guaranteed jobs, arguing for "programs of compensatory opportunity" (1963: 123). Although the empirical data provided by Alexander about the economic status of black people in the US shed new light on the economic status and behavior of a large subgroup of the American population, this knowledge ended up in the economics discipline's proverbial drawer. It took until 2021 for her economic work to be published and made fully available (Banks, 2021). As feminist economists have experienced again and again, for data and facts to be counted and assessed as "scientific facts," they need to be backed up by power, influence, and support within the discipline. This was clearly something the work of Anna Julia Cooper, Ida B. Wells-Barnett, and Sadie Alexander, among others, did not possess in large enough quantities.

The generations of women who reached adulthood at the beginning of the twentieth century took the opportunities available to obtain a higher education, a job, and a career in economics and other academic fields, as well as in journalism and politics. Eleanor Roosevelt, as US First Lady, brought her network of highly qualified friends to the dinner table. One of her friends, Frances Perkins, became Secretary of Labor in Franklin Roosevelt's (FDR) administration from 1933 to 1945. By handing FDR a list of social and economic policies she would like to put in place – and then doing just that – Perkins effectively became "the Woman behind the New Deal," the title of her biography (Downey, 2009). Perkins put her name on, for instance, the Social Security Act of 1935 and the Fair Labor Standards Act of 1938 (Ware, 1981). Eleanor Roosevelt wrote a daily column, "My Day," and various books (e.g., *It's Up to the Women*, published in 1933) that dealt head-on with the difficult issues of her time. She was a liberal who believed in the capitalist system, while at the same time recognizing the severe problems of poverty, economic hardship and of racism that the black community faced. Her work on the 1948 Universal Declaration of Human

Rights and the foundation of the Commission on the Status of Women contributed substantially to the development of an analytical framework based on human rights that would later be used by feminist and development economists.

In the 1980s and 1990s, feminist economists in Europe focused their work in large part on public policymaking, conducting large-scale research projects for national governments as well as for the European Commission, for instance with the aim of supporting women's labor force participation and a redistribution of income between men and women through taxation, benefits, and income transfers (see, e.g., Rossilli, 2000). After the economic crisis of 2008/9, the European Commission and many European member states in its wake, chose austerity measures that had a significantly negative impact on policies supporting gender equality (see, e.g., Bettio et al., 2013; Karamessini and Rubery, 2014).

Over the same period in the US, economists, inspired by Reaganomics and the rational expectations theory of economist Robert Lucas, turned away from such social policy research. In its place there was a move to a more "scientific research" model, which resulted in a further increase in mathematical modeling. Feminist economists responded with critical theoretical analyses and epistemological debates. Moving in the opposite direction, however, were Heidi Hartmann and others, who founded the Institute of Women's Policy Research (IWPR) in Washington that provided a continuous stream of information in the form of data and briefs about women's economic status and feminist issues.

Along with the further increase in the monetization and marketization of work formerly conducted in the household, over the twentieth and early twenty-first centuries the role of the state expanded to include provision of those goods and services that could only be produced as public goods. Feminist economists realized in the early 1990s that there was gender bias in the process of public policymaking itself. This meant that both the social policies aimed at women and children, as well as the more general economic, housing, and trade policies, were biased against women in their design, operation, and impact. In 1995, Debbie Budlender in South Africa and Rhonda Sharp in Australia started initiatives to evaluate gender biases in local and government budgets.

Gender-responsive budgeting (GRB) recognizes the budget as one of the most important tools available to local and national governments. By working with civil servants involved in the budget process and by analyzing and assessing the impact of gender biases in the budget process, policies were evaluated and analyzed on gender bias, monitored and evaluated on their effectivity, and improvements were proposed and implemented. These proposals followed the budget cycle and became part of effective administrative and budgeting processes in countries in Africa, Europe, and South-East Asia (see, e.g., Budlender, 2000). The UNDP accepted this approach and began training civil servants to include gender awareness in their programs and policy development. In 2018 the South African government announced its intention to "ensure the development and implementation of a Gender-Responsive Planning, Budgeting, Monitoring, Evaluation and Auditing Framework in South Africa." In the US, GRB initiatives are notoriously scarce. Though an effective tool for improving the budgeting process, GRB, in which many feminist economists and grassroots initiatives are involved (e.g., the Women's Budget Group in the UK), is a rather time- and energy-intensive endeavor. Such initiatives may have to continue, however, until the basic principles of GRB have become integrated into the education and training of civil servants worldwide.

Care services as public goods, local and global

The marketization and monetization of women's productive activities formerly conducted in the household were considerably hampered by the fact that these activities and their value had hardly been recognized by economists and politicians. This led to surprises for economists when women, married women in particular, were pushed and pulled into the labor market. Since the assumption was that they had been inactive and considered as "stay at home" mothers, now the need and demand for their unpaid household production became visible and these goods and services became available, carrying substantially higher costs. Part of the goods and services formerly undertaken in the household, however, were provided neither by the private sector nor by the public sector. We will focus here on women's economic writings and economists' writing on government policies in the area that became conceptualized as "care work," closing this chapter off with sections on the environment and on the South.

Early on, women economic writers and economists had already mentioned the inefficiency of married women cooking each day individually for their husband and children. Charlotte Perkins Gilman, who took differences between women and men and the sexual division of work as a given, proposed to take "this great race-function of cooking," cleaning, and the raising of children out of the home to be taken over by trained professionals, thereby freeing women as economic agents, which she thought would support them to achieve "the much better fulfilment of their duties as wives and mothers to the vast improvement in health and happiness of the human race" (1998 [1898]: 119). Gilman had community kitchens in mind and high-quality childcare centers. What actually happened was that when a profit could be made, entrepreneurs stepped in and sold their goods and services to individual households. The food and restaurant industry are now, at least in the US, an important part of the service economy, selling among other things pre-cooked food to individual households.

By enabling and expecting women to earn a wage and become economically independent, the transitional household model has – in the US – taken the place of the traditional, male wage-earner household. The public goods required to support working women have, however, materialized slowly, if at all, which has led to increased pressure on women, married women with children in particular, who also aimed at having, and were expected to have, a full-time job. The government has consistently been under attack over more than four decades and turned itself, initiated by and with the support of mainstream economists, into the provider of last resort, prioritizing production for profit. Only in those cases where otherwise dire needs, misery, and death could not be prevented did the government step in, providing public education, healthcare, elderly care, and food stamps. As such, the transitional household model is closely connected to the single parent household. The single parent household is, after all, a transitional household without the presence of a male wage earner, which is one of the main reasons why these family groups are so overrepresented among poor households (see, e.g., Albelda, 2013; Albelda et al., 2005).

Although in Europe and many other countries in the world, states do take (at least some) responsibility for the costs of care work formerly conducted in the household – for instance in the form of paid maternity/parental leave and quality childcare – in the US, federal and state provision for parental leave and childcare arrangements remains very limited. Especially in Europe, there emerged in the 1980s a widespread and lively academic debate about the economic and social impacts of the change in household pattern from the male wage-earner model to the transitional/single parent model and the possibilities for a more egalitarian household model. Feminist sociologists, political scientists, and economists contributed theoretical and empirical research, initially focusing on social policies. The European Commission pressured individual member states to increase the labor force participation of (married) women, leaving it up to nation-states to decide on (and pay for) what were perceived as "social arrangements." Large-scale country comparisons based on quantitative research enabled economists such as Jane Lewis, Jill Rubery, and Janneke Plantenga to investigate the impacts of taxation systems, wage increases, and the number of months of paid maternity leave on women's participation in the labor market. On the basis of this research, they provided policy proposals, such as making work-related expenses for secondary income earners (costs of childcare, workspace at home, etc.) tax-deductible, which would recognize and remove historical hurdles. Articles by these and other authors on specific countries were brought together in, for example, Jane Lewis's edited works, *Women's Welfare, Women's Rights* (1983) and *Women and Social Policies in Europe* (1993).

Even though in the US the push for women to get paid jobs was much stronger than, for instance, in Germany, the Netherlands, or Spain, the dominant standard economic perception that raising children was part of the private sphere and the primary responsibility of the mother remained strong. By the 1990s, a literature emerged about the costs and impact of various social and economic arrangements in Western industrialized countries. Gøsta Esping-Anderson's *The Three Worlds of Welfare Capitalism* (1990) distinguished three types of welfare state: the liberal (the US and the UK), the corporatist-statist (e.g., Germany), and the social democratic (Nordic countries). In his analysis, he initially did not address the role of women and gender. Diane Sainsbury (1996) responded, addressing the implications of the different kinds of welfare states for women, broadening the research to include the economic structure of states, their gendered structures and impacts on both women and men. Sainsbury distinguishes between various aspects of a welfare state (e.g., the proportion of GDP devoted to social purposes, the level of benefits, population covered, type of financing, etc.) and describes the US, the UK, the Netherlands, and Sweden as prototypical welfare states.

The strong focus on the market-oriented approach in the US to providing goods and services that are essentially public goods has been problematic with respect to women, children, and the environment. This came to the fore in 2020 during the COVID-19 pandemic. Women lost their jobs and/or were leaving the labor market in unprecedented numbers, due to a lack of quality childcare and flexibility in the work place. In the fall of 2019, women outnumbered men in the US labor market, which means that their place in that market has changed fundamentally. This will make dealing with issues that hamper women's engagement in paid – and unpaid – work essential.

Control of waste and conservation of the natural environment

Where the control of waste and conservation of the natural environment are concerned, feminist economists, ecological economists, and other heterodox economists have explained the serious limitations of an economy that exploits production factors and dumps workers and waste back into the household and the environment when their use is exhausted. This process of the externalization of costs and ignoring the real costs of production to keep prices low is problematic on many levels. That it is unsustainable becomes clear as pandemics and climate change have come to impact us directly.

Based on the many critiques of the GDP index of economic growth, the new indices that have been developed – e.g., the Human Development Index (HDI), the Happiness Index, the Gender Equality Measure (GEM), and the Gender Equality Index (GEI) – demand a reorientation on the broader goals of the economy and society of policymakers and economists. The international community led by the UN set up a set of shared goals for the global economy and society at large that started in 2000 and ran until 2015: the Millennium Development Goals (MDGs). Gender equality and the empowerment of women was the third MDG, which came behind "ending world poverty" and "achieving universal primary education." As a follow-up, in 2015 the UN presented seventeen Sustainable Development Goals (SDGs) for 2030, of which "gender equality" is the fifth. Feminist economists, like Radhika Balakrishnan, Director of the Center for Women's Global Leadership, requested that gender concerns should also be integrated in other MDGs. Overall, the SDGs are more interconnected than the MDGs. Governments are required to report annually on progress made on all these goals, including gender equality. Governments have also become increasingly aware of their crucial role in the process of countering climate change, or at least of containing the increase in global temperatures. The lack of voice of young people in our societies and the invisibility of later generations in our economic models are clearly deficiencies that need to be addressed.

International economic policies

Backed by Milton Friedman's arguments for a limited government, Robert Lucas's rational expectations theory, and an increasing support for Friedrich Hayek's notion that that government's "interference with the markets" was costly, harmful, and at best useless, the economics discipline moved away from policy research and toward mathematical modeling and theory development. This had two main impacts, the first being that fewer and fewer economists were involved in policymaking, but instead chose other careers, such as in the financial sector. The second was the strengthening of the idea that mathematical models were scientific and thus universally applicable. As such, they were used to back-up and direct the policies of the IMF and World Bank on development countries' lending practices.

Internationally, the application of standard economic models was widespread under the regime referred to as "the Washington Consensus": the sharing of norms, values, theories, and mathematical models between the IMF, the World Bank and the US Treasury – all located in the center of Washington, DC – informing the approach and policies of international financial institutions. Based on these models, these institutions imposed austerity policies on countries in the South (so-called structural adjustment programs, SAPs). These contained conditions such as budget cuts for their governments, devaluation of their currency to support their exports (thereby hampering domestic industries), deregulation of corporations in terms of legal protection of workers, and privatization of public services; all this to enable and guarantee that states could pay off their debts and open up their economies to international corporations and competition.

When what turned out to be the last international women's conference, the Fourth World Conference on Women, convened by the United Nations, took place in Beijing in 1995, the Beijing Platform of Action was decided upon. This declaration and plan set the stage for feminist policy debates on the international stage for the decades that followed. At the Third World Conference on Women in Nairobi and the Fourth in Beijing, feminists from the South had critiqued the one-sided economic approach and also white liberal women's agenda of focusing on increasing women's labor force participation as a means to economic independence. They had demanded that attention be paid, among other things, to the specific impacts of these policies in the South, where women ended up in informal jobs with low pay, and few protections and benefits. The Beijing Platform of Action centers around gender equality and economic justice for women, for women in the South in particular.

Instead of "gender equality" or "gender equity," some prefer the term "women's empowerment." To operationalize "women's empowerment" so that success (or failure) could be assessed, the 2007 World Bank's Gender Equality Plan defined women's empowerment as "making markets work for women (at the policy level) and empowering women to compete (at the agency level)." The feminist economist Naila Kabeer, on the other hand, conceptualized women's empowerment in economic terms that were broader than those of the World Bank. Women's empowerment is a dynamic process, according to Kabeer (1999), in which women improve their ability to make important life choices, taking into account the availability of resources as preconditions, agency as an aspect of process, and women's achievements as a measure of outcomes.

Feminist economists have articulated severe critiques on the SAPs and have done extensive work to integrate gender into macroeconomic and trade policies, taking women and, for instance, unpaid household work into account (see, e.g., Elson and Çagatay, 2000; van Staveren et al., 2007). To further women's empowerment internationally, Radhika Balakrishnan, James Heintz, and Diane Elson (2016) argue for establishing feminist economic arguments within the human rights framework.

9

Findings, Feminist Economics, and Further Explorations

Introduction

Economics remains a male-dominated field. The percentage of women economics students both in Europe and in the US has been slowly increasing, from 30 percent in the 1970s to 35 percent of the total number of economics students today. In the US, the number of assistant, associate, and full professors is also growing. Over the period 1994 to 2020, the percentage of assistant professors increased from 25 percent to 31 percent. Over this same period, there was close to a doubling of the percentage of associate professors in economics departments from 14.5 percent to 28 percent and more than a doubling of full professors, from 7 percent to almost 15 percent (CSWEP, 2020). This means, however, that women economists still do not have sufficient representation and voice to contribute fully to decision-making about the direction of the field in economics. This, of course, applies even more strongly with regards to women economists of color (Bueno and Bueno, 2020).

This chapter provides an overview of the findings in the earlier chapters, a brief introduction to the emergence of feminist economics as a new approach to economics, and some explorations of possible directions with respect to women economists and the feminist debates on economic issues.

Findings and conclusions from earlier chapters

By putting women economic writers and economists center stage, it became clear that these authors wrote for an audience of women and girls, activists and politicians. Political economists, on the other hand, wrote predominantly for legislators, the government, entrepreneurs, and other economists. This affected the language, concepts, and focus of both women and men economists. As men dominated women both in the political realm and at home, those in power did not consider this one-sidedness in economic science, which resulted from the limitations that went with a male-only perspective, problematic.

Taking a woman's perspective provides us with a different narrative about economic development, a clear view on the limits of the male perspective in economic thinking, and indicates a set of aspects that have been neglected in economic thinking. The large majority of the works discussed in this book are not referred to in the economics discipline or in the history of economics. We have seen that, over the centuries, women's contributions to economic debates outside and inside the discipline increased in number, although the lack of references to their work and the underappreciation of the topics they addressed remained.

Over time, gender as a marker determining one's opportunities and behavior has, to some extent, decreased in importance for upper-class women. By the end of the twentieth century, for instance, a substantial number of women economists were engaged in mainstream economic research. Discrimination may have impacted these women's experience, and probably still will do so, but has less clearly determined their choice of topic or method of research. Since the history of exclusion of women's economic writing has stretched out over many decades, if not centuries, taking gender as a basis for selecting these writers was justified as we focused on a context in which gender largely determined women's life experiences and in which women were excluded from œconomia, political economy, and later economics. After women gained access to social, political, and economic institutions, the gap between the topics addressed by men and women decreased, but it has still not fully disappeared. Below, some of the findings that have come to light in terms of differences with the traditional history of economic thought are highlighted.

1. Œconomia as a predecessor of political economy and economics

Œconomia, or the study of household management, appeared to be a full-fledged predecessor of political economy, one that centered around the efficient running of a household. In the early texts, women figured as central agents whose attitude, skills, connections, and experience made a large difference to the wealth of the household. We uncovered a literature that developed in the seventeenth and eighteenth centuries and dealt with how to run a household well. These texts included knowledge about efficient allocation of resources, chemistry, biology, medicine, spinning, weaving, furniture maintenance, conservation, cooking, and hiring and supervising personnel. With the monetization and marketization of production that formerly took place in the household, this study of household management became reduced to what was taught as "home economics" in high schools and colleges.

2. Women's agency in the household and marriage

Marriage was conceived by most women economic writers as a legal and economic institution that played a central role in determining (and limiting) women's economic agency. With the emergence of industrial society and the legal changes that occurred in England, the rest of Europe, and later in the US, the agency of married women in particular was severely reduced, and the economic dependence on their husband reinforced this. Whereas the inequality of legal rights has by now for the most part been dealt with in the Western world, the economic dependence of women on men is still a major issue. This is mainly due to the unequal division of care and financial responsibilities in the household and the ongoing discrimination in the labor market. The overrepresentation of single parent households – mostly women – among poor households reflects this.

The exclusion of household management in economic thinking and the shift toward the focus on individuals and social classes as basic units of analysis in political economy have not been gender-neutral, as they have taken place in a context in which legal changes were put in place that excluded women from the public realm. It made women invisible, or perhaps even nonexistent – in legal terms as well as in economic analysis. The household, or the family, became understood as a pre-capitalist institution and, as such, not subject to economic laws. When Economics replaced Political Economy, claimed a scientific status, and pursued the mathematical reasoning and quantitative approach used in the hard sciences, the male "individual" came to be seen as a generic central unit of analysis, similar to the atom in physics. The only way to pay attention to and analyze women's issues, concerns, interests, and behavior was to apply this approach – the economic method, according to Gary S. Becker – to women's issues, while claiming that this approach itself was value-neutral or "value free."

3. Shifting boundaries between household production and monetarized and marketized activities

The process of monetization and marketization of goods and services formerly produced in the household started with, and is an inherent part of, the industrialization of Western Europe and the US. This process has importantly contributed to what has been perceived as the increase in wealth or economic growth, while an ongoing debate, if not fight, has been taking place about whether these products and services should be provided by the public sector or by the private sector. Along with this, we see the reconceptualization of women's activities in the household as "consumption." Technological development brought about efficiency gains together with a range of new jobs and professions, on the one hand; the increase in the consumption of goods with an increasingly short life span led to a substantial decline in the efficient use of resources and added to waste and pollution, on the other. This process of monetization and marketization is still going strong, and although approaching its physical limits, thus far, there is little indication that this tendency is being reversed or stopped.

4. Women's legal control over their body, children, earnings, and capital

With the change in legal rights, and a strengthening of gender ideology over the nineteenth century, most women economic writers resisted the patriarchal and gender-value system based on economic chivalry and the cult around motherhood. The bourgeois moral system that developed alongside the growth of industrial society enabled middle- and higher-class men to contribute to society and decision-making about its direction – but severely limited women in the process. Over the nineteenth century, things changed for the better, but economic institutions, including economic science, still today contain aspects and remnants of these sexist and misogynic norms, values, and practices, as they do racist norms and values that negatively impact women of color. Women's underrepresentation in the growing financial and tech industries and in economic science can be perceived as a historical remnant of gender and racial hierarchies and at the same time as a way these hierarchies are being reproduced.

5. Women's role in and writing on education

Women have long fought for education as a fundamental right. Sound training and study enabled women to obtain the skills to get a job, earn a living, become economically independent, know their rights, defend themselves legally, control their own assets, and contribute to science and society at large. This, notwithstanding the fact that in many instances education has also been used by governments as a tool to estrange children from their history and culture. In a compa-rable way, the teaching of economic theories that excluded women's experiences, history, and interests, in particular those of people of color, contributed to the colonialization of the minds of women (of color). They were trained in a perspective and understanding of the economy, which was presented as a value-free scientific approach, even as this approach at the same time made their specific histories and interests invisible.

Women economic writers perceived education as starting from a very early age and encompassing all aspects of a person, including moral strength and skills required to lead a good and responsible life. In political economy and later economics, education, its impor-tance for individuals and its role in the economy, became reduced to either a consumer good and/or an investment in a career with higher earnings later in life. As raising and educating (younger) children was assigned to women, the relevance of education, particularly of younger children, has not been fully recognized in economics. Differences in children's potential therefore became understood not as resulting from differences in attention, love, and resources acces-sible during the first years of a child's life, but as inherited talents or merit.

6. Exploitation and discrimination in production

Processes of dispossession, perceived as foundational for the later accumulation of capital – such as the enclosure movement, slavery, and the legal arrangement of "feme covert" – did not end with the onset of industrialization but continued. The appropriation of the produce of women's (slave) labor, land, and capital was a considerable source for the accumulation of capital, contributing to the devel-opment of wealth in industrial countries. The externalization of costs in terms of time spent, low wages, and the extraction of resources and pollution impacted the most vulnerable in society in particular.

Women took an active part in the abolitionist and socialist movements by teaching, lecturing, writing, and starting and running communities; their own movement was founded halfway through the nineteenth century. The demands for wage increases, minimum wages, and equal wages for equal work go way back, in some cases about a century, in others for more than two. In the debate about equal pay for equal work that started at the end of the nineteenth century, most male economists took an ahistorical approach, ignored earlier women's research and writing on the topic, and argued that women earned less because the produce of their work was less valuable. Women economists, on the other hand, argued that part of these pay differences were historical practices that had assigned this kind of production to women and people of color, and that a lack of training on the job, promotion, and discrimination played a substantial role in causing the gender and racial wage gaps. This debate would reoccur in the 1960s following similar lines. More recently, mainstream economists are recognizing that institutional discrimination and occupational segregation do play a substantive role in the reproduction of gender and racial wage gaps.

Although scarcely documented, women have been active as entrepreneurs throughout the industrial era, often as co-workers in their husband's business and as small business owners and retailers. Women's economic writing about the financial industry and economic crises has been from a more recent date as women have long been effectively excluded from this industry.

7. Consumption from the perspective of the consumer, budgeting, and financial literacy

The separation between production and consumption was importantly based on the gender of the person who conducted the activity and its location; when done in the home and carried out by women, productive activities became over time increasingly invisible or perceived as consumption, while men's activities outside the home for wages or profit or for the state became perceived as production.

Consumption in economics has mainly been conceptualized from the perspective of the market: what is bought and how much is paid for these goods and services? The consumer's preferences were taken as a given, instead of explained, and derived from how consumers spent their incomes. Women economists restructured the field of household management by dividing it into (a) household administration, (b) consumption decision-making, (c) marketing, and (d) the remnants of home economics. Overall, women economists assigned a more active role to consumers than mainstream economists and argued that they be trained so they could become knowledgeable, efficient, and responsible consumers.

The shift in focus in economic science from production to consumption turned the circular process of raising children, production, maintenance, consumption, waste reduction, care of the sick and elderly, care of the dead, and care of the land into an ahistorical linear process that focused on goods; goods were produced, distributed over markets, and, satisfying limitless wants, destroyed in the consumption process.

8. Shifts in household models: from the male wage earner to the transitional and egalitarian model

The emergence of the male wage-earner model took time, reaching its zenith by the end of the nineteenth century. The transitional household model, in which the wife took up the role of financial provider alongside her role as care provider, emerged with the rise of middle-class women's participation in the labor force. This model became increasingly dominant in the 1960s and 1970s, and was strengthened by the decline in men's wages in the 1970s and the increase in women's wages, along with a steep growth of single parent households due to increased divorce rates.

When women returned to studying economic science in larger numbers than ever before in the 1960s and 1970s, they conducted research in support of the transitional household model, pointing out the issues and vulnerabilities faced by single parent households. The demand for the valuation of unpaid household production resulted in the inclusion of this kind of production in growth indices, policy research and proposals, gender-responsive budget initiatives, and research on care work. As the policy discussion focused on increased female labor force participation, policy proposals in support of sharing household tasks and putting an end to the sexual division of labor in the household came practically to a stand-still.

9. Care activities

Those activities that were formerly excluded from most economic theorizing, but that were constitutive of the home and family life have become increasingly monetized and marketized over the twentieth century. Feminist economists have taken it upon themselves to develop tools to measure the value of unpaid household production or unpaid care work and the conceptualization and inclusion of care activities in terms of dependency relations (Jochimsen, 2004) or as activities motivated by care, commitment, and altruism (Folbre, 1991). The marketization and monetization of care work led to a strong price increase for these products and services. What ensued were often informal and mostly low paid jobs for women, which added to the overall income inequality and created more hurdles for these women to have children and raise them.

Those with the financial means to do so solve these problems on an individual basis by employing documented and undocumented workers from countries in the South and the former USSR. These women take up part of the care activities such as raising children and domestic work like cooking and cleaning. Instead of demanding high-quality childcare provided by the state, these households choose the market option and join the global care chain that redistributes income between the North and the South – but at the cost of draining away the care of at least one of the parents from families in the South, mostly the mother.

10. Minimization of waste and conservation of the environment

While farmers used to have a direct interest in maintaining a healthy environment and supporting the commons, and while women, in running their household, were trained to make efficient use of resources and materials, the incentives in industrial agriculture and society at large changed over the centuries. The tradition and literature of household management spent ample time and space to describe methods to reduce waste, reuse materials, adjust clothes, conserve and store food, and improve the use of resources. The increasing externalization of costs to the natural environment, the shift toward an economy based on consumption, and economic concepts that claim that consumer desires are without limits has led to a situation in which about 20 percent of the food purchased in the US is never consumed, clothes are made to last shorter and shorter time periods, repairing products has been taken over by replacing them with new goods, and the production of waste vastly outweighs the recycling of resources. The focus in mainstream economics on the functioning of markets, instead of on production and distribution in relation to the social and natural environment, contributes to keeping the unsustainable character of this economic behavior invisible.

11. State provision of public goods and services formerly produced by the household

In the process of monetization and marketization of goods and services formerly provided by households, those goods and services that can and have to be considered as public goods were to some extent, but not fully, provided by the state. In relation to education, for instance, this process professionalized education but also shifted the focus from educating the person toward preparation for the labor market. The provision of childcare services is still very much debated today: should these be provided through the private sector or by the public sector? In the meantime and by default, it is assumed that households, and women in particular, will take care of the work that needs to be done, even though the amount of time and energy needed to do this has been cut down to the bare bone.

In the twentieth century, private and public large-scale research projects aiming at documenting the wealth and economic health of the population provided women with opportunities to obtain, develop, and apply research skills. These research projects pursued questions that the women involved considered relevant, and they were thus able to provide data that showed facts about poverty levels, wages, and work circumstances of women that went against the dominant economic theory and backed up demands for changes in legislation. As discrimination turned out not to disappear by itself, it seemed that government policies were required to counter bias in the economy, in the budget process, in the labor market, and, in particular, in the distribution of resources. The state has a distinct role in the economy to provide public goods and services that the household is no longer expected and able to provide. When society does not want employers to cut back working hours for workers and parents particularly and/or increase their wages, the employer or the government needs to provide these goods and services.

12. Excluding women from economic science and from the history of economic thought

The exclusion of women from political economy (both as contributors and as topics of research) over the first few centuries of its existence importantly set the direction and laid the foundation of what is now known as "the economy" and "economics." The impact has been that topics, issues, and traits associated with women were relegated to the margins at best, and this importantly structured the direction of the development of the history of economic thought. Women's interests (as well as those of children, the elderly, the disabled, and the sick) were not brought to the fore, let alone addressed; besides these groups, people who were not Western European/Caucasian healthy males were "othered," seen and described as deviating from what was "normal" or "standard." The lack of attention for the production in the household, the moral quality of economic decision-making, and the education of children are just a few examples here. The interests of women of color, black women more particularly, still lack full acknowledgment. Since "future generations" have, according to the gender ideology, been perceived as "a women's issue," their concerns and interests are not well represented either, which increasingly translates into a lack of concern about the future of the planet.

Economics from a feminist perspective

When the extremely low representation of women in economics had become a concern for the American Economic Association (AEA), the Committee for the Status of Women in the Economic Profession (CSWEP) was founded, in 1971. CSWEP has been reporting on the progress made by women in economics every year since 1993.

When feminist economists started their research in the 1970s they initially faced a situation in which basic data on the economic position of women were not available. Data on, for instance, unemployment, pensions, co-working entrepreneurs, labor supply, had to be gathered for the first time. To explain women's economic experiences, feminist economists applied (extensions of) institutionalist, Marxist, and (post-)Keynesian analysis to address non-traditional economic issues like women's unemployment and lower wages, women's labor supply, discrimination practices, and the economic value of domestic work. Concepts that were based on male experience as, for instance, in labor market theory needed to be adjusted and extended to fully address the experience of women. In labor economics, to stay with the example, this meant that the choice between hours of labor and hours of leisure to explain male labor market participation had to be changed into a choice between hours of paid labor, leisure, and housework to explain women's labor market behavior. By the beginning of the 1990s, a group of feminist economists found these theories fundamentally lacking, most of which was due to the fact that hierarchical and sexist notions of gender were ingrained in the definition of the basic concepts in these theories (Nelson, 1992; Ferber and Nelson, 1993; Kuiper and Sap et al., 1995). Feminist economists did not stop at critiquing economic concepts and theories. They also analyzed economic methods and the underlying epistemological approaches that supported the scientific claims of these theories, and they made inquiries into the scientific basis of arguments used to dismiss feminist economic research as "political," "partial," or simply as "irrelevant" and not "core to the field" (see, e.g., Explorations, in *Feminist Economics*, 1997). In the meantime, the International Association for Feminist Economics (IAFFE) was founded in 1992 with the aim of supporting and stimulating research on women's economic issues, the role of gender in the economy more broadly, and the impact of gender (and also race and class) on the field of economics (Ferber and Nelson, 2003).

Feminist economics, or feminist political economy, does not fit any of the traditional categories of subfield in economics, although they are perceived as such by some people. Most subfields are based on either a theoretical approach, like post-Keynesian or neo-institutionalist economics, or focus on an aspect of economic reality, such as neuroeconomics. Feminist economics, on the other hand, perceives economic science as a social institution and recognizes that hierarchical notions of gender, race, class, age, health, and location have, over the centuries, become fundamentally ingrained in economic theory. In their research, feminist economists criticize mainstream and other economic theories, and develop new concepts, theories, and perspectives that transcend the traditional male-oriented approaches, especially where these have been found severely lacking and misrepresenting reality. Feminist economists also broaden the focus of economic research to fully include and address the economic behavior of cis-women, nonbinary and transpersons, people of color, and people in the South. Not being wedded to one specific economic theoretical approach or method, feminists conduct research in fields ranging from microeconomics, macroeconomics, public policy, and development economics to finance, methodology, and the history of economic thought (see, e.g., Humphries, 1995; Peterson and Lewis, 1999; Figart and Warnecke, 2013; Elias and Roberts, 2018; Barker and Kuiper, 2010, 2020; Jacobsen, 2020; Berik and Kongar, 2021).

The issue of underrepresentation of women in economics has been reoccurring in the media and addressed as a problem on a regular basis over the past few decades. This can in part be explained by a nasty process of discrimination and exclusion. It can also in part be explained by a strengthening of the position of women in the field. The response in the field to the first female Nobel Prize winner Elinor Ostrom in 2009 induced, for instance, Gary Becker to question the scientific character of today's economics. In 2010, CSWEP addressed a full issue of its Newsletter to discrimination against women in the economic discipline. The conclusion was that discrimination was less severe than in previous decades but that it was still alive and well. The research conducted by Alice H. Wu (2017) put numbers on the level of sexism toward women economists and showed, using quantitative

analysis, that the main economics job search list for young economists referred to women candidates negatively and in terms of their
appearance, whereas the references to men were mostly to their
professional qualities. At the Allied Social Sciences Associations
(ASSA) of 2018, on the wave of the #MeToo movement, the issue
of sexual harassment in the discipline elicited a lively discussion,
particularly with respect to the very low representation of women of
color in the field. Things are clearly moving. Let's now explore some
of the directions and possible paths into the future.

Explorations

This book ends in 2020. Women in the US, the UK, and most
countries worldwide have now full or strongly improved access to
higher education and universities. In the US and Western Europe,
more girls than boys receive a Master's degree. This, however, does
not mean they have equal access to higher management positions in
the private sector, the public sector, or, for that matter, in economic
departments. Access to the position of full professor in economics
is still limited, and for women of color the hurdles are even higher.
Over the past several decades, some feminist economists have finally
reached positions of power in the discipline, but not yet in the critical
mass that would lead to a change in its culture. It still remains
difficult, for instance, to obtain tenure in most economic departments
while openly conducting feminist economic research.

Women of color are standing up, speaking out about the difficulties they face when they choose a career as economist. The group
Radical Feminist Political Economists was founded to put pressure
on the members of IAFFE, the AEA, and on the discipline at large to
recognize the gender and race discrimination that was still occurring
in the field and to put in place policies to counter this. There is a
response. The Board of the AEA decided, under pressure of an Open
Letter signed by hundreds of feminist and other economists, to start
a second monitored job site. Economics departments are pressed
to address issues of diversity and inclusion and programs became
available for hiring people of color in particular. Acknowledgment
and acceptance of the fact that diversity adds to objectivity and that
tunnel vision is a serious threat to objective knowledge production
will need time, though, and a stronger commitment from economists.
The deeply ingrained dominance of mainstream economics that has
close ties with vested social and economic interests forms in itself a
bastion against broader theoretical change. There is a tendency for

those who are not interested in transforming academic institutions to start new institutes and organizations outside academia, such as the Institute for New Economic Thinking, Rethinking Economics – and others do both.

In the face of current crises such as global warming, pandemics, authoritarian tendencies, and large-scale migration, economic science faces huge challenges. This means that the necessity and possibility of fast and fundamental changes in the economic system need to be expected and to be addressed – changes that mainstream economics is particularly ill-equipped to deal with. Of course, there will be a strong tendency to keep on along the established paths, extending the "pluralist approach to economics," which means applying mainstream economics to a wide variety of topics and theoretical extensions to accommodate such research. With respect to women's and people of color's issues, this would mean the application of neoclassical research on issues such as wage gaps, unemployment, and discrimination, as is done in the fields of gender economics and family economics.

More innovative approaches will acknowledge the historical and fundamental role that gender, race, class, location, and the relationship with nature have played in the development of the economy and economic thought, and will work toward including these in encouraging new understandings of economic and sustainable development. This book shows, for instance, that limiting the history of economic thought to an internalist approach to the field which only includes established academic voices within the debates reproduces the exclusionary practices and institutional discrimination that have been an inherent part of academia for too long. When we want to understand the emergence, content, and role of the economic concepts and theories that are used to describe the way societies have dealt with the provision, organization, and efficient use of its resources in a changing world, we cannot afford to limit our views in this way.

Feminist economists are becoming more and more vocal. While obtaining a stronger foothold in the discipline and beyond, they can use their voices to both engage in research and debates in the economics discipline and support and share knowledge with other movements, streams of knowledge, and experience, such as those particularly concerned and interested in class, LGBTQ+ issues, antiracism, international inequality, and sustainable development. That will enable them to look for better answers to old issues and unprecedented problems and to base these on facts, scientific analysis, and sound and inclusive debates.

References

Abbott, Edith (1907). *Women's Work and Wages: A Phase of Life in an Industrial City*, by Edward Cadbury, M. Cécile Matheson, and George Shann. Book review: *Journal of Political Economy*, 15(9): 563–565. https://www.journals.uchicago.edu/doi/10.1086/251366.

Abbott, Edith (1910). *Women in Industry. A Study in American Economic History*. New York: Appleton and Comp.

Abbott, Edith, and Breckinridge, Sophonisba (1917). *Truancy and Non-Attendance in Chicago Schools. A Study of the Social Aspects of the Compulsory Education and Child Labor Legislation of Illinois*, Chicago, IL: University of Chicago Press.

Abbott, Edith, with Breckinridge, Sophonisba (1936). *The Tenements of Chicago 1908–1935*. Chicago, IL: University of Chicago Press.

Agarwal, Bina (1992). The Gender and Environment Debate. *Feminist Studies*, 18(1): 119–158.

Agarwal, Bina (1994). *A Field of One's Own. Gender and Land Rights in South Asia*. New York: Cambridge University Press.

Agarwal, Bina (2010). *Gender and Green Governance*. New Delhi: Oxford University Press.

Albelda, Randy (2013). Low-wage Mothers on the Edge in the US. In Deborah M. Figart and Tonia L. Warnecke, eds., *Handbook of Research on Gender and Economic Life*. Northampton, MA: Edward Elgar, pp. 257–272.

Albelda, Randy, Himmelweit, Susan, and Humphries, Jane, eds. (2005). *The Dilemmas of Lone Motherhood*. London: Routledge.

Alexander, Sadie Tanner Mossell (1930). Negro Women in Our Economic Life. In Nina Banks, ed., *Democracy, Race, and Justice. The Speeches and Writings of Sadie T.M. Alexander*. New Haven, CT: Yale University Press, pp. 52–57.

Alexander, Sadie Tanner Mossell (1934). The Economic Status of Negro

Women. In Nina Banks, ed., *Democracy, Race, and Justice. The Speeches and Writings of Sadie T.M. Alexander*. New Haven, CT: Yale University Press, pp. 65–72.

Alexander, Sadie Tanner Mossel (1963). New Tempos – New Concepts. In N. Banks, ed. *Democracy, Race, and Justice. The Speeches and Writings of Sadie T.M. Alexander*. New Haven, CT: Yale University Press, pp. 117–126.

Amott, Teresa, and Matthaei, Julie (1991). *Race, Gender, and Work. A Multicultural Economic History of Women in the United States*. Boston: South End Press.

Antilla, Susan (2003). *Tales from The Boom-Boom Room. The Landmark Legal Battles that Exposed Wall Street's Shocking Culture of Sexual Harassment*. New York: HarperCollins.

Antonopoulos, Rania, and Hirway, Indira, eds. (2009). *Unpaid Work and the Economy: Gender, Time Use and Poverty in Developing Countries*. New York: Palgrave Macmillan.

Aslanbeigui, Nahid, and Summerfield, Gale (2000). The Asian Crisis, Gender, and the International Financial Architecture. *Feminist Economics* 6(3): 81–103.

Assassi, Libby (2009). *The Gendering of Global Finance*. Basingstoke: Palgrave Macmillan.

Astell, Mary (1695). *A Serious Proposal to the Ladies for the Advancement of their True and Greatest Interest. By a Lover of her Sex. Part I*. London.

Astell, Mary (1697). *A Serious Proposal to the Ladies. Wherein a Method is Offer'd for the Improvement of their Minds. Part II*. London.

Astell, Mary (1700). *Some Reflections upon Marriage, Occasion'd by the Duke and Duchess of Mazarine's Case; which is also considered*. London.

Atkinson, Mabel (1987 [1914]). The Economic Foundations of the Women's Movement. In Sally Alexander, ed., *Women's Fabian Tracts*. London, pp. 256–282.

Austen, Jane (1986 [1811]). *Sense and Sensibility*. New York: Barnes and Noble.

Austen, Jane (1813). *Pride and Prejudice*. Cambridge: Heffer and Sons.

Baillie, Grisell (1911). *The Household Book of Lady Grisell Baillie, 1692–1733*. Notes and introduction by R. Scott-Moncrieff. Edinburgh: Scottish History Society.

Balakrishnan, Radhika, Heintz, James, and Elson, Diane (2016). *Rethinking Economic Policy for Social Justice*. New York: Routledge.

Banks, Nina, ed. (2021). *Democracy, Race, and Justice. The Speeches and Writings of Sadie T.M. Alexander*. New Haven, CT: Yale University Press.

Barbauld, Anna (1791). *Epistle to William Wilberforce, Esq. on the Rejection of the Bill for Abolishing the Slave Trade*. Repr. in E. Kuiper, ed., *Women's Economic Thought in the Eighteenth Century*, vol. 3. New York: Routledge, 2014, pp. 469–477.

Barker, Drucilla K., and Feiner, Susan F. (2004). *Liberating Economics. Feminist Perspectives on Families, Work, and Globalization*. Ann Arbor: Michigan University Press.

Barker, Drucilla K., and Kuiper, Edith, eds. (2010). *Feminist Economics. Critical Concepts*. London: Routledge.

Barker, Drucilla K., and Kuiper, Edith (2020). Feminist Economics. In S. Crasnow and K. Intemann, eds., *The Routledge Handbook for Feminist Philosophy of Science*. London: Routledge, pp. 355–367.

Bauer, Dale M. (2020). *Nineteenth-Century American Women's Serial Novels*. Cambridge: Cambridge University Press.

Bebel, August (1988 [1879]). *Women in the Past, Present and Future*. Repr. with an introduction by Moira Donald. London: Zwan Publications.

Becker, Gary S. (1957). *The Economics of Discrimination*. Chicago, IL: University of Chicago Press.

Becker, Gary S. (1964). *Human Capital. A Theoretical and Empirical Analysis, with Special Reference to Education*, New York: NBER.

Becker, Gary S. (1965). A Theory of the Allocation of Time. *The Economic Journal*, 75(299): 493–517.

Becker, Gary S. (1981). *A Treatise on the Family*. Cambridge, MA: Harvard University Press.

Beecher, Catharine Esther (1851). *The True Remedy for the Wrongs of Woman. With a History of an Enterprise Having that for its Object*. Boston, MA: Phillips, Simpson.

Beecher, Catharine Esther (1856 [1841]). *A Treatise on Domestic Economy. For the Use of Young Ladies at Home and at School*, rev. ed. New York: Harper & Row.

Beeton, Isabella Mary (1861). *Mrs. Beeton's Book of Household Management*. London: Jonathan Cape.

Benería, Lourdes (2003). *Gender, Development and Globalization*. London: Routledge.

Benería, Lourdes, and Sen, Gita (1981). Accumulation, Reproduction, and Women's Role in Economic Development: Boserup Revisited. *Signs: Journal of Women and Culture in Society*, 7(2): 279–298.

Bentham, Jeremy (1789). *Introduction to the Principles of Morals and Legislation*. London: Payne and Son.

Berg, Maxine (2005). *Luxury and Pleasure in Eighteenth-Century Britain*. Oxford: Clarendon Press.

Bergeron, Suzanne (2004). *Fragments of Development*. Ann Arbor: University of Michigan Press.

Bergmann, Barbara (1974). Occupational Segregation, Wages and Profits, When Employers Discriminate by Race or Sex. *Eastern Economic Journal*, 1(2): 103–110.

Bergmann, Barbara (1986). *The Economic Emergence of Women*. New York: Basic Books.

Berik, Günseli, and Kongar, Ebru, eds. (2021). *The Routledge Handbook of Feminist Economics*. London: Routledge.

Besant, Annie (1877). *The Law of Population: Its Consequences, and Its Bearing upon Human Conduct and Morals*. London: Freethought Publishing.

Bettio, Francesca et al. (2013). *The Impact of the Economic Crisis on the Situation of Women and Men and on Gender Equality Policies*. Synthesis Report. Brussels: European Union.

Bigg, Ada Heather (1894). The Wife's Contribution to Family Income. *The Economic Journal*, 4(13): 51–58.

Blackstone, William (1765–69). *Commentaries on the Laws of England*, 4 vols. Worcester, MA: Isaiah Thomas.

Blanchard, Olivier (1996). *Macroeconomics*. Pearson.

Blau, Francine, and Ferber, Marianne A. (1986). *The Economics of Women, Men, and Work*. Englewood Cliffs, NJ: Prentice Hall.

Blau, Francine D., and Kahn, Lawrence M. (1992). The Gender Earnings Gaps: Some International Evidence. Working Paper. Cambridge, MA: NBER.

Blau, Francine D., and Kahn, Lawrence M. (2017). The Gender Wage Gap: Extent, Trends and Explanations. *Journal of Economic Literature*, 55(3): 789–865.

Bodichon, Barbara Leigh Smith (1854). *A Brief Summary, in Plain Language, of the Most Important Laws Concerning Women: Together with a Few Observations Thereon*. Repr. in C. Lacey, ed., *Barbara Leigh Smith Bodichon and the Langham Place Group*. London: Routledge & Kegan Paul, 1987, pp. 23–35.

Bodichon, Barbara Leigh Smith (1857). *Women and Work*. Repr. in C. Lacey, ed., *Barbara Leigh Smith Bodichon and the Langham Place Group*. London: Routledge & Kegan Paul, 1987, pp. 36–73.

Bodichon, Barbara Leigh Smith (1860). Middle-Class Schools for Girls. Repr. in C. Lacey, ed., *Barbara Leigh Smith Bodichon and the Langham Place Group*. London: Routledge & Kegan Paul, 1987, pp. 74–83.

Bodkin, Ronald G. (1999). Women's Agency in Classical Economic Thought: Adam Smith, Harriet Taylor Mill, and J.S. Mill. *Feminist Economics*, 5(1): 45–60.

Booth, Charles (1903). *Life and Labour of the People in London*. London: Macmillan.

Boserup, Ester (1970). *Women's Role in Economic Development*. London: Allen and Unwin.

Boserup, Ester (1993 [1965]). *The Conditions of Agricultural Growth: The Economics of Agrarian Change Under Population Pressure*. London: Routledge.

Boucherett, Jessie (1864). On the Cause of the Distress Prevalent among Single Women, *The English Woman's Journal*, February. Repr. in C. Lacey, ed., *Barbara Leigh Smith Bodichon and the Langham Place Group*. London: Routledge & Kegan Paul, 1987, pp. 268–272.

Bradley, Martha (1758). *The British Housewife: or, the Cook, Housekeeper's, and Gardiner's Companion*. Prospect Books.

Breckinridge, Sophonisba, and Abbott, Edith (1912). *The Delinquent Child and the Home. A Study of the Delinquent Wards of the Juvenile Court of Chicago*. New York: Russell Sage.

Brooke, Emma (1895). *Transition. A Novel*. Philadelphia, PA: J.B. Lippincott.

Brooke, Emma (1898). *A Tabulation of the Factory Laws of European Countries in so far as they Relate to the Hours of Labour, and to Special Legislation for Women, Young Persons, and Children*. London: Grant Richards.

Brooke, Emma (2015 [1894]). *A Superfluous Woman*, ed. Barbara Tilley. Brighton: Victoria Secrets.

Brown, Jenny (2019). *Birth Strike. The Hidden Fight over Women's Work*. Oakland, CA: PM Press.

Brown, Karin, ed. (2008). *Sophie de Grouchy Letters on Sympathy (1798): A Critical Edition*. Letters translated by James E. McClellan III. Philadelphia, PA: American Philosophical Society.

Browne, Irene, ed. (1999). *Latinas and African American Women at Work: Race, Gender, and Economic Inequality*. New York: Russell Sage.

Brundtland, Gro Harlem (1987). *Our Common Future*. New York: Oxford University Press.

Budlender, Debbie (2000). The Political Economy of Women's Budgets in the South. *Feminist Economics*, 28(7): 365–378.

Bueno, Carycruz M., and Bueno, Cruz Caridad (2020). Corona, the Great Exposer: How the Pandemic has exacerbated Inequalities in American Society. *The Minority Report – American Economic Association*, 13(Winter): 1–5.

Burke, Edward (1790). *Reflections on the Revolution in France and on the Proceedings in Certain Societies in London Relative to that Event*. London: J. Dodsley.

Burney, Frances (1778). *Evelina, or a Young Lady's Entrance into the World*. London: Thomas Lowndes.

Burney, Frances (1782). *Cecilia; or, Memoirs of an Heiress*. London.

Burney, Frances (1796). *Camila: or, a Picture of Youth*. London.

Butler, Judith (1990). *Gender Trouble*. New York: Routledge.

Cadbury, Edward, Matheson, M. Cécile, and Shann, George (1906). *Women's Work and Wages: A Phase of Life in an Industrial City*. London: Fischer Unwin.

Carlyle, Alexander (1973). *Anecdotes and Characters of the Times*, ed. James Kinsley. London: Oxford University Press.

Carson, Rachel (1962). *Silent Spring*. New York: Houghton Mifflin Comp.

Cartwright, Mrs. (1777). *Letters on Female Education, Addressed to a Married Lady*. London: Edward and Charles Dilly. Repr. in E. Kuiper ed., *Women's Economic Thought in the Eighteenth Century*, vol. 2. New York: Routledge, 2014, pp. 114–137.

Chapone, Hester Mulso (1773). *Letters on the Improvement of the Mind, Addressed to a Young Lady*. London: J. Walter. Repr. in E. Kuiper ed., *Women's Economic Thought in the Eighteenth Century*, vol. 1. New York: Routledge, 2014, pp. 588–613.

Chapone, Sarah Kirkman (1735). *The Hardship of the English Laws in Relation to Wives. With an Explanation of the Original Curse of Subjection Passed upon the Woman. In an Humble Address to the Legislature*. London. Repr. in E. Kuiper ed., *Women's Economic Thought in the Eighteenth Century*, vol. 3. New York: Routledge, 2014, pp. 177–243.

Chassonery-Zaïgouche, Cléo (2019). Is Equal Pay Worth It? Beatrice Potter Webb's, Millicent Garrett Fawcett's and Eleanor Rathbone's Changing Arguments. In Kirsten Madden and Robert W. Dimand, eds., *The Routledge Handbook of the History of Women's Economic Thought*. London: Routledge, pp. 129–149.

Châtelet, Émilie du (2009 [1779]). Discourse on Happiness. In Judith P. Zinsser, ed., *Du Châtelet, Émilie, Selected Philosophical and Scientific Writings*, trans. Isabelle Bour and Judith P. Zinsser. Chicago, IL: University of Chicago Press.

Chudleigh, Mary Lee (1701). *The Ladies Defence: or, The Bride-Woman's Counsellor Answer'd: A Poem. In a Dialogue Between Sir John Brute, Sir William Loveall, Melissa, and a Parson*. London: John Deeve.

Cicarelli, James, and Cicarelli, Julianne (2003). *Distinguished Women Economists*. London: Greenwood Press.

Clark, Alice (1919). *Working Life of Women in the Seventeenth Century*. London: Routledge.

Clark, John Bates (1899). *The Distribution of Wealth. A Theory of Wages, Interest, and Profits*. New York: MacMillan.

Clery, Emma (2017). *Jane Austen. The Banker's Sister*. London: Biteback Publishing.

Cobbe, Frances Power (1862). What Shall We Do With Our Old Maids? Repr. in C. Lacey, ed., *Barbara Leigh Smith Bodichon and the Langham Place Group*. London: Routledge & Kegan Paul, 1987, pp. 354–377.

Colander, David, and Klamer, Arjo (1987). The Making of an Economist. *Journal of Economic Perspectives*, 1(2): 95–111.

Cole, Margaret (1953). *Robert Owen of New Lanark*. New York: Oxford University Press.

Collet, Clara (1898). The Collection and Utilization of Official Statistics Bearing on the Extent and Effects of the Industrial Employment of Women. *Journal of the Royal Statistical Society*, 61(2): 219–260. Repr. in D.K. Barker and E. Kuiper, ed., *Feminist Economics*. Vol. I: *Early Conversations*. London: Taylor & Francis, 2010, pp. 250–290.

Collet, Clara (1911). *Women in Industry*. London: Women's Print.

Collier, Mary (1739). *The Woman's Labour*. https://www.eighteenthcentury-poetry.org/works/pco62-w0010.shtml

Collins, Patricia Hill (2000). *Black Feminist Thought. Knowledge, Consciousness, and the Politics of Empowerment*. New York and London: Routledge.

Condorcet, Marie-Jean Antoine Nicolas Caritat, Marquis de (1822). *Esquisse d'un tableau historique des progrès de l'esprit humain [Sketch for a Historical Picture of the Progress of Human Kind]*. Paris: Masson and Sons.

Cooper, Anna Julia (2016 [1892]). *A Voice from the South*. Mineola, NY: Dover Publications.

Copeland, Edward (1995). *Women Writing about Money. Women's Fiction in England 1790–1820*. Cambridge: Cambridge University Press.

Cornell Law School (2021). Legal Capacity of Married Persons Act. Legal Information Institute. https://www.law.cornell.edu/women-and-justice/resource/legal_capacity_of_married_persons_act.

Crenshaw, Kimberlé (1993). Demarginalizing the Intersection of Race and Sex: A Black Feminist Critique of Antidiscrimination Doctrine, Feminist Theory and Antiracist Politics. *University of Chicago Legal Forum*, 1989(1): 139–167.

CSWEP (2020). CSWEP Survey and Annual Report. American Economic Association. https://www.aeaweb.org/about-aea/committees/cswep/about/survey.

D'Aelders, Etta Palm (1791). Etta Palm d'Aelders Proposes a Network of Women's Clubs to Administer Welfare Programs in Paris and Throughout France. Repr. in D.G. Levy, H. B. Applewhite, and M. D. Johnson, eds.,

Women in Revolutionary Paris 1789–1795. Urbana: University of Illinois Press, 1979, pp. 68–71.

Dall, Caroline Healey (1860). *"Women's Right to Labor,"* or, *Low Wages and Hard Work: in Three Lectures, Delivered in Boston.* Boston, MA: Walker, Wise, & Co.

Dall, Caroline Healey (1972 [1867]). *The College, the Market, and the Court; or Women's Relation to Education, Labor, and the Law.* New York: Arno Press.

Dalla Costa, Mariarosa, and James, Selma (1972). *The Power of Women and the Subversion of the Community.* Bristol: Falling Wall Press.

Daubié, Julie-Victoire (1993 [1866]). *La Femme pauvre au XIXe siècle.* Paris: Côté-femmes.

Davidoff, Leonore, and Hall, Catherine (1987). *Family Fortunes: Men and Women of the English Middle Class 1780–1850.* Chicago. IL: Chicago University Press.

Davis, Angela (1981). *Women, Race, and Class.* New York: Random House.

Deere, Carmen Maria, and Doss, Cheryl (2006). The Gender Asset Gap: What Do We Know and Why Does It Matter? *Feminist Economics*, 12(1–2): 1–50.

Defoe, Daniel (1719). On the Education of Women. English Essays from Sir Philip Sidney to Macaulay. Modern History Sourcebook. https://sourcebooks.fordham.edu/mod/1719defoe-women.asp.

Dimand, Robert (1995). The Neglect of Women's Contributions to Economics. In Mary Ann Dimand, Robert W. Dimand, and Evelyn L. Forget, eds., *Women of Value. Feminist Essays on the History of Women in Economics.* Cheltenham: Edward Elgar, pp. 1–24.

Dimand, Robert, Dimand, Mary Ann, and Forget, Evelyn L., eds. (2000). *A Biographical Dictionary of Women Economists.* Cheltenham: Edward Elgar.

Downey, Kirstin (2009). *The Woman Behind the New Deal. The Life and Legacy of Frances Perkins: Social Security, Unemployment Insurance, and the Minimum Wage.* New York: Anchor Books.

Drumgoold, Kate (1988 [1898]). *A Slave Girl's Story.* In Annie Burton et al., *Six Women: Slave Narratives.* New York: Oxford University Press, pp. 105–154.

Duck, Stephen (1736). *The Thresher's Labour.* https://www.eighteenthcentury poetry.org/works/o4741-w0030.shtml.

Dymski, Gary, and Floro, Maria (2000). Financial Crisis, Gender, and Power: An Analytical Framework. *World Development*, 38: 1269–1283.

Eckhardt, Celia Morris (1984). *Fanny Wright. Rebel in America.* Cambridge, MA: Harvard University Press.

Edgeworth, Francis, Y. (1922). Equal Pay to Men and Women for Equal Work. *The Economic Journal*, 32: 431–457.

Edgeworth, Francis Y. (1923). Women's Wages in Relation to Economic Welfare. *The Economic Journal*, 33: 487–495.

Edgeworth, Maria (1800). *Castle Rackrent.* London.

Edgeworth, Maria, and Edgeworth, Robert Lovell (1796). *The Parent's Assistant; or Stories for Children.* London: Macmillan.

Edgeworth, Maria, and Edgeworth, Robert Lovell (1815 [1798]). *Practical Education*, 2nd ed. Boston: Wait and Sons.

Ehrenreich, Barbara, and Hochschild, Arlie Russell (2002). *Global Woman.*

Nannies, Maids, and Sex Workers in the New Economy. New York: Holt and Comp.

Ehrenzweig, Albert A. (1959). Contractual Capacity of Married Women and Infants in the Conflict of Laws. *Minnesota Law Review*, 811.

Ekelund, Robert B., and Hébert, Robert F. (1997). *A History of Economic Theory and Method*, 4th ed. New York: McGraw-Hill.

Ekerwald, Hedvig (2016). Alva Myrdal and the Role of Politics in the Transformation of Sweden in the 1930s. In S. Eliaeson, L. Harutyunyan, and L. Titarenko, eds., *After the Soviet Empire*. Leiden: Brill Publishers, pp. 108–132.

Elias, Juanita, and Roberts, Adrienne, eds. (2018). *Handbook on the International Political Economy of Gender*. Cheltenham: Edward Elgar.

Elson, Diane, ed. (1991). *Male Bias in the Development Process*. Manchester: Manchester University Press.

Elson, Diane (2002). International Financial Architecture: A View from the Kitchen. *Femina Politica*, 11(1): 26–37.

Elson, Diane, and Çagatay, Nilüfer (2000). The Social Content of Macroeconomic Policies. *World Development*, 28(7): 1347–1364.

Elson, Diane, and Pearson, Ruth (1981). "Nimble Fingers Make Cheap Workers": An Analysis of Women's Employment in Third World Export Manufacturing. *Feminist Review*, 7: 87–107.

Engels, Friedrich (1972 [1884]). *The Origin of the Family, Private Property, and the State*. London: Pathfinder.

England, Paula (1982). The failure of human capital theory to explain occupational segregation. *Journal of Human Resources*, 17(30): 358–370.

Erickson, Amy Louise (2005). Coverture and Capitalism. *History Workshop Journal*, 59: 1–16.

Esping-Anderson, Gøsta (1990). *The Three Worlds of Welfare Capitalism*. Princeton: Princeton University Press.

Fawcett, Millicent Garrett (1874). *Tales in Political Economy*. London: Macmillan.

Fawcett, Millicent Garrett (1892). Mr. Sidney Webb's Article on Women's Wages. *The Economic Journal*, 2: 173–176.

Fawcett, Millicent Garrett (1911 [1870]). *Political Economy for Beginners*, 10th ed. London: Macmillan.

Fawcett, Millicent Garrett (1918). Equal Pay for Equal Work. *The Economic Journal*, 28(109): 1–6.

Federici, Silvia (2012 [1975]). Wages Against Housework. In S. Federici. *Revolution at Point Zero: Housework, Reproduction, and Feminist Struggle*. Brooklyn: Autonomedia, pp. 11–18.

Federici, Silvia (2014). *Caliban and the Witch. Women, the Body and Primitive Accumulation*. New York: Autonomedia.

Feiner, Susan F., and Roberts, Bruce (1990). Hidden by the Invisible Hand. Neoclassical Economic Theory and the Textbook Treatment of Race and Gender. *Gender and Society*, 4(2): 159–181.

Ferber, Marianne A., and Nelson, Julie A., eds. (1993). *Beyond Economic Man: Feminist Theory and Economics*. Chicago, IL: University of Chicago Press.

Ferber, Marianne A., and Nelson, Julie A. (2003). *Feminist Economics Today. Beyond Economic Man.* Chicago. IL: University of Chicago Press.

Ferguson, Moira (1985). Mary Collier 1689/90–after 1759. In M. Ferguson, ed., *First Feminists: British Women Writers, 1578–1799.* New York: The Feminist Press, pp. 257–265.

Figart, Deborah M., and Warnecke, Tonia L. (2013). *Handbook of Research on Gender and Economic Life.* Cheltenham: Edward Elgar.

Figart, Deborah M., Mutuari, Ellen, and Power, Marilyn (2001). *Living Wages, Equal Wages: Gender and Labor Market Policies in the United States.* New York: Routledge.

Fine, Cordelia (2010). *Delusions of Gender.* London: Norton.

Folbre, Nancy (1982). Exploitation Comes Home: A Critique of Marxian Theory of Family Labor. *Cambridge Journal of Economics*, 6(4): 317–329.

Folbre, Nancy (1991). The Unproductive Housewife: Her Evolution in Nineteenth-Century Economic Thought. *Signs*, 16(2): 245–255.

Folbre, Nancy (1994). *Who Pays for the Kids? Gender and the Structures of Constraints.* New York: Routledge.

Folbre, Nancy (2008). *Valuing Children. Rethinking the Economics of the Family.* Boston, MA: Harvard University Press.

Folbre, Nancy (2009). *Greed, Lust and Gender: A History of Economic Ideas.* Cambridge: Cambridge University Press.

Folbre, Nancy (2020). *The Rise and Decline of Patriarchal Systems. An Intersectional Political Economy*, London: Verso.

Forget, Evelyn L. (1999). *The Social Economics of Jean-Baptiste Say: Markets and Virtue.* London: Routledge.

Forget, Evelyn L. (2000). Margaret Gilpin Reid (1896–1991). In Robert W. Dimand, Mary Ann Dimand, and Evelyn L. Forget, eds., *A Biographical Dictionary of Women Economists.* Cheltenham: Edward Elgar, pp. 357–362.

Fraser, Nancy (1992 [1990]). Rethinking the Public Sphere: A Contribution to the Critique of Actually Existing Democracy. In Craig Calhoun, ed., *Habermas and the Public Sphere.* Cambridge, MA: MIT Press, pp. 109–142.

Friedan, Betty (1963). *The Feminine Mystique.* New York: W.W. Norton.

Gaskell, Elizabeth (1855). *North and South.* London: Walter Scott.

Gaskell, Elizabeth (1996 [1863]). *Sylvia's Lovers.* London: Penguin Classics.

Gaskell, Elizabeth (1906 [1864–6]). *Wives and Daughters.* London: Smith, Elder and Co.

Gensemer, Susan H. (2000). Virginia Penny (b. 1826). In Robert W. Dimand, Mary Ann Dimand, and Evelyn L. Forget, eds., *A Biographical Dictionary of Women Economists.* Cheltenham: Edward Elgar, pp. 330–334.

George, Susan (1988). *A Fate Worse than Debt. A Radical Analysis of the Third World Debt Crisis.* Harmondsworth: Penguin Books.

Gilman, Charlotte Perkins (1899 [1892]). *The Yellow Wallpaper.* Boston, MA: Small, Maynard and Co.

Gilman, Charlotte Perkins (1998 [1898]). *Women and Economics: A Study of the Economic Relation Between Men and Women as a Factor in Social Evolution*, ed. S. L. Meyering. Boston, MA: Small, Maynard and Co.

Godwin, William (1798). *Memoirs of the Author of A Vindication of the Rights of Woman*. London: Johnson.

Goldin, Claudia (1990). *Understanding the Gender Gap. An Economic History of American Women*. New York: Oxford University Press.

Gottman, Felicia (2011). Du Châtelet, Voltaire, and the Transformation of Mandeville's Fable. *History of European Ideas*, 38(2): 218–232.

Gouges, Olympe de (1791). *Déclaration des Droits de la Femme et de la Citoyenne*. Paris. Trans. and repr. as *The Declaration of the Rights of Women*. In D. Levy, H. Branson Applewhite, and M. Durham Johnson, eds., *Women in Revolutionary Paris 1789–1795*. Selected documents, translated with notes and commentary by the editors. Urbana: University of Illinois Press, 1980, pp. 87–96.

Griffin, Susan (1978). *Women and Nature. The Roaring Inside Her*. New York: Harper & Row.

Grimké, Sarah (1838). *Letters on the Equality of the Sexes and Other Essays*. Boston, MA: Isaac Knapp. Repr. with an introduction by Elizabeth Ann Bartlett. New Haven/London: Yale University Press, 1988.

Groenewegen, Peter, ed. (1994). *Feminism and Political Economy in Victorian England*. Cheltenham: Edward Elgar.

Groenewegen, Peter (1995). *A Soaring Eagle: Alfred Marshall 1842–1924*. Cheltenham: Edward Elgar.

Groenewegen, Peter (2002). *Eighteenth-century Economics: Turgot, Beccaria and Smith and Their Contemporaries*. London: Routledge.

Grossbard-Shechtman, Shoshana (1984). A Theory of Allocation of Time in Markets for Labour and Marriage. *The Economic Journal*, 94(376): 863–882.

Grouchy de Condorcet, Sophie de (1798). *Lettres à C[abanis], sur la théorie des sentiments moraux*. Translated into French from the 7th edition of Adam Smith's *Theory of Moral Sentiments*. Paris: F. Buisson 1792.

Gustafsson, Siv S., and Meulders, Danièle E. (2000). *Gender and the Labour Market. Econometric Evidence of Obstacles to Achieving Equality*. London: Macmillan.

Habermas, Jürgen (1989 [1962]). *The Structural Transformation of the Public Sphere: An Inquiry into a Category of Bourgeois Society*. Cambridge, MA: MIT Press.

Hameln, Glückel von (1920 [1715–17]). *The Memoirs of Glückel of Hameln*, trans. Marvin Lowenthal. Berlin.

Hammond, Claire Holton (2000a). Edith Abbott (1875–1957). In Robert W. Dimand, Mary Ann Dimand, and Evelyn L. Forget, eds., *A Biographical Dictionary of Women Economists*. Cheltenham: Edward Elgar, pp. 1–8.

Hammond, Claire Holton (2000b). Sophonisba Breckinridge (1866–1948). In Robert W. Dimand, Mary Ann Dimand, and Evelyn L. Forget, eds., *A Biographical Dictionary of Women Economists*. Cheltenham: Edward Elgar, pp. 81–89.

Hardenberg, H. (1962). *Etta Palm: Een Hollandse Parisienne, 1743–1799*. Assen: Van Gorcum.

Harding, Sandra (1995). Can Feminist Thought Make Economics More Objective? *Feminist Economics*, 1(1): 7–32.

Hartley, James E. (2008). *Mary Lyon. Documents and Writings*. South Hadley, MA: Doorlight Publications.

Hartmann, Heidi I. (1976). Capitalism, Patriarchy, and Job Segregation by Sex. *Signs, Journal of Women in Culture and Society*, 1(3): 137–170.

Hartmann, Heidi I. (1979). The Unhappy Marriage of Marxism and Feminism: Towards a More Progressive Union. *Capital and Class*, 3(2): 1–33.

Harvey, David (2003). *The New Imperialism*. Oxford: Oxford University Press.

Harvey, Karen (2012). *The Little Republic. Masculinity and Domestic Authority in Eighteenth-Century Britain*. Oxford: Oxford University Press.

Hays, Mary (1996 [1796]). *Memoirs of Emma Courtney*, ed. Eleanor Rose Ty. New York: Oxford University Press.

Hays, Mary (1798). *Appeal to the Men of Great Britain on Behalf of Women*. London: J. Johnson.

Heckscher, Eli F. and Ohlin, Bertil (1991). *Heckscher–Ohlin Trade Theory*, trans. and ed. Harry Flam and M. June Flanders. Cambridge, MA: MIT Press.

Heilbroner, Robert (1999 [1981]). *The Worldly Philosophers. The Lives, Times, and Ideas of the Great Economic Thinkers*. New York: Touchstone.

Henderson, Willie (1995). *Economics as Literature*. London: Routledge.

Hertz, Noreena (2001). *The Silent Take Over. Global Capitalism and the Death of Democracy*. New York: HarperCollins.

Hertz, Noreena (2004). *IOU. The Debt Threat and Why We Must Defuse It*. London: Fourth Estate.

Himmelweit, Susan, and Simon Mohun (1977). Domestic Labour and Capital. *Cambridge Journal of Economics*, 1(1): 15–31.

Hochschild, Arlie Russell (2012). *The Outsourced Self. What Happens When We Pay Others to Live Our Lives for Us*. New York: Henry Holt.

Hochschild, Arlie Russell, with Machung, Anne (1989). *The Second Shift. Working Parents and Revolution at Home*. New York: Viking Press.

Holcombe, Lee (1983). *Wives and Property. Reform of the Married Women's Property Law in Nineteenth-Century England*. Toronto: University of Toronto Press.

Holt, Alix (1977). Introduction. In Alix Holt, ed., *Alexandra Kollontai. Selected Writings*. New York: Norton, pp. 13–27.

Horrell, Sara and Humphries, Jane (1995). Women's Labour Force Participation and the Transition to the Male-Breadwinner Family, 1790–1865. *The Economic History Review*, 8(1): 89–117.

Hoyt, Elizabeth (1928). *The Consumption of Wealth*. New York: Macmillan.

Hoyt, Elizabeth (1938). *Consumption in Our Society*. New York/ London: McGraw–Hill.

Hume, David (1985 [1739]). *A Treatise of Human Nature*. London: Penguin Books.

Humphries, Jane (1977). Class-Struggle and the Persistence of the Working-Class Family. *Cambridge Journal of Economics*, 1: 241–258.

Humphries, Jane, ed. (1995). *Gender and Economics*. Cheltenham: Edward Elgar.

Hunt, E.K., and Lautzenheiser, Mark (2011). *History of Economic Thought. A Critical Perspective*, 3rd ed. New Delhi: PHI Learning.

Hutcheson, Francis (2004 [1726]). *An Inquiry into the Original of our Idea of Beauty and Virtue*. Indianapolis, IN: Liberty Fund.

Hutchins, Elizabeth Leigh (2020 [1907]). Home Work and Sweating: The Causes and the Remedies. In Sally Alexander, ed., *Women's Fabian Tracts*, vol. VII. London: Routledge, pp. 33–52.

Hutchins, Elizabeth Leigh (2020 [1911]). The Working Life of Women. In Sally Alexander, ed., *Women's Fabian Tracts*, vol. VII. London: Routledge, pp. 164–178.

Hutchins, Elizabeth Leigh, and Harrison, Amy (1911). *A History of Factory Legislation*. London: King and Son.

Hutchins, Elizabeth Leigh, with Mallon, James J. (1915). *Women in Modern Industry*. London: Bell and Sons. Repr. Wakefield, England: E.P. Publishing, 1978.

Ivory, Christine (2000). Julie-Victoire Daubié (1824–74). In Robert W. Dimand, Mary Ann Dimand, and Evelyn L. Forget, eds., *A Biographical Dictionary of Women Economists*. Cheltenham: Edward Elgar, pp. 125–129.

Jacobs, Jo Ellen, and Payne, Paula Harms, eds. (1998). *The Complete Works of Harriet Taylor Mill*. Bloomington: Indiana University Press.

Jacobs, Harriet (2001 [1861]). *Incidents in the Life of a Slave Girl*, ed. Joselyn T. Pine. Mineola, NY: Dover Publications.

Jacobsen, Joyce (2020). *Advanced Introduction to Feminist Economics*. Cheltenham: Edward Elgar.

Jennings, Ann (1990). On the Possibility of a Feminist Economics: The Convergence of Institutional and Feminist Methodology, *Journal of Economic Issues*, 24(2): 613–622.

Jevons, William S. (1883). Married Women in Factories. In *Methods of Social Reform, and Other Papers*. London: Macmillan, pp. 156–179.

Jevons, William S. (1965 [1871]). *The Theory of Political Economy*. New York: August Kelley.

Jochimsen, Maren (2004). *Careful Economics. Integrating Caring Activities and Economic Science*. Dordrecht: Kluwer Academic Publishers.

Justman, Stewart (1993). *The Autonomous Male of Adam Smith*. Norman: University of Oklahoma Press.

Kabeer, Naila (1999). Resources, Agency, Achievements: Reflections on the Measure of Women's Empowerment. *Development and Change*, 30: 435–464.

Karamessini, Maria, and Rubery, Jill, eds. (2014). *Women and Austerity. The Economic Crisis and the Future of Gender Equality*. London: Routledge.

Keller, Evelyn Fox (1985). *Reflections on Gender and Science*. New Haven, CT: Yale University Press.

Kern, William (1998). Maria Edgeworth and Classical Political Economy. *Newsletter CSWEP* (Winter): 9, 19.

Keynes, John Maynard (1933). *Essays in Biography*. London: Macmillan.

Kim, Marlene ed. (2007). *Race and Economic Opportunity in the Twenty-First Century*. London: Routledge.

Kollontai, Alexandra (1920). *Communism and the Family*. London.

Kollontai, Alexandra (1971 [1926]). *The Autobiography of a Sexually*

Emancipated Communist Woman, trans. Salvator Attansio. https://www. marxists.org/archive/kollonta/1926/autobiography.htm.

Krugman, Paul (2009). How Did Economists Get It So Wrong? *New York Times*, September 6.

Kuiper, Edith (2001). The Most Valuable of All Capital: A Gender Reading of Economic Texts. Tinbergen Institute Research Series. https://www. semanticscholar.org/paper/The-most-valuable-of-all-Capital1%3B-a-gender-reading-Kuiper/6c0301490d51d54b487805ff26f555773 06dfe38.

Kuiper, Edith (2003). The Construction of Masculine Identity in Adam Smith's *Theory of Moral Sentiments* (1759). In D.K. Barker and E. Kuiper, eds., *Towards a Feminist Philosophy of Economics*. London: Routledge, pp. 45–60.

Kuiper, Edith, ed. (2014). *Women's Economic Thought in the Eighteenth Century*. Routledge Major Work Series, 3 vols. London: Routledge.

Kuiper, Edith, and Robles-García, Claudia (2012). The Economic Experiences and Views of Elizabeth Montagu, the Queen of the Bluestockings. Paper Presented at the Annual Conference of the International Association of Feminist Economics, Barcelona, Spain.

Kuiper, Edith, and Springer, Adrienne (2013). Navigation Technique of a Female Philosophe. Paper presented at Women's Studies Conference, Marist College, Poughkeepsie, NY.

Kuiper, Edith, and Sap, Jolande C.M., with Feiner, Susan F., Ott, Notburga, and Tzannatos, Zafiris, eds. (1995). *Out of the Margin. Feminist Perspectives on Economics*. London: Routledge.

Kyrk, Hazel (1923). *A Theory of Consumption*. Boston, MA: Houghton Mifflin.

Kyrk, Hazel (1953). *The Family in the American Economy*. Chicago, IL: University of Chicago Press.

Kyrk, Hazel, Monroe, Day, Brady, Dorothy S., Rosenstiel, Colette, and Rainboth, Edith Dyer (1941). *Family Expenditures for Housing and Household Operations. Five Regions*. Washington, DC: US Department of Agriculture.

Lacey, Candida Ann (1987). Introduction. In C.A. Lacey, ed., *Barbara Leigh Bodichon and the Langham Place Group*. London: Routledge & Kegan Paul, pp. 1–16.

Lambert, Anne-Thérèse, marquise de (1729). *New Reflections on the Fair Sex*, trans. J. Lockman. London: Prevost and Lewis.

Lambert, Anne-Thérèse, marquise de (1748). *Oevres de Madame la Marquise de Lambert*. Amsterdam.

Lambert, Anne-Thérèse, marquise de (1749). *The Works of the Marchioness de Lambert. Containing Thoughts on Various Entertaining and Useful Subjects. Reflections on Education, on the Writings of Homer and on Various Public Events of the Time. Carefully Translated from the French*. London: William Owen.

Landry, Donna (1990). *The Muses of Resistance: Laboring-Class Women's Poetry in Britain 1739–1796*. Cambridge: Cambridge University Press.

Lee, Jarena (2019 [1836]). *Religious Experience and Journal of Mrs. Jarena Lee: Giving an Account of her Call to Preach the Gospel*. Philadelphia, PA: Pantianos Classics.

Lewis, Jane, ed. (1983). *Women's Welfare, Women's Rights*. London: Croom Helm.

Lewis, Jane, ed. (1993). *Women and Social Policies in Europe: Work, Family, and the State*. Cheltenham: Edward Elgar.

Lewis, Susan I. (2009). *Unexceptional Women, Female Proprietors in Mid-Nineteenth-Century Albany, New York 1830–1885*. Columbus: Ohio State University.

Libby, Barbara (1990). Women in the Economics Profession: 1900–1940. Factors in Declining Visibility. *Essays in Economic and Business History*, 8: 121–130.

Lobdell, Richard A. (2000). Hazel Kyrk (1886–1957). In Robert W. Dimand, Mary Ann Dimand, and Evelyn L. Forget, eds., *A Biographical Dictionary of Women Economists*. Cheltenham: Edward Elgar, pp. 251–253.

Lochhead, Marion (1948). *The Scots Household in the Eighteenth Century. A Century of Scottish Domestic and Social Life*. Edinburgh: Moray Press.

Lucas, Linda, ed. (2007). *Unpacking Globalization: Markets, Gender, and Work*. Plymouth: Lexington Books.

Luxemburg, Rosa (2003 [1913]). *The Accumulation of Capital*, trans. Agnes Schwarzschild. London: Routledge.

Maas, Harro (2016). *Letts* Calculate: Moral Accounting in the Victorian Period. *History of Political Economy*, 48(suppl.): 16–43.

McCarthy, Helen (2020). *Double Lives. A History of Working Motherhood*. London: Bloomsbury.

McDonald, Deborah (2004). *Clara Collet 1860–1948: An Educated Working Woman*. London: Routledge.

McElroy, Marjorie B., and Horney, Mary J. (1981). Nash-Bargained Household Decisions: Toward a Generalization of the Theory of Demand. *International Economic Review*, 22(2): 333–349.

Madden, Kirsten (2002). Female Contributions to Economic Thought, 1900–1940. *History of Political Economy*, 34(1): 1–30.

Madden, Kristen, and Persky, Joseph (2021). Anna Doyle Wheeler on the Conditions for Gender Equality. Paper presented at the Annual Conference of the International Association for Feminist Economics (IAFFE), June 22–25, Quito, Ecuador (virtually).

Madden, Kirsten, and Dimand, Robert W., eds. (2019). *The Routledge Handbook of the History of Women's Economic Thought*. London: Routledge.

Madden, Kirsten, Seiz, Janet, and Pujol, Michèle, eds. (2004). *A Bibliography of Female Economic Thought to 1940*, 2nd ed. London: Routledge.

Malthus, Thomas (1970 [1798]). *An Essay on the Principle of Population*. London: Penguin Books.

Mandeville, Bernard (1924 [1714]). *The Fable of the Bees: or, Private Vices Publick Benefits*. Oxford: Oxford Clarendon Press.

Mankiw, N. Gregory (1997). *Principles of Microeconomics*. Stanford, CA: Cengage Learning.

Manser, Marilyn, and Brown, Murray (1979). Bargaining Analysis of Household Decisions. In C.B. Lloyd, E.S. Andrews, and C.L. Golroy, eds., *Women in the Labor Market*. New York: Columbia Press.

Marcet, Jane H. (1824 [1816]). *Conversations on Political Economy, in which the Elements of that Science are Familiarly Explained*, 5th ed. London: Longman, Hurst, Rees, Orme, Brown, and Green.

Marcet, Jane H. (1833). *John Hopkins's Notions on Political Economy*. Boston.

Marcet, Jane H. (1851). *Rich and Poor*. London: Longman, Brown, Green, and Longman.

Marshall, Alfred (1890). *Principles of Economics*. London: Macmillan.

Marshall, Alfred (1897). The Old Generation of Economists and the New. *The Quarterly Journal of Economics*, 11 (2): 115–135.

Marshall, Alfred (1907). The Social Possibilities of Economic Chivalry. *The Economic Journal*, 17(65): 7–29.

Marshall, Alfred, and Paley Marshall, Mary (1879). *The Economics of Industry*. London: Macmillan.

Martin, Bonnie (2016). Neighbor-to-Neighbor Capitalism. Low Credit Network and the Mortgaging of Slaves. In S. Beckert and S. Rockman, eds., *Slavery's Capitalism. A New History of American Economic Development*, Philadelphia: University of Pennsylvania Press, pp. 107–121.

Martineau, Harriet (1834). *Illustrations of Political Economy*, 9 vols. London: Charles Fox.

Martineau, Harriet (1838). *How to Observe Morals and Manners*. London: Knight and Co.

Martineau, Harriet (1962 [1837]). *Society in America*, ed. Seymour Martin Lipset. Garden City, NY: Anchor Books.

Maupin, Joyce (1964). *Labor Heroines. Ten Women Who Led the Struggles*. Berkeley, CA: Union Wage.

Meadows, Donella H., Meadows, Dennis L., Randers, Jørgen, and Behrens, William W., III (1972). *The Limits to Growth*. Washington, DC: Universe Books.

Meadows, Donella H., Randers, Jørgen, and Meadows, Dennis L. (2004). *Limits to Growth. The 30-Year Update*. White River Junction, VT: Chelsea Green Publishing.

Mellor, Mary (1997). *Feminism and Ecology*. Cambridge: Polity.

Mellor, Mary (2010). The Future of Money. From Financial Crisis to Public Resource. OAPEN. http://library.oapen.org/handle/20.500.12657/30777.

Merchant, Caroline (1980). *The Death of Nature. Women, Ecology, and the Scientific Revolution*. New York: Harper and Row.

Mies, Maria (1986). *Patriarchy and Accumulation at the World Scale. Women in the International Division of Labour*. London: Zed Books.

Mies, Maria, with Vandana Shiva (1988). *Ecofeminism*. London: Zed Books.

Mill, John Stuart (1848). *Principles of Political Economy*. London.

Mill, John Stuart, with Mill, Harriet Taylor (1997 [1869]). *The Subjection of Women*. Mineola, NY: Dover Publications.

Mill, John Stuart (2008 [1873]). *Autobiography*. Rockville, MA: Arc Manor.

Mill, Harriet Taylor (1851). The Enfranchisement of Women. *Westminster Review*.

Miller, P.J. (1972). Women's Education, "Self-improvement" and Social Mobility: A Late Eighteenth-century Debate. *British Journal of Educational Studies*, 20(3): 302–314.

Mincer, Jacob (1962). Labor Participation of Married Women. A Study of Labor Supply. In H. Gregg Lewis, ed., *Aspects of Labor Economics*. NBER. Princeton: Princeton University Press, pp. 63–105.

Minsky, Hyman (1982). *Can "It" Happen Again?* Armonk, NY: M.E. Sharpe.

Minsky, Hyman (1992). The Financial Instability Hypothesis. Working Paper no. 74. The Jerome Levy Economics Institute of Bard College.

Mintz-Habib, Nazia (2016). *Biofuels, Food Security, and Development Economics*. London: Routledge.

Mitchell, Natalie (2020). A Girl's Song: Recounting Women and the Nantucket Whaling Industry, 1750–1890. Williams Honors College, Honors Research Projects, 1017. https://ideaexchange.uakron.edu/honors_research_projects/1017.

Montagu, Elizabeth Robinson (1769). *An Essay on the Writings and Genius of Shakespear, compared with the Greek and French Dramatic Poets. With Some Remarks upon the Misrepresentations of Mons. de Voltaire*. London: Dodsley.

More, Hannah (1795–8). *Cheap Repository Tracts*. London: J. Marshall and R. White.

More, Hannah (1796). *The Apprentice turned Master; Or, the Second Part of the Two Shoemakers. Shewing How James Stock from a Parish Apprentice became a creditable Tradesman*. Oxford Text Archive. http://ota.ox.ac.uk/id/3847.

Murray, Judith Sargent (1798). *The Gleaner. A Miscellaneous Production in Three Volumes*. Boston, MA: Thomas and Andrews.

Myrdal, Alva, and Klein, Viola (1968 [1956]). *Women's Two Roles. Home and Work*. 2nd ed. London: Routledge & Kegan Paul.

Nelson, Julie A. (1992). Gender, Metaphor, and the Definition of Economics. *Economics and Philosophy*, 8(1): 103–125.

Nelson, Julie A. (1993). The Study of Choice or the Study of Provisioning? Gender and the Definition of Economics. In Marianne A. Ferber and Julie A. Nelson, eds., *Beyond Economic Man*. Chicago, IL: University of Chicago Press, pp. 23–36.

Nelson, Julie A. (1995). *Feminism, Objectivity and Economics*. London: Routledge.

Nelson, Julie A. (2014). The Power of Stereotyping and Confirmation Bias to Overwhelm Accurate Assessment: The Case of Economics, Gender, and Risk Aversion. *Journal of Economic Methodology*, 21(3): 211–231.

Nelson, Julie A., and Power, Marilyn (2018). Ecology, Sustainability, and Care: Developments in the Field, *Feminist Economics*, 24(3): 80–88.

Nettl, J.P. (1969 [1966]). *Rosa Luxemburg*, abridged ed. Oxford: Oxford University Press.

Noble, David F. (1992). *A World Without Women. The Christian Clerical Culture of Western Science*. Oxford: Oxford University Press.

Nyland, Chris, and Heenan, Tom (2003). William Thompson and Anna Doyle Wheeler: A Marriage of Minds on Jeremy Bentham's Doorstep. In Robert Dimand and Chris Nyland, eds., *The Status of Women in Classical Economic Thought*. Cheltenham, UK: Edward Elgar, pp. 241–261.

O'Brien, K. (2009). *Women and Enlightenment in Eighteenth-Century Britain*. Cambridge: Cambridge University Press.

Ostrom, Elinor (1990). *Governing the Commons: The Evolution of Institutions for Collective Action.* Cambridge: Cambridge University Press.

Ott, Notburga (1992). *Intrafamily Bargaining and Household Decisions.* New York: Springer.

Ott, Notburga (1995). Fertility and Division of Work in the Family. In Edith Kuiper and Jolande Sap, with Susan F. Feiner and Notburga Ott, eds., *Out of the Margin. Feminist Perspectives on Economics.* London: Routledge, pp. 80–99.

Paley Marshall, Mary (1896). Conference of Women Workers. *The Economic Journal*, 6(21): 107–109.

Paley Marshall, Mary (1947). *What I Remember.* With an Introduction by G.M. Trevelyan, Cambridge: Cambridge University Press.

Parkes, Bessie Rayner (1860). Statistics as to the Employment of the Female Population of Great Britain. Repr. in C. Lacey, ed., *Barbara Leigh Smith Bodichon and the Langham Place Group.* London: Routledge & Kegan Paul, 1987, pp. 174–179.

Parkes, Bessie Rayner (1862). The Balance of Public Opinion in Regard to Women's Work. Repr. in C. Lacey, ed., *Barbara Leigh Smith Bodichon and the Langham Place Group.* London: Routledge & Kegan Paul, 1987, pp. 200–205.

Parreñas, Rhacel Salazar (2001). *Servants of Globalization: Women, Migration, and Domestic Work,* Stanford, CA: Stanford University Press.

Parsons, Elizabeth, and Tadajewski, Mark (2013). Pioneering Consumer Economist: Elizabeth Hoyt. *Journal of Historical Research in Marketing*, 5(3): 334–350.

Patten, Eileen (2016). Racial, Gender Wage Gaps Persist in US Despite Some Progress. Pew Research Center, July 1. https://www.pewresearch.org/fact-tank/2016/07/01/racial-gender-wage-gaps-persist-in-u-s-despite-some-progress/.

Penny, Virginia (1862). *The Employments of Women: A Cyclopaedia of Women's Work.* Boston, MA: Walker, Wise & Co.

Perelman, Michael (2000). *The Invention of Capitalism. Classical Political Economy and the Secret History of Primitive Accumulation.* Durham, NC: Duke University Press.

Perkins, A.J.P., and Wolfson, Theresa (1939). *Frances Wright: Free Enquirer.* London: Harper & Row.

Perkins, Ellie, ed. (1997). Women, Ecology, and Economics: New Models and Theories. Special Issue. *Ecological Economics*, 20(2).

Perkins, Ellie, and Kuiper, Edith, eds. (2005). Explorations: Feminist Ecological Economics. *Feminist Economics*, 11(3): 107–150.

Perry, Ruth (2005). Mary Astell and Enlightenment. In S. Knott and B. Taylor, eds., *Women, Gender and Enlightenment.* London: Palgrave Macmillan.

Peterson, Janice, and Lewis, Margaret, eds. (1999). *The Elgar Companion to Feminist Economics.* Cheltenham: Edward Elgar.

Peterson, V. Spike (2003). *A Critical Rewriting of Global Political Economy.* London: Routledge.

Pietilä, Hilkka (2002). *Engendering the Global Agenda. The Story of Women and the United Nations.* Geneva: UN Nongovernmental Liaison Service.

Piketty, Thomas (2014). *Capital in the Twenty-First Century*. Cambridge, MA: Harvard University Press.

Pinchbeck, Ivy (1930). *Women Workers and the Industrial Revolution 1750–1850*. London: Frank Cass and Co.

Pisan, Christine de (1982 [1405]). *Book of the City of Ladies*. New York: Persea Books.

Poovey, Mary (1998). *A History of the Modern Fact. Problems of Knowledge in the Sciences of Wealth and Society*. Chicago, IL: University of Chicago Press.

Pott-Buter, Hettie A. (1992). *Facts and Fairy Tales about Female Labor, Family and Fertility, A Seven-Country Comparison, 1850–1990*. Amsterdam: Amsterdam University Press.

Power, Marilyn (2004). Social Provisioning as a Starting Point for Feminist Economics. *Feminist Economics*, 10(3): 3–19.

Prince, Mary (1997 [1831]). *The History of Mary Prince. A West Indian Slave. Related by Herself*, ed. Moira Ferguson. Ann Arbor: University of Michigan Press.

Pujol, Michèle (1989). Economic Efficiency or Economic Chivalry? Women's Status and Women's Work in Neo-classical Economics. PhD Thesis, Simon Fraser University, National Library Canada.

Pujol, Michèle (1992). *Feminism and Anti-Feminism in Early Economic Thought*. Cheltenham: Edward Elgar.

Radcliffe, Ann (1999 [1791]). *The Romance of the Forest*. Oxford: Oxford University Press.

Rand, Ayn (1985 [1957]). *Atlas Shrugged*. New York: Signet.

Rand, Ayn (1993 [1943]). *The Fountainhead*. New York: Signet.

Rathbone, Eleanor F. (1917). The Remuneration of Women's Services. *The Economic Journal*, 27(105): 55–68.

Raworth, Kate (2017). *Doughnut Economics. Seven Steps to Think Like a 21st Century Economist*. White River Junction, VT: Chelsea Green Publishers.

Reeve, Clara (1792). *Plans of Education; with Remarks on the System of Other Writers. In a Series of Letters between Mrs. Danford and her friends*. London: Hookham and Carpenter.

Reeves, Maud Pember (1912). Family Life on a Pound a Week. In Sally Alexander, ed., *Women's Fabian Tracts*, Women's Source Library, Vol. VII, London: Routledge, pp. 200–223.

Reid, Margaret G. (1934). *Economics of Household Production*. New York: J. Wiley and Sons.

Reis, Elizabeth (2009). *Bodies in Doubt: An American History of Intersex*. Baltimore, MD: John Hopkins University Press.

Rendall, Jane (1987). Virtue and Commerce: Women in the Making of Adam Smith's Political Economy. In E. Kennedy and S. Mendus, eds., *Women in Western Political Philosophy, Kant to Nietzsche*. Brighton: Wheatsheaf Books, pp. 44–77.

Ricardo, David (1911 [1817]). *The Principles of Political Economy and Taxation*. London: Everyman's Library.

Richards, Earl Jeffrey (1982). Introduction to *Book of the City of Ladies* by Christine de Pizan. New York: Persea Books, pp. xix–li.

Rippon, Gina (2019). *The Gendered Brain. The New Neuroscience that Shatters the Myth of the Female Brain*. London: Bodley Head.

Robinson, Harriet Hanson (2021 [1898]). *Loom and Spindle*. Middletown, DE: Forgotten Books.

Robinson, Joan (1962). *Economic Philosophy*. London: C.A. Watts.

Robinson, Joan (1969 [1933]). *The Economics of Imperfect Competition*, 2nd ed. London: Macmillan.

Roosevelt, Eleanor (2017 [1933]). *It's Up to the Women*. New York: Nation Books.

Ross, Ian S. (1995). *The Life of Adam Smith*. Oxford: Clarendon Press.

Rossilli, Mariagrazia, ed. (2000). *Gender Policies in the European Union*. Berlin: Peter Lang.

Rostek, Joanna (2021). *Women's Economic Thought in the Romantic Age. Towards a Transdisciplinary Herstory of Economic Thought*. London: Routledge.

Rousseau, Jean-Jacques (2016 [1755]). *A Discourse on Inequality*. New York: Philosophical Library.

Rowntree, B. Seebohn (1901). *Poverty, A Study of Town Life*. London: Macmillan.

Sainsbury, Diane (1996). *Gender Equality and Welfare States*. Cambridge: Cambridge University Press.

Samuelson, Paul (1948). *Economics. An Introductory Analysis*. New York: McGraw-Hill.

Sanger, Margaret (1914). *Family Limitation*. Publisher not identified. https://babel.hathitrust.org/cgi/pt?id=udel.31741115153472&view=1up&seq=6.

Sanger, Margaret (2005 [1920]). *Woman and the New Race*. New York: Cosimo.

Sargent, Lydia, ed. (1981). *Women and Revolution. The Unhappy Marriage of Marxism and Feminism*. London: Pluto Press.

Scharf, Lois (1980). *To Work and To Wed. Female Employment, Feminism, and the Great Depression*. London: Greenwood Press.

Schaw, Janet (1927 [n.d.]). *Journal of a Lady of Quality. Being the Narrative of a Journey from Scotland to the West Indies, North Carolina, and Portugal, in the Years 1774 to 1776*, ed. E. Walker Andrews with Charles McLean Andrews. New Haven, CT: Yale University Press.

Schiebinger, Londa (1989). *The Mind Has No Sex? Women in the Origins of Modern Science*. Cambridge, MA: Harvard University Press.

Schreiner, Olive (1911). *Women and Labor*, 7th ed. New York: Stokes Company.

Schröder, Hannelore (1989). Inleiding en commentaar [Introduction and comments]. In Olype de Gouges, *Verklaring van de Rechten van de Vrouw en Burgeres* (1791). [Declaration of the Rights of Woman and Burgheress]. Kampen: Kok Agora.

Schumpeter, Joseph A. (1954). *History of Economic Analysis*, ed. E. Boody Schumpeter. London: Routledge.

Schumpeter, Joseph A. (2008 [1942]). *Capitalism, Socialism, and Democracy*. 5th ed. New York: Harper & Row.

Schuurman, Anna Maria van (1659 [1638]). *The Learned Maid, or Whether a Maid May Be a Scholar*, trans. Clement Barksdale. London: Redmayne.

Scott, Joan W. (1988). *Gender and the Politics of History.* New York: Columbia University Press.

Scott, Sarah Robinson (1762). *A Description of Millennium Hall, and the Country Adjacent; Together with the Characters of the Inhabitants, and Such Historical Anecdotes and Reflections, as May Excite in the Reader Proper Sentiments of Humanity; and lead the Mind to the Love of Virtue.* London: J. Newbery. Repr. in E. Kuiper ed., *Women's Economic Thought in the Eighteenth Century.* London: Routledge, 2014, pp. 407–439.

Senior, Nassau William (1830). *Three Lectures on the Rate of Wages.* London: John Murray.

Shah, Sumitra (2006). Sexual Division of Labor in Adam Smith's Work. *Journal of the History of Economic Thought,* 28(2): 221–241.

Skemp, Sheila L. (1998). Judith Sargent Murray, Introduction. In S.L. Skemp, ed., *Judith Sargent Murray. A Brief Biography with Documents.* New York: Bedford Books, pp. 1–122.

Smith, Adam (1976 [1776]). *An Inquiry into the Nature and Causes of the Wealth of Nations.* Oxford: Oxford University Press.

Smith, Adam (1984 [1759]). *Theory of Moral Sentiments,* ed. D.D. Raphael and A.L. MacFie. Indianapolis, IN: Liberty Fund.

Smith, Florence M. (1966 [1916]). *Mary Astell.* New York: AMS Press.

Smith, Mrs. (1810). *The Female Economist; or, A Plain System of Cookery: For the Use of Families.* London.

Sockwell, William D. (2000). Barbara Bodichon (1827–91). In Robert W. Dimand, Mary Ann Dimand, and Evelyn L. Forget, eds., *A Biographical Dictionary of Women Economists.* Cheltenham: Edward Elgar, pp. 53–56.

Spencer, Herbert (1851). *Social Statics; or The Conditions Essential to Happiness Specified and the First of Them Developed.* London: John Chapman.

Spencer, Herbert (1900 [1862]). *First Principles.* 6th ed. London: Williams and Norgate.

Stage, Sarah, and Vincenti, Virginia B., eds. (1997). *Rethinking Home Economics. Women and the History of a Profession.* Ithaca, NY: Cornell University Press.

Stern, Andrea Minna (2020). Forced Sterilization Policies in the US Targeted Minorities and Those with Disabilities – and Lasted into the 21st Century. The Conversation. https://theconversation.com/forced-sterilization-policies-in-the-us-targeted-minorities-and-those-with-disabilities-and-lasted-into-the-21st-century-14d3144.

Strang, John (1856). *Glasgow and its Clubs; or Glimpses of the Condition, Manners, Characters, and Oddities of the City, during the Past and Present Century.* Glasgow: Griffin.

Tadajewski, Mark (2013). Helen Woodward and Hazel Kyrk. *Journal of Historical Research in Marketing,* 5(3): 385–412.

Talbot, Marion, and Breckinridge, Sophonisba Preston (1912). *The Modern Household.* Boston: Whitcomb and Barrows.

Tarbell, Ida M. (1904). *The History of the Standard Oil Company.* New York: Macmillan.

Taylor, Barbara (2005). Feminists versus Gallants: Manners and Morals in

Enlightenment Britain. In S. Knott and B. Taylor, eds., *Women, Gender and Enlightenment*. New York: Palgrave Macmillan, pp. 30–52.

Terrell, Mary Church (1898). The Progress of Colored Women: An Address Delivered Before the National American Women's Suffrage Association. Columbia Theater, Washington, DC. 19 February. Repr. in D.K. Barker and E. Kuiper, eds., *Feminist Economics, Critical Concepts in Economics*. London: Routledge, 2010, pp. 113–119.

Thompson, E.P (1966 [1963]). *The Making of the English Working Class*. New York: Alfred Knopf.

Thompson, William, and Wheeler, Anna Doyle (1825). *Appeal of One Half of the Human Race, Women, Against the Pretensions of the Other Half, Men, to Retain them in Political and thence in Civil and Domestic Slavery; in Reply to a Paragraph of Mr. Mill's Celebrated "Article on Government."* London: Longman.

Thomson, Dorothy Lampen (1973). *Adam Smith's Daughters*. New York: Exposition Press.

Thorne, Alison Comish (2000). Elizabeth Ellis Hoyt (1893–1980). In Robert W. Dimand, Mary Ann Dimand, and Evelyn L. Forget, eds., *A Biographical Dictionary of Women Economists*. Cheltenham: Edward Elgar, pp. 215–219.

Tollec, Agnès le (2020). Finding a New Home (Economics) Towards a Science of the Rational Family 1924–1981. Doctoral thesis, ENS Paris-Saclay.

Tonna, Charlotte Elizabeth (1843). The Little Pin-Headers. In C.E. Tonna, *The Wrongs of Women*, Part III. London: Dalton. Repr. in D.K. Barker and E. Kuiper eds., *Feminist Economics. Critical Concepts*. London: Routledge, 2014, pp. 60–67.

Trautwein, Hans-Michael (2000). Marie Dessauer (b. 1901). In Robert W. Dimand, Mary Ann Dimand, and Evelyn L. Forget, eds., *A Biographical Dictionary of Women Economists*. Cheltenham: Edward Elgar, pp. 138–140.

Tribe, Keith (1978). *Land, Labour and Economic Discourse*, London: Routledge & Kegan Paul.

Trimmer, Sarah (1787). *The Œconomy of Charity; or, an Address to Ladies Concerning Sunday-Schools; The Establishment of Schools of Industry under Female Inspection; and the Distribution of Voluntary Benefactions. To which is added an Appendix, containing an account of the Sunday-schools in Old Brentford*. London: J. Longman.

Tristan, Flora (1983 [1843]). *The Workers' Union*, trans. and with an introduction by Beverly Livingston. Chicago: University of Illinois Press.

Truth, Sojourner (1993 [1850]). *The Narrative of Sojourner Truth*, ed. M. Washington. New York: Vintage Books.

Ulrich, Laurel Thatcher (1990). *A Midwife's Tale. The Life of Martha Ballard. Based on Her Diary 1785–1812*. New York: Alfred Knopf.

UNDP (1995). *Human Development Report 1995*. New York: Oxford University Press.

van Staveren, Irene (2002). Global Finance and Gender. In Jan Aart Scholte with Albrecht Schnabel, eds., *Civil Society and Global Finance*. London: Routledge, pp. 228–246.

van Staveren, Irene, Elson, Diane, Grown, Caren, and Çagatay, Nilüfer, eds. (2007). *The Feminist Economics of Trade*. London: Routledge.

van Velzen, Susan (2003). Hazel Kyrk and the Ethics of Consumption. In D.K. Barker and E. Kuiper, eds., *Toward a Feminist Philosophy of Economics*. New York: Routledge, pp. 38–55.

Veblen, Thorstein (1899). *The Theory of the Leisure Class*. New York: Macmillan.

Wakefield, Priscilla (1798). *Reflections on the Present Condition of the Female Sex; with Suggestions for Its Improvement*. London: Johnson, Darton and Harvey.

Ware, Susan (1981). *Beyond Suffrage*. Cambridge, MA: Harvard University Press.

Waring, Marilyn (1988). *If Women Counted. A New Feminist Economics*. New York: Macmillan.

Webb, Beatrice Potter (1896). Women and the Factory Acts. In Sally Alexander ed., *The Fabian Tracts*, vol. VII. London: Routledge, pp. 17–32.

Webb, Beatrice Potter (1909). *The Minority Report of the Poor Laws Commission* (Parts I and II), London.

Webb, Beatrice Potter (1919). *The Wages of Men and Women: Should they be Equal?* London: Fabian Society.

Webb, Beatrice Potter (1979 [1926]). *My Apprenticeship*. Cambridge: Cambridge University Press.

Webb, Sidney (1891). The Alleged Differences in the Wages Paid to Men and Women for Similar Work. *The Economic Journal*, 1(4): 635–662.

Wells-Barnett, Ida B. (2018 [1892]). *Southern Horrors: Lynch Law in All Its Phases*. Paris: Alpha Editions.

Wells-Barnett, Ida B. (2021 [1895]). *The Red Record. Tabulated Statistics and Alleged Causes of Lynching in the United States*. With an introduction by Frederick Douglass. Middletown, DE: Cavalier Classics.

Williford, Miriam (1975). Bentham on the Rights of Women. *Journal of the History of Ideas*, 36(1): 167–176.

Wollstonecraft, Mary (1787). *Thoughts on the Education of Daughters, with Reflections on Female Conduct in the More Important Duties of Life*. London: Johnson.

Wollstonecraft, Mary (1792). *A Vindication of the Rights of Woman. With Strictures on Political and Moral Subjects*. London: J. Johnson.

Wollstonecraft, Mary (2008 [1788]). *Mary: A Fiction*. London: Dodo Press.

Wood, Ellen Meiksins (1999). *The Origin of Capitalism. A Longer View*. London: Verso.

Woodward, Helen (1926). *Through Many Windows*. New York and London: Harper & Row.

Woolf, Virginia (1929). *A Room of One's Own*. London: Hogarth Press.

World Bank (2001). *Engendering Development. Through Gender Equality in Rights, Resources, and Voice*. Washington DC: Oxford University Press.

Wright, Angela (2013). *Britain, France and the Gothic, 1764–1820. The Import of Terror*. Cambridge: Cambridge University Press.

Wright, Frances (1821). *Views of Society and Manners in America. A Series of*

Letters from that Country to a Friend in England. During the Years 1818, 1819, and 1820. London: Longman, Hurst, Rees, Orme, and Brown.

Wright, Frances (2020 [1855]). *Memoir of Frances Wright. The Pioneer Woman in the Cause of Human Rights*, ed. Amos Gilbert. Cincinnati: Longley Brothers.

Wu, Alice H. (2017). Gender Stereotyping in Academia: Evidence from Economics Job Market Rumors Forum. PhD. thesis, University of California, Berkeley.

Xenophon (2021). *Œconomicus*, trans. B.J. Hayes. Andesite Press.

Young, Brigitta (2013). Gender, Debt, and the Housing/Financial Crisis. In Deborah M. Figart and Tonia L. Warnecke, eds., *Handbook of Research on Gender and Economic Life*. Northampton, MA: Edward Elgar, pp. 378–390.

Young, Brigitta (2018). Financialization, Unconventional Monetary Policy, and Gender Inequality. In Juanita Elias and Adrienne Roberts, eds., *Handbook on the International Political Economy of Gender*. Cheltenham: Edward Elgar, pp. 241–251.

Zetkin, Clara (1915). Women of the Working People. In P.S. Foner, ed., *Clara Zetkin: Selected Writings*. New York: International Publishers, pp. 130–132.

Zetkin, Clara (1932). Fascism Must Be Defeated. In Philip S. Foner, ed., *Clara Zetkin: Selected Writings*. New York: International Publishers, pp. 170–175.

Zetkin, Clara (1984 [1893]). Women's Work and the Trade Unions. In Philip S. Foner, ed., *Clara Zetkin: Selected Writings*. New York: International Publishers, pp. 51–59.

Zinsser, Judith P. (2006). *Daring Genius of the Enlightenment, Émilie du Châtelet*. New York: Penguin Books.

Zinsser, Judith P., ed. (2009). *Émilie du Châtelet. Selected Philosophical and Scientific Writings*, trans. Isabelle Bour and Judith P. Zinsser. Chicago, IL: University of Chicago Press.

Index

women's wealth 81, 85, 86–8
see also black people especially
 women; enslaved people,
 especially women
Universal Declaration of Human
 Rights, UN 153–4
universities 36, 37, 61
upper classes *see* social class
USSR 117, 147
utopian socialism 47, 64

value
 and consumption 130, 132, 140
 and women's labor 95–6, 99, 166
value neutrality 34, 164
value-in-exchange/value-in-use 101
Veblen, Thorstein 133
Victorian times 132
violence to women 50, 52, 57–8, 95
Voltaire 26, 29
voting rights 38, 58, 145
 United Kingdom 40, 41, 48, 74

wage control 45
wage equality 40, 166
 and black people 58, 125–9
 and discrimination of women 110,
  126–7, 128, 138–9
 and employment opportunities for
  women 108, 109, 122, 124–5,
  126–7
  access to professions 65, 122
 and gender equality 58, 122–9, 168
 and government policies 110, 146,
  169
 and income distribution 14–15, 115
 and motherhood 127, 128
 and neoclassical economic theory
  125–6, 127, 128
wage labor system 115, 117–22
wage-earners, secondary 114, 151,
 157
wages, minimum 151
wages of men 119, 167
wages of women 5–6, 96, 151–2, 167
 low wages 6, 109, 115, 122, 126,
  133
 single women 122, 150

wages, subsistence 5, 114, 124, 125
Wakefield, Priscilla 2, 14, 43–4, 64,
 86, 108, 122
Waring, Marilyn 24
Washington Consensus 159
waste prevention 59
waste production 143, 158, 168
Waterloo Bridge, London 103
wealth 35, 135
 women's 77–91, 102, 133–4, 165
  and black people 83, 89
  and dependency of women 78, 79
  and social class 80, 83–4
  and trust 80–1, 86
  and United States 81, 85, 86–8
Webb, Beatrice Potter 70, 101, 119,
 151
 and government policies 66, 146,
  148, 149
 and wage equality 123, 125
Webb, Sidney 70, 119, 123, 126
welfare programs/services 110, 152,
 169
welfare state 129, 146–7, 150, 157
Wells-Barnett, Ida B. 57–8, 153
Wheatley, Phyllis 54
Wheeler, Anna Doyle 46
white women 6, 55, 58
Williams, Helen Maria 56
witch hunts 19
Wollstonecraft, Mary 81, 146
 and education of children 13, 69
 and education of women 41, 62,
  64
 and property rights 12, 50
 and voting rights 40, 41
Women's Department, USSR 117
women's movement 6, 51, 99, 115,
 166
 and black people 57, 58
women's rights 38–9, 96
 Women's Rights Convention 52, 54
Woodhull, Victoria 86
Woodward, Helen 15, 139
Woolf, Virginia 85
work, unpaid 140, 147
 definition 23
 men's 24